BURN YOUR SH*T

BURN YOUR

SHIT

THE LIFE-CHANGING
MAGIC OF RITUALS

LORI DYAN

Collins

Published by Collins, an imprint of HarperCollins Publishers Ltd

First edition

HarperCollins books may be purchased for educational, business, or
sales promotional use through our Special Markets Department.

HarperCollins Publishers Ltd
Bay Adelaide Centre, East Tower
22 Adelaide Street West, 41st Floor
Toronto, Ontario, Canada
M5H 4E3

www.harpercollins.ca

Library and Archives Canada Cataloguing in Publication

Title: Burn your sh[i]t : the life-changing magic of rituals / Lori Dyan.
Other titles: Burn your shit
Names: Dyan, Lori, author.
Description: First edition. | On title page "[i]" appears as an illustration in the form of a match.
Identifiers: Canadiana (print) 20240321278 | Canadiana (ebook) 20240324110 |
ISBN 9781443471558 (softcover) | ISBN 9781443471565 (ebook)
Subjects: LCSH: Self-actualization (Psychology) | LCSH: Ritual. | LCGFT: Self-help publications.
Classification: LCC BF637.S4 D93 2024 | DDC 158.1—dc23

Chapter opener images from Adobe Stock

Printed and bound in the United States of America
24 25 26 27 28 LBC 5 4 3 2 1

For Luka and Maia, who guided me to myself.
And for all of the Grandmothers who came before me . . .

CONTENTS

◇◇◇

Introduction 1

1. WTF Is a Ritual? 5
2. Don't Bring a Knife to a Gunfight (Getting Clear on Your Gear) 19
3. Clean Up on Aisle Six! (Cleansing with Sage, Sound, & Crystals) 57
4. Moon Magic 101 (Lunar Rhythms) 73
5. It's Time to Burn Your Sh*t (Full Moon Rituals) 85
6. Manifesting for Dummies (New Moon Magic Ritual) 115
7. Rise & Shine (How to Start & End Your Day with Intention) 137
8. Birthdays and New Year's and Divorce, Oh My! (Easy Rituals for Any Occasion) 189
9. A Merka-*what?* (The Potency of Sacred Geometry) 229
10. Angels & Devils (Connecting with Spirit & Ditching Your Demons) 243
11. Writing Wild & Cutting Cords (Tapping Into & Protecting Your Energy) 259
12. Circles & Spells (The Power of Women Gathering) 277

Conclusion 293
Acknowledgments 295

INTRODUCTION

◇◇◇

When I held my first tarot deck over thirty years ago, I had no idea those cards would become the crux of my career or how my readings would affect people—I'm not that kind of psychic. Tarot opened the door to what existed beyond my limited vision: I learned about the power of crystals and visualization; I discovered astrology that dug deeper than *Cosmopolitan* magazine's monthly horoscopes; and I became aware of energy, symbolism, and spells. Most importantly, I realized that the common through-line for everything we do is ritual. Rituals are woven throughout our days (and nights) like a gossamer thread; they're crucial not just for making magic but for living life.

As a seeker and a teacher, rituals are my spiritual roadmap. They're practical tools I've used my entire life for self-discovery, healing, and empowerment. I can access rituals whenever I need them, and I invite you to join me so you can experience their impact yourself.

I've been doing rituals for three decades as a facilitator and a participant, in person and online. I've set fire to limiting beliefs from a rooftop in Manhattan and torched bad habits in the back of a small-town nail salon. I've lit a match to relationships on a Mexican beach and buried negative self-talk in the ground. And every month, rain or shine or snow—So. Much. Snow.—I turn up on Instagram Live from my front porch in Canada, showing people how to harness the power of the Full Moon with a ritual I've spent years perfecting (and that, like me, remains a work in progress). I call this experience "Burn Your Sh*t" because the word *ritual* can sound witchy and intimidating for some people, just like *ceremony* can seem too formal and *practice* too homework-ish. Whatever you call it, the empowerment and unburdening that people feel afterward is immense and undeniable.

But burning your sh*t is just the beginning.

As I often like to say, once you've pulled the weeds, you can start planting seeds, which is where the power of the New Moon comes in. My New Moon Magic workshop is a masterclass in manifesting, inspired by my tarot mentor, who is a legit witch. This online event sells out every month, and many clients repeat it because they've experienced the potency of New Moon energy firsthand and want more.

As much as I adore La Luna, this book goes beyond Moon ceremonies to help you build a ritual toolbox and guide you on a spiritual detox. In addition to explaining the importance (and prevalence) of rituals in our lives, I'll show you how to clear your physical and energetic space, create an altar (spoiler: a rock from your garden can be an altar, so no pressure), tap into your intuition, protect your energy, and so much more. From the five-minute morning routine that can change your life to the easiest way to kill (or at least quiet) your inner critic, this book gives you step-by-step instructions, prompts, scripts, and explanations (and you'll also find a QR code on page 303 that will lead you to online recordings of me guiding you through various rituals).

My approach to modern rituals is accessible, engaging, and—most importantly—profoundly effective. This book provides a framework to support your well-being for the moment you're in, demystifying rituals so you can create lasting change for yourself whenever you feel the urge. The majority of the rituals I've included can be done solo, and most of them don't have to cost a thing. (You can always add extra *oomph* with altars and crystals if you want to indulge— Chapter 2 is dedicated to ceremonial gear.)

Rituals give you agency over your journey and healing; they're an essential component of self-care, helping you understand the world and your place in it. Whether you do yours alone or with a group of like-minded souls, rituals allow you to step into your potential and make your own magic. They give you an opportunity to discover who you are as well as envision who you're ready to become and the work that needs to be done to get you there.

This is the book I wish I'd had years ago, and the one I've been asked and called to write. Thank you for reading it.

CHAPTER 1

WTF IS A RITUAL?

When was the last time you attended a parade, concert, or playoff game? Did you ever pledge allegiance to a flag, raise your glass for a toast, or knock on wood (just in case)? Congratulations, you're already a ritual pro! We're just adding rocks, fire, and intention to the mix. Rituals don't have to be weird, complex, or mystical. Cauldrons aren't required, and you don't need to join a coven (although, if you're doing rituals with a couple of friends, you kinda already have one).

The word *ritual* may bring to mind voodoo dolls or seances, but rituals are actually ingrained in our daily lives, in every culture on Earth. From christenings to cremations and everything in between—graduations, weddings, birthdays, bachelorettes—we treat rituals with reverence, even if we can't articulate why.

Whether it's a tea ceremony in Japan, a political inauguration in Finland, or simply eating the red Skittles first, our lives are marked by rituals. They can be elaborate and life-affirming, like Mexico's Día de los Muertos (Day of the Dead), which celebrates the living by joyfully honoring those who've passed. Or they can be romantic and awe-inspiring, such as Thailand's Yi Peng Lantern Festival, where thousands of paper lanterns are launched under a Full Moon to mark the end of monsoon season and to pay respect to Buddha. But rituals can also be simple and practical, like taking three deep breaths when you're stuck in traffic or grabbing Starbucks every morning on your way to work. One person's morning routine is another's ritual.

While the importance of any ritual is rooted in the distinctly personal meaning we give to it, it's critical to acknowledge that rituals don't determine outcomes; they simply support them.

Rituals, especially the ones contained in this book, are meant to give you clarity when required, provide an anchor during turbulent times, and be a conduit to your inner wisdom. Be wary of any ritual that forces you to become so superstitious or rigid that you can't function without it—that's drifting into obsession, which can be more restrictive than supportive. Practiced with balance, rituals are flexible and adaptive tools you can use to boost whatever you apply them to, in any area of your life.

CAN'T STOP, WON'T STOP (WHY WE NEED RITUALS)

◇◇◇

Unlike a habit or routine, rituals are internally motivated and require conscious effort to provide a sense of purpose—and we've been doing them since the beginning of time. Our African ancestors were carrying out rituals over 70,000 years ago, when their lives literally depended on the cohesion and kinship that rituals provide. By coming together in ceremony, they formed a core community with shared rules, beliefs, and values. Society was created and maintained through rituals.

Early rituals demonstrate a powerful capacity for symbolic thought, which is a defining feature of our species. Regardless of the literal intention behind a ritual—from mundane and realistic to utterly fantastic—the performance of ritual itself offers collective benefits. I'm not endorsing the sacrificing of virgins, I'm just saying that rituals have been a powerful force in human societal evolution because they work.

The sacrificial offerings that unified early humans were a form of communal worship that evolved into organized religion, and the basic tenets of religion are still reinforced today through the rituals used to ignite spiritual introspection, such as prayer or fasting. Although we've been expressing our humanity through rituals for thousands of years, for many of us rituals aren't part of a particular religion—they're a way of life. We express our humanity through rituals.

We no longer have to lean on them for our physical survival, but rituals are here to stay. Legendary composer Ludwig van Beethoven couldn't start his day without a cup of coffee that he meticulously brewed himself with precisely sixty beans. And while this might seem slightly fastidious, millions of people around the world engaged in their own personal coffee ritual this morning (maybe you were one of them).

Former president Barack Obama had to go on the record to dispel the myth (reported in the *New York Times*) that he allowed himself a nightly snack of exactly seven lightly salted almonds. His famous self-discipline made the rumor easy to believe, along with the fact that his wife, Michelle, started it (as a joke with the Obamas' chef regarding the former president's healthy eating). He didn't deny that almonds were part of his evening ritual; it was the quantity that was in dispute (he'll splurge on twelve if he's feeling particularly reckless . . . or hungry).

According to science, Beethoven and Obama might have been on to something. In 2013, researchers from Harvard and the University of Minnesota discovered that when we engage in rituals before eating or drinking, the flavors are enhanced. The simplest rituals, like dunking your Oreo in milk before every bite, can heighten your enjoyment. The power of ritual is so strong that even *carrots* were perceived as more delicious after participants knocked on the table before eating them. Interestingly, watching passively as someone else performs a ritual, such as a sommelier uncorking a bottle of wine, does *not* affect the consumer's pleasure in drinking it (the sommelier, on the other hand, absolutely delights in it). We have to be mindfully engaged in a ritual to feel the effects from it, so even taking a brief moment to bow your head in acknowledgment of the meal you're about to eat will intensify your pleasure: you're fully present in the moment and that jacks up your enjoyment (even for a handful of almonds).

Rituals are routines infused with loving intention. When you combine a habit with something that makes you happy, a ritual (and life hack) is born. Monotonous tasks can become joyful, or at least tolerable, if you get a little creative. I tackled my hang-ups about money and scarcity by establishing a monthly date with my finances: I set the mood at an assigned time with some candles and soothing music; grab a glass of rosé or cup of tea (depending on the season); and settle into my comfiest chair before opening my laptop to look at my budget. I'm basically seducing my moolah. Because I consciously cultivate a particular vibe, financial planning no longer fills me with dread.

A ritual stirs our emotions, spurring us to act. Habits become sacred because of the significance we assign to them. The key is awareness—rituals require intention and focus, which is exactly what makes them so effective. A 2020 study published by the National Library of Medicine shows that participating in rituals lowers levels of stress and chronic anxiety. They ground us in the present moment and prevent us from marinating in the past (which often causes depression) or fixating on the future (which usually induces anxiety). We instinctively look to rituals as a way to provide stability during unpredictable times because they bring calm to chaos, help us concentrate, and bolster our confidence so we can face our fears.

RITUALS HELP US KEEP OUR COOL

◇◇◇

Anxiety is heightened when our brains can't find patterns, and rituals offer reassurance and comfort. We're hardwired to look for patterns as a means for our survival because they introduce order to the unpredictable nature of life. From avoiding poisonous plants to preparing for the changing seasons, patterns help us make sense of the world, and rituals create patterns where none existed (which is why our ancestors honoring python-shaped rocks isn't all that different from singing the national anthem). Even if we think they're goofy, our mental health gets a huge assist from rituals. A 2017 University of Toronto study confirmed that ritualistic behavior had a positive effect despite participants' negative assumptions. Whether it's an Indigenous group dancing before a big hunt or grandma blowing on dice at the craps table in Vegas, we instinctively look to rituals when the stakes are high or outcomes seem beyond our control.

Even if a ritual looks wacky on the outside, it can still be useful on the inside. After a particularly brutal breakup in my twenties, I swore off romance and was prepared to die alone until my friendly neighborhood witch (and tarot mentor) Erica gave me a red "passion candle" to burn while repeating a specific affirmation (she called it a spell) to attract love. Did this ritual immediately deliver a dude to my doorstep? Nope. Did it make me feel better at that moment? Absolutely. Did that in turn get me to a place emotionally and energetically to welcome a healthy romantic relationship? Unclear . . . but it definitely didn't hurt. There are different paths to growth, comfort, and healing. As long as you don't become obsessive-compulsive, rituals won't make things worse. It doesn't have to be practical to be purposeful; if a ritual eases anxiety, it's a win.

We're soothed into a state of flow when we perform rituals—and you don't need a direct connection between a ritual and a goal for the desired outcome to be realized. Rituals give you agency in high-pressure situations, or whenever you feel uncertain, by clarifying your intentions, restoring your confidence, and fortifying your beliefs. Think of any quirks you carry out before a big test, job interview, or first date. Do you use a certain pencil, give yourself a pep talk, or wear your lucky undies? Attaching a specific meaning to a ritual is enough to achieve the intended result. Psychologists call it "positive performance expectation"; I call it "manifesting" (more on this in Chapter 6).

Using rituals to anchor ourselves in the present moment and cultivate inner calm improves performance. In 2003, the *Journal of Sport Behavior* published research by psychologists that showed rituals don't guarantee specific results but can induce a state of serenity that allows people to perform at their peak. Working in the metaphysical space for over thirty years, I've witnessed (and experienced) the intangible power of rituals and their immeasurable value. Rituals help us access our intuition, tap into a higher wisdom, and connect to the energy of the Divine* so we can step into our potential.

---

* Throughout this book I use the words *Divine, Source, Universe, Higher Power,* and *Creator* interchangeably. They all refer to the energy that is greater than ourselves.

RITUALS GET SH*T DONE

◇◇◇

When we embed them in our daily lives, rituals put us into a specific mindset in order to reach our goals. I'm an example of this. When writing this book about rituals, I sat at my desk, in my office, during my dedicated book-writing time. I lit my book-writing candle and put in my book-writing earplugs. I wore my book-writing socks and chewed my book-writing gum. I didn't consciously set out to create a writing ritual—it evolved naturally as a way to get myself in the zone to write. Rituals help shape our self-perception and actualize our future. When I'm in my space with my candle and earplugs and socks and gum, I am a writer. We forge our identities, align with our purpose, and set ourselves up for success with rituals.

The COVID-19 pandemic proved that rituals aren't a luxury; they're a necessity. We look to rituals for comfort and connection, and quarantine denied both when we needed them most. But even when stuck at home, people found ways to adapt their most cherished rituals, like getting married on Zoom or watching concerts from cars. We also created new rituals—online family game nights or standing on a balcony banging pots with spoons—to give us the sense of community we crave.

Both of my kids graduated during quarantine, and their schools went above and beyond to make these days special, despite the circumstances (full disclosure: my son was *thrilled* to wear shorts and crocs with mismatched socks to his drive-thru graduation). As a tarot reader, I initially worried that my business would plummet during the pandemic because the majority of my readings were done in person, but my career actually skyrocketed with group readings. I was hired for virtual corporate events, wedding showers, birthday parties, and even blind dates.

Rituals link us to the collective, and in today's increasingly fragmented society, we need them more than ever. Participating in a group ritual can generate a specific state of shared excitement known as collective effervescence, a concept coined by sociologist Émile Durkheim in 1912. Anyone who's been to a Pride parade or watched the Olympics at a sports bar knows this feeling. Our primal urge to gather in sacred ways that connect, heal, and transform is constantly evolving.

I started doing my Burn Your Sh*t Full Moon ritual on Instagram Live during the COVID-19 pandemic because I had nowhere else to do it. What began as a few friends and clients joining me for twenty minutes of burning away our fears and doubts quickly turned into an anticipated global gig. And although quarantines are (hopefully) a thing of the past, people from all over the world still show up to burn stuff every month. My Woo Woo Crew (as I like to call them) tunes in from Kenya, Kuwait, Norway, Panama, and Australia to seek solace with me under the Full Moon. It doesn't matter if I burn sh*t on your behalf, you participate on your own as I'm doing it, or you simply lurk on the sidelines watching—you will benefit from this experience because we are all invested in it. When I burn something for a person in Spain and you feel it like you wrote it yourself, you're releasing just as much as the person who wrote it.

Burn Your Sh*t connects you to the energy of the collective, reassuring you that you're not alone and empowering you to be a cocreator of your life. All of this from a ritual rooted in the unknown with no proof that it actually works (it totally works). Rituals like this create a sense of belonging and continuity that act as the glue of culture. They are a fundamental part of what makes us human.

RITUALS CONNECT US
TO THE DIVINE

◇◇◇

As important as rituals are for unifying us in celebration, they're even more crucial during times of loss. Rituals play an essential role in death and dying; they become our compass as we navigate grief. Across cultures, religions, communities, and families, people gather with others to find comfort as they mourn; rituals are a balm for broken hearts. Indigenous cultures in North America consider death to be a natural transition back to the spirit world, and families gather to help facilitate that journey. Tobacco and sacred medicines may be burned, with speeches given about the dying person and his/her/their wishes. A repenting ritual is often performed to assist in releasing the person's spirit through prayer, smudging, pipe ceremonies, and sacred songs (similar to the last rites of Christian faiths).

When a person dies, mourning rituals take many forms—from a boisterous Irish wake to the solemnity of sitting Shiva—but they all serve to guide us in honoring those who've passed and allow us to feel the support of our community, which is vital in helping us process our pain as we adjust to the void left behind.

Our spiritual well-being is strengthened by rituals because they allow us to be in conversation with ourselves as well as the people and world around us, both seen and unseen. You can write a letter of forgiveness to a past lover, ask for Divine guidance while meditating, or clear your psyche with a sound bath—when you do these types of rituals by yourself, there's a sense that you aren't alone. Where there is disconnection from Source, there is separation from Self.

We all yearn for meaning in our lives—whether we're consciously aware of it or not—and many of us spend our lives (and a lot of money) seeking to fill this longing in our souls with something deeper. When we're disconnected from a Higher Power, we can fall into habits of escapism, like scrolling social media, bingeing Netflix, shopping impulsively, or snacking mindlessly (just me?). Escaping in these ways only exacerbates the feeling deep inside us that something is missing. The good news is that reconnection is possible—and rituals are the key.

Acknowledging a Higher Power using rituals helps you refrain from seeking validation or fulfillment from others and instead start loving yourself, expressing who you truly are, and elevating to your potential. Simple rituals become a sacred spiritual practice when you attune to this otherworldly energy. They're an opportunity for introspection in a time when social media demands that we live our lives virtually—instead of liking TikTok videos on autopilot, you can connect to your soul with a ritual.

Infusing your life with ritual allows you to slow down and live more intentionally—these soul offerings calibrate you to the energy of the Divine. They provide a cosmic reset, inviting ease and healing into your world and softening the hard edges of daily life. A sacred practice holds you together when things fall apart, and the smallest ritual can cushion your fall and support you in getting back up again. You're more connected to your inner wisdom and less reliant on seeking answers or validation from external sources (your mother, your boss, Instagram ads for belly fat–reduction teas).

True transformation occurs beyond our brains, in a place so deep and vast that it can't be explained with logic but is undeniably felt on a soul level. The Universe is waiting to guide you, but you must be fully present in order to receive that support. When you tap into its energy with rituals, you shift into a flow state that transcends winning a race or acing a test. Life gets easier in ways you can't explain—things suddenly fall into place, answers appear out of nowhere, and you find yourself in the right place at the perfect time.

Rituals are the secret sauce to living a life of purpose, intention, and abundance. You can customize them to meet you where you're at in any given moment—from fueling your body to finding your soulmate. I've learned over the years that rituals, tarot, and any other beliefs or practices we employ are all different paths to self-actualization.

Aligning with the Universe as you connect with others and yourself will transform your life into a work of art.

CHAPTER 2

DON'T BRING A KNIFE TO A GUNFIGHT (GETTING CLEAR ON YOUR GEAR)

You've decided to do a ritual . . . now what? You can transform a simple ritual into a sacred spiritual practice with the right tools. Tools infuse routines with meaning and inject cosmic kerosene into intentions. Whether you're a seasoned practitioner or ceremonial newbie, your equipment focuses and directs your energy in symbolic as well as practical ways.

Each item in your ritual toolkit serves a purpose, so before you spend the rent going wild on Etsy, consider what works for you. It's taken me decades to collect the tools of my trade, and they continue to evolve alongside me. For example, wands have been used by healers around the world since ancient times because their elongated, cylindrical shape gathers and directs energy in a straight line. I made an elaborately decorated wand (I call it a talking stick) covered in feathers and crystals that I use in ceremonial circle gatherings. But before I had my wand, I used a twig from my backyard (and, in a pinch, a tube of lipstick).

From an energetic standpoint, the intentions we set through ritual are deepened when they're supported in tangible ways. Similar to countless religious and healing practices, the objects we incorporate into our rituals are often tied to the four natural elements: Earth, Air, Water, and Fire. The four elements can be found in the four suits of tarot, the medicine wheel of Indigenous traditions, and the Hindu philosophy of Ayurveda (to name a few). From ancient Greek philosophers to modern Wiccans, the four elements are foundational principles of life that comprise the world around us. Spirit (or Space) is often evoked as a fifth element, but I view Spirit as an all-encompassing presence that we connect with through the four elements. Whether you work with four elements or five, what matters most is that the elements you choose resonate with you.

Including the elements enriches your connection to any ceremony. A lit candle brings in the transformational element of Fire. Soaking in a Moon bath incorporates Water, the most purifying element. The smoke of burning incense represents Air—the engine that powers everything by connecting us to the universal life force of breath. And the grounding energy of Mother Earth can be found in crystals that symbolize the circle of life. Traditional smudging incorporates all four elements: the shell holding the smoldering sage represents Water, sage comes from the Earth, Fire is found in the burning, and the resulting smoke encompasses the Air. (More on sage in Chapter 3.)

Your rituals and tools are an extension of you; whatever infuses meaning into your practice is appropriate. You might gravitate toward a particular crystal because it resonates with your objective in a specific way or you may incorporate incense because it smells pretty—your gear is the perfect fusion of fashion and function, guaranteed to spice up any ceremony and make it feel like your own. As with everything in this book (and life), take what is meaningful to you and leave the rest. Have fun experimenting. You may realize that candles aren't really your thing, but palo santo is your superpower.

Whatever you end up using in your rituals, make sure there's a method to your magic; spend time considering the intention behind the tools you choose.

BOUGIE VERSUS BASIC (LET YOUR FRYING PAN BE YOUR CAULDRON)

◇◇◇

Just like kneeling to pray at church is no weirder than burning old love letters, the space you create and tools that you use in a ritual can be as simple or elaborate as you want. Your energetic offerings can include rare resins and crystals harvested in Bali, or you can arrange some sticks from your backyard by your bedside. You already have everything you need to start doing profound rituals right now.

This chapter is meant to inspire and guide you through the various accessories you can incorporate into your rituals. If you want to invest in your ritual practice by purchasing carefully curated adornments, there are things to know before you buy, which I'll get into in the pages that follow. Or your intention can be supported with thoughtfully collected items that are free, found, or pre-owned—they're all means to the same end. Please don't pressure yourself to buy specific things or stress about the perfect conditions before you perform a ritual. Awareness and intention are all you really need.

I've burned my sh*t under a Full Moon on a tropical beach using a cast iron cauldron, but I've also done it on my front porch during a Canadian snowstorm with a Dollar Store ashtray—both were impactful in their own way. While I don't *require* accessories for a ritual, it feels auspicious to light a candle or set out some crystals to do one. Our feelings are fueled when we seduce our senses with beautiful or yummy-smelling accessories. Layering different components can enhance your ritual experience (kind of like how wearing a cute outfit can make working out a bit more tolerable).

DON'T BE FOOLED BY THE ROCKS THAT I GOT (CRYSTALS 101)

◇◇◇

Did you know Adele calms her nerves with crystals while performing? Or that Victoria Beckham's fashion collection featured secret pockets in the pants made specifically to hold crystals? And that NBA star Dennis Rodman was once accused of stealing a 400-pound amethyst crystal from a yoga studio?

Crystals have been having a moment for a few years now, and although you can find them everywhere, it's important to know what to look for (and, more importantly, what to avoid) when you work with crystals.

But, like, how do they work? Every animate and inanimate object has a unique vibrational frequency—the result of atoms and molecules moving—that can be measured in hertz (Hz). The frequency of a human body is unstable and easily altered, ranging from 4 to 15 Hz. The Earth vibrates at a base frequency of 7.83 Hz. Whether a crystal is grown in a lab or comes from the ground, it has an incredibly stable frequency that never shifts because it is formed in a defined and repeating geometric pattern of molecules, with some crystals vibrating at over 32,000 Hz. Crystals are fixed while we are in flux.

The higher your vibrational frequency, the cleaner and clearer you feel—physically, emotionally, and spiritually. Because our frequencies are not fixed (like a crystal or, for that matter, a chair or umbrella), our vibes are easily influenced by the energy around us. Think about how you feel physically after eating an apple versus a hotdog, or the emotional impact of a hug versus an argument. What (and who) we interact with will have an impact on us—and this is where crystals come in.

All crystals (based on their size, shape, and type) have a stable frequency and signature vibration that never changes. A rule in physics states that when two frequencies are put together, the stronger, more stable vibration will dominate, causing any mutable frequencies to align with it. That's how these stones work with humans: a crystal's fixed and consistent vibration—as well as the inherent qualities of its unique frequency—influences our more pliant energetic field, and our lower vibration adjusts to match it. When you come into contact with a crystal, its vibration interacts with the vibrations of the cells in your body.

The energy emitted by crystals doesn't decompose like organic matter over time, which is why they're so prevalent in modern technology (like the silicon used in computers). The oldest dated material on the planet is a 4.4-billion-year-old crystal, and humankind has been drawn to the power of ceremonial crystals for thousands of years. From preparing for battle to repelling evil, our ancestors turned to crystals for guidance, luck, healing, and spiritual connection. In 1880, French physicist Pierre Curie (Marie Curie's husband) created electricity when applying pressure to quartz, topaz, and tourmaline. This phenomenon, called the piezoelectric effect, is why crystals are used in modern technology, like satellites and cell phones. Today, crystals have even made their way into our skincare routines, with jade face rollers and ruby-infused exfoliants purported to smooth and nourish skin.

Even if you doubt the efficacy of a crystal's energetic properties (but why would you?), the meaning you imbue in a stone makes it work in a ritual. Selecting a crystal with certain energetic properties—manifesting luck, soothing a broken heart, igniting courage—centers you in what you require in that moment. Crystals are a talisman that offer empowerment, protection, or connection by igniting something within us, like motivation, reassurance, or relief. Even if it's due to a placebo effect, crystals still make people feel better. (Also, let's not knock the placebo effect—it's real. Pharmaceutical studies have shown that administering placebo medication activates parts of our brain to release natural pain-relieving chemicals into the body.)

Rock Shopping

When it comes to buying crystals, don't worry about picking the perfect stone—let your intuition bring the right crystal to you. Long gone are the days where you could find only a smattering of stones at that one yoga studio that reeked of patchouli. If possible, visit a store (in person or online) that specializes in gems and take your time exploring what they have to offer. The impact of your rituals will be deepened and your intentions can be clarified as you shop for crystals. Ideally, you should buy from a merchant who knows where their crystals come from and how they're mined. Raw crystals look more like rocks than the shiny tumbled crystals that catch our eye, but raw crystals are often more powerful because they haven't been treated and stripped of their potency. That said, I have both in my collection. You can also buy crystals in the shape of a point or pyramid (I'll expand on Sacred Geometry in Chapter 9), and they vary in size from tiny chips to a massive geode, which is a crystal hidden inside a rock, like a geological Kinder Surprise.

It's good to have a sense of what you want to accomplish with the help of your crystal beforehand. Do you need to focus on a project? Do you want to boost your luck? Are you grieving a loss? Getting a sense of what you need from your stone will help you with your purchase while clarifying your intentions. Google will find you millions of articles about which stones align with whatever chakra or astrological sign, but that stuff is often a marketing gimmick rather than a rule—you'll instinctively be drawn to certain crystals, so let your gut be your guide. If you're in a physical store, do some crystal speed-dating—pick up a stone and wrap your hands around it, noticing how it makes you feel physically, emotionally, and energetically. A lot of crystals are multipurpose, so you don't have to invest in dozens of different types. Grab a few stones that speak to you, and you'll be good to go.

Every crystal has its own distinct characteristics and spiritual properties, and you can choose a stone based on your mood, preference, or need. If you want to work with crystals but aren't sure where to begin, the following are some great starter stones:

Clear Quartz

Clear quartz is like the quarterback of your crystal team, amplifying the vibrational properties of every stone around it. As the name suggests, it's clear in color and, while it may not look as snazzy as a sparkly piece of pyrite, clear quartz does a lot of heavy energetic lifting. This champion healer is easily programmable with any and all intentions, fostering the focus and motivation you need to realize them. It can also purify a person or place, making it a great healing crystal. If you buy only one stone, make it a clear quartz.

Amethyst

Amethyst is another MVP, and it's extremely popular because it's so gorgeous and versatile. Ideal for cosmic connections and deeply divine sleep, amethyst transmutes negative vibes, leaving you feeling calm and grounded—perfect for tapping into your intuition or connecting with the spiritual realm. Its vibrant violet hues make amethyst the perfect crystal to display in your space, as stunning as it is powerful.

Citrine

Citrine is all about that money, honey. A beautiful, sunny stone of abundance, citrine is a manifesting powerhouse (it's also known as the merchant's stone) that can be applied to any area of life that you're ready to expand. Its golden orange and yellow tones make it a pretty addition to any rock collection, but citrine's confident, empowering, and optimistic energy are what make it an energetic toolbox essential.

Smoky Quartz

Smoky quartz is a workhorse that gets in there to get the job done. Are you feeling anxious? Carry a piece of smoky quartz. Do you need protection? Smoky quartz has your back (and front). Is there energetic smog surrounding you? Smoky quartz is like smokeless sage, transforming your negative energy (and that of your space) into something more positive. Share whatever your intention is with smoky quartz and let your rock do the rest.

Black Obsidian

Black stones may look ominous, but they are the ultimate energetic bodyguards—and black obsidian is the leader of the pack. It repels negativity and envelops you in the protective energy of the Earth while fortifying you in your truth. Black obsidian balances the energies around it, acting as crowd control for chaotic vibes. This serious stone means business, helping you call in confidence and stability when you need it most.

Rose Quartz

Dim the lights and crank up the Sade: rose quartz is here to be your personal Cupid. But this gentle pink stone is about so much more than sexy times. Rose quartz wants you to fall in love with *yourself*. Its calm, soothing energy encourages you to commit to your personal growth and can help heal the ache of any heart. Whether you're grieving a relationship that ended or a person who passed, rose quartz brings you peace and compassion as you recover.

Selenite

Selenite is the Molly Maid of crystals, cleaning everything in its path. The extraordinarily high vibes emanating from this otherworldly wonder make it the perfect energetic booster for all of your other crystals. Selenite encourages you to move forward with calm confidence and leave the past behind, which aligns beautifully with the Burn Your Sh*t Full Moon ritual (and, fun fact, selenite is named after Selene, Goddess of the Moon). Let your selenite work its magic, clearing out bad vibes to restore peace and power.

Some crystals are better suited for specific intentions, objectives, or needs than others. Here's a brief primer to help you decide what will work best for you.

For calm: If you find yourself drowning in dread or paralyzed by doubt, grab some kyanite, aquamarine, blue lace agate, or fluorite. These stress-soothers quiet an anxious mind, allowing calm energy to enter. When insomnia strikes, reach for howlite, lepidolite, or moonstone to ease your sleep struggles.

For courage: To face life's challenges with confidence and clarity, try carrying around a tiger's eye, amazonite, or garnet. You'll get a boost of energetic strength from these motivating stones as they support you when times get tough.

For healing: Your mind, body, and spirit will benefit from the nurturing vibes offered by hematite, pink opal, and amber. The uplifting, tranquil energy of these stones will support you in navigating illness, grief, and pain. Amethyst and clear quartz are also outstanding stones to help you heal.

For love: Nothing beats the harmonious, loving frequency of rose quartz when it comes to matters of the heart, but red jasper, kunzite, and rhodochrosite come close. They all promote empathy, compassion, and loving tenderness for others and, most importantly, for yourself. If your libido needs a boost, your best bet is to stock up on carnelian.

For abundance: If you're ready to make your own luck and manifest abundance, stick some jade, pyrite, or green aventurine in your wallet. These stones invite prosperity into your life by dissolving self-doubt and fortifying a growth mindset. And remember, you can't go wrong with the ultimate money-magnet stone, citrine.

For protection: If your black obsidian needs backup, get your hands on some shungite, malachite, or black tourmaline to banish toxic vibes. Whether you need protection from the electromagnetic waves from your computer or the salty mojo from your mother-in-law, these powerful stones are like spiritual armor, helping you feel safe. (Pro tip: Soak these babies in brown rice overnight to remove the energetic sewage they absorb in the call of duty, and then toss the rice.)

How you work with your crystals is up to you. You can arrange them on your altar if you have one (we'll get to altars in a minute), or spread them around your space. Put one (or more!) by your bedside, at your office, in your living room, or anywhere that feels stagnant. Intuitively select a few and stick them in your car, your purse, or even your bra. Try placing one on a certain part of your body or sit quietly as you hold it (crystals make great meditation buddies). Buy a crystal pendant to beautify your altar or to use as a divination tool in your rituals (more on this in Chapter 11). Some people throw a few rose quartz crystals in their bath to soak in the stone's calm, loving energy. Others get their crystal fix with amethyst-infused water bottles. But please, for the love of Goddess, don't go plopping crystals directly into water you'll be drinking, because many of them are toxic in raw form or if they break. Malachite, for example, is 57 percent copper and can cause diarrhea if ingested to excess (no crystal is worth potentially crapping your pants in public). A safer and more powerful way to turbocharge your rocks is to create a crystal grid, putting them in an intentional pattern that boosts the frequency and gives extra healing or protection to a person, place, or thing (I'll expand on crystal grids in Chapter 9).

One of the easiest—and most powerful—ways to connect with the vibrational frequency of a crystal is to wear it as jewelry, close to your skin. This is how I prefer to absorb their energy, and I turned to an expert to help find the best stone for me. I chose a store that specialized in matching rare crystals with a person's energy, where they do a vibrational analysis to match you with your stone (like Harry Potter's magic wand choosing him). During the analysis, I closed my eyes as the sales associate held up a few options. For the first crystal, I felt nothing. The second one elicited a few tingles in my tummy.

The third one nearly knocked me off my chair. Of course, it was the most expensive of the three (I hadn't spent that much money on myself since buying a plane ticket to Australia thirty years earlier). My best friend reminded me how transformative *that* investment had been and held my hand as I pushed through the nausea to pay for my necklace. The crystal I chose (or rather, the one that chose me) is called scapolite, and it's breathtaking. When I first placed it around my neck, I felt energy radiating through my chest with such intensity that I had to wear the pendant backward for a few hours to acclimate. I was informed that scapolite is a motivating crystal of achievement and transformation, excellent for stimulating self-discipline and overcoming self-sabotage. It helps release old karma and baggage so a new path can be forged with determination and confidence.

My stunning scapolite changed my life. I wore it every day, and it became part of my signature style, like my glasses or red lipstick. I finally finished writing my first book (one that I'd been working on for a few years). I redid my website and started booking media appearances. My confidence in my work skyrocketed as my profile elevated exponentially. This piece of jewelry expanded my expectations of what I'm worth and what is possible. It opened the door for more abundance to enter my life because I showed myself (and the Universe) that I was a worthy investment. I've since added to my collection, and each piece has brought me to a new place, professionally and personally.

You can have five crystals or five hundred. They might adorn a beautiful ring or sit loose in a bowl. The key to connecting with their power lies in the intentions you set for them—give your crystals a job to do. Whether they're being tasked with supporting you in your healing, manifesting your desires, or just feeling happier, your crystals benefit from being programmed with a purpose. If you skip this step, don't worry—their vibrations will still impact you. But when you assign a crystal a certain role in a particular aspect of your life, you're encouraging and enhancing the alignment of your frequencies. Besides, you aren't so much activating the power within your stones as you are clarifying your goals for *yourself.* Your intentions will likely change over time, so be sure to let your crystals know there's a change in plan as you continue to co-create in a new direction.

Again, these are only suggestions. If you simply want a beautiful display of crystals that make your heart light up every time you see them, that's fantastic. There is no right or wrong way to work with crystals. Cleansing and charging them, however, is another matter . . .

Crystal Care

Although they're just sitting there, your crystals are working hard and will need a little R&R from time to time. Clearing (also known as *cleansing* or *charging*) works to rebalance and replenish the stone's energetic integrity. Crystals conduct and absorb energy. For example, citrine conducts abundant, generative energy while rose quartz is a conductor for loving energy. Other crystals, such as black obsidian, absorb negative energy. We have interactive energetic exchanges with our crystals, which is why we have to clear them on a regular basis. Crystals are electromagnetic oscillators, and their natural frequency can get knocked off kilter when exposed to energies with a higher amplitude, such as the electromagnetic fields of a computer or energy released during a healing session (it's like radio interference). Clearing brings a crystal's vibration back to its natural state.

Holding crystals under running tap water for a few minutes or sticking them in a bowl of sand reintroduces the natural elements, as does placing crystals on an open windowsill to let them bask in a cool breeze or resting them near a lit candle's fiery glow. But you have to be mindful of how the elements might affect your crystals.

While moldavite is cleansed and charged by the Sun, amethyst, sapphire, celestite, smoky quartz, rose quartz, fluorite, citrine, and howlite aren't fans of direct sunlight (you don't have to hide them away, just keep them off windowsills). If you're using water to clean your crystals, make sure they can handle it—more porous crystals will weaken and break if they hang out in water (anything ending in -*ite* generally doesn't like water, including malachite, pyrite, calcite, hematite, fluorite, and selenite). Fortunately, you can easily clean your crystals with other crystals—selenite is the gold standard because it's self-cleaning *and* self-charging, readily available, and fairly affordable. Place crystals on top of a selenite slab (they range in size from a postage stamp to a pizza box) or buy a selenite lamp (similar to a Himalayan salt lamp) and gather your crystals around its gentle warmth. Citrine and amethyst are also energetic vacuum cleaners that remove vibrational debris from their crystal companions.

Smudging and sound rituals (see Chapter 3) are both great ways to rebalance your crystals, but you can also stick them in a bowl of brown rice for a few days to absorb negative energy (like a cell phone that's been dropped in water). Some people recommend doing this with salt, but I would never do so because it can be too abrasive on the stone's energy (like wiping off mascara with nail polish remover). Salt may cause a crystal to crack, and the composition of certain stones (such as sodalite, which contains aluminum, or pyrite, which contains sulfur) can be harmful to bare skin. Same goes for sticking gems in soil: too many variables (such as excessive moisture in the ground) could mess with them. I'll sometimes place my crystals on the surface of an indoor plant's soil, but I much prefer to harness the energy of La Luna by putting them under a Full Moon (sometimes outside, but usually inside on a window ledge because: Canada). The

Moon's energy is strong enough to find them even when it's hiding behind clouds or not within view of your stones. Once you get the hang of cleansing your crystals with one method, experiment with other ways to see what works best for you. Regardless of how you do it, the intentional act of tending to your crystals goes a long way in cultivating a lifelong love affair.

Some crystals get along better than others, so it's important to consider how you store them (assuming they're not always on display or stuck in your bra). I have dozens of crystals that I've collected over the years scattered around my home, so storage really isn't an issue for me. If you have a crystal obsession (and listen, I get it!), you can store them until needed, rotate them based on the season (or mood) you're in, or bring them out only during rituals. Keep them in breathable containers, wooden bowls, cloth pouches, or jewelry boxes. Buy storage containers with dividers from a craft store and organize them by color, type, or even intention (this can get tricky with multipurpose stones). If you're brand new to crystals, consider starting a little photo album on your phone to easily identify your stones, taking a picture of the stone alongside the identification card that comes with it. Taking the time to categorize your stones can help you avoid frustration down the road as your collection grows (I know from experience).

What if you spend all that time choosing and sorting and charging the ultimate crystal for every occasion and then one *gulp* breaks? Let's say you get a little overzealous with the smudge stick and knock a stone off your altar? Or you fumble trying to put on your favorite crystal pendant? What if you wake up one morning to find one stone just kind of snapped in half? Reader, I have experienced all of these things and, let me tell you, I was devastated (not to mention freaked out) every time.

First things first: a broken crystal does not equal a curse, bad luck, or an omen of any kind. The only negative about a crystal breaking is how crappy it makes you feel when it happens. Also, ditch any guilt you're feeling if you broke your crystal. Part of that gem's role might be reminding you that you're a human being doing the best you can and mistakes happen, presenting you with an opportunity to practice forgiveness.

Rather than being a cause for concern, a broken stone can be a positive indicator that the crystal has completed the job or intention that you assigned to it. Maybe it was filled to capacity from absorbing and transforming the negative energy (from you or your environment) and splitting open signaled the completion of that crystal's cycle. Perhaps your stone's time with you was simply over.

However your crystal may break, you have a few options: keep using it, glue it back together, or say goodbye. When my pendant broke, the stone was fractured and too fragile to wear, but I kept it tucked away to use as a pendulum (more on those in Chapter 11). It kind of felt like I was retiring a champion thoroughbred to enjoy its remaining days in the ease of greener pastures. I've never tried gluing a broken crystal, but if you attempt it, make sure you (carefully!) use a superglue rather than a hot glue gun or crafting glue.

My preferred method of dealing with a broken crystal is to say goodbye with (of course!) a ritual. In the past I've buried crystals in my yard, but I live in the 'burbs, where the soil quality is crappy, so I've started going on little hikes in the woods for my crystal release ritual. I find a nice secluded spot, dig a little hole in the ground with the spoon I bring from my kitchen, hold my crystal to my heart as I express my gratitude for all it has done for me, and then nestle it into the hole and cover it with dirt, returning the stone to its Earthly home. By infusing this situation with ceremonial energy, I'm paying respect not only to my hard-working crystal but also to its creator, Mother Earth. A ritual to say goodbye also helps me process any emotions, such as sadness or guilt.

I was very freaked out the first time one of my crystals cracked in half on its own. Many years ago, in the *very* early days of Google, I was searching random stuff one night when I couldn't sleep and ended up reading about serial killers, weird sex cults, and all sorts of other garbage nobody should read (especially in the middle of the night). I woke up the next day in a cloud of gloom. My limbs felt heavy, and I was on the verge of tears, consumed with a sense of hopelessness, which is very unlike me. I dragged myself to the kitchen and there on the table beside my still-open laptop was my favorite crystal (a lapis lazuli the size of a golf ball) broken into two pieces.

Lapis lazuli promotes calm and loving vibes, but it's also fiercely protective. When provoked with negative energy, its inner mama bear comes out. I didn't know any of this when I first saw my busted stone. All I knew was that my prettiest crystal was broken, just like me and everything else in the world (did I mention I was marinating in despair?). I called a friend who specializes in crystals, and she assured me that my lapis lazuli had simply done its job (and done it well) by sucking up most of the negative vibes I'd summoned with my late-night googling. By cracking open, my crystal also served to get my attention and point out that I likely needed a thorough energetic cleansing to clear away any residual darkness. She advised me to thank my stone before burying it, take a cleansing sea-salt bath, and smudge my space—and also to step away from Google. It worked: the next day I felt more like myself and vowed to stay off the internet after midnight (which I managed to do . . . until Instagram was invented).

As with any ritualistic tool, the more you work with your crystals and understand their characteristics, the more strategically you can use them. When you pair a crystal with a ritual, you give that crystal a purpose. And it's not the crystal doing all the work; it's simply one of nature's divine tools helping you to tune in to your own intuition, recalibrate your vibrational frequency, and make your own magic.

COUNTING CARDS (INCORPORATING ORACLE & TAROT DECKS)

◇◇◇

I read tarot cards for a living, so they're an obvious component of my rituals, but you don't need to be a professional reader to incorporate tarot into yours.

Every challenge or opportunity can be highlighted or informed through the cards, and you can use tarot, oracle, or even a standard poker deck. The teachings of tarot in particular have guided us for centuries because tarot is rooted in archetypes that reflect the human experience (that's why their meanings resonate with all of us). Each card you pull tells a different story, and together they tell the story of you. But tarot and oracle cards don't tell you what to do; they're more like a conversation starter between you and your intuition. Rather than giving predictions, they deliver messages from your soul.

You don't have to memorize every single card—just grab a deck and start pulling! I still don't know the names and numbers of most of the Minor Arcana cards in my deck (that I've had for *over thirty years*). If you asked me to describe the Seven of Wands, I have no clue what it looks like. But if you *show me* the Seven of Wands, I'll talk about it for hours. When it comes to cartomancy, it's about learning the story (not memorizing definitions). You'll eventually develop a dialogue with your deck, and your interpretations will be just as relevant as the standard interpretations.

An easy way to introduce cards into your life is to pick one every morning. Knock the deck (it's like an energetic palate cleanser) and give it a good shuffle, and then cut the cards in half with your nondominant hand, which is a shortcut to your intuition. Ask yourself, *What do I need to know today?* and choose one card. Take a moment to really look at the imagery and consider how it makes you feel. Journal your first impressions before consulting the little how-to booklet that comes with your deck, and then put the card aside and go about your day. At bedtime, pick up your card and reflect on how its meaning or message showed up in your day. This is a fun and easy way to learn about your cards. You can also pull a card to start or end any ritual. I usually finish with a card, like taking a little party favor from the experience.

You might use one deck or have a whole collection to choose from. Let your intuition guide you. The basics of tarot can be found in the guide that comes with your deck, but if you want to delve deeper, get your hands on a book written by a proven and established tarot reader. (Spoiler: My second book will be that book!) However you choose to work with the cards and whichever deck you choose, remember: you aren't abdicating responsibility of your life to a piece of paper. Tarot and oracle cards are a tool that empowers you to make the best decision for yourself—what you do with the information is up to you.

WHAT'S THAT SMELL? (INCORPORATING HERBS, OILS, & OTHER BOTANICALS)

◇◇◇

The act of burning herbs to clear and cleanse energy is deeply rooted in cultures around the world. You'll learn how to smudge in Chapter 3, but you need to know what you're working with before you get to work.

People commonly turn to sage for cleansing rituals—for good reason. Plants and herbs have been burned in purification ceremonies for centuries, and a 2007 study in India found that the smoke of medicinal herbs reduced airborne bacteria in confined spaces by 94 percent, with the antibacterial effects lasting up to 24 hours. Although sage wasn't included in the 2007 study, it has a well-documented history of helping people feel better and gain clarity, and was used in ancient Greece and Rome as a traditional herbal remedy. Recent research suggests that white sage contains compounds known to activate the receptors in our brains responsible for lowering stress, boosting mood levels, and mitigating pain.

Respect the Ritual

Smudging ceremonies are most commonly associated with North American Indigenous cultures, and for centuries, First Nations people have been (and continue to be) persecuted as they fight to preserve their language and culture. To see sacred ceremonies commodified into a vacuous trend is offensive and hurtful; therefore, it's essential that non-Indigenous people take the time to learn the deeper meaning of these practices before undertaking them, honoring the history and people behind the ceremony.

If you're non-Indigenous, you can still appreciate and partake in ceremonies like smudging provided you're culturally conscious. Purchase sage that was harvested sustainably (preferably from an Indigenous seller), acknowledge the origin of the ritual, and thank the Creator as you honor the importance of the ceremony. Sacred medicines are viewed by Indigenous cultures as gifts from the Creator to support the healing of our mind, body, and spirit. Protocols may vary, but the ceremonies typically share similar tools, methods, and principles as a means of releasing negative energies while promoting spiritual healing.

Now, before you go rummaging in the spice rack, be aware that the sage we smudge with is very different from what we use to season chicken. The *Salvia* plant family contains over 900 varieties of sage (its name comes from the Latin word meaning "to save" or "to heal"), but dried white sage is most commonly used in smudging ceremonies. You can buy dried white sage wrapped in a bundle (also called a smudge stick) or as loose leaves. Either will produce the necessary smoke, but the tightly packed leaves in smudge sticks can be tricky to light (and keep lit). When I smudge, I untie the sage bundle and burn the loose leaves so the air can get at them more easily, allowing for a stronger burn. Elders also suggest that crumbling the leaves activates the plant's natural healing powers, so I gently break up the leaves with my hands before starting. Both methods work—it's a matter of personal preference and availability rather than right or wrong.

Heads up: sage smells *a lot* like marijuana. If you'd rather your home not smell like a college frat party, sage sprays are an option. You can also combine other dried plants with your sage (more on that in a bit). In 2016, Australian researchers published a study confirming that the smoke from the burning of sacred mixtures can improve your cognitive health, while research out of Brazil documents the effectiveness of these traditional remedies for heightening your mood. If you're mixing sage leaves with other aromatics, make sure you purchase them from a reliable source to avoid a toxic blend.

Smoke on its own moves out the energetic goo, but combining the unique energy of other plants enhances the cleansing qualities of the smoke. You can burn the dried plants on their own or add them to a smudge stick or fireproof bowl filled with sage (Chapter 3 gives you all the details about smudging). Consider adding a few of the following botanicals to your smudging ritual:

Cedar is one of the most sacred medicines in Indigenous culture, commonly used in smudge ceremonies to bless a new home. It acts as a purifier to chase away negative energy to make room for something better.

Juniper was burned in ancient temples during purification rituals and is known today for clearing out anxious energy while drawing in prosperity.

Lavender has a history of being burned to clear the air in infirmaries; its gentle and calming fragrance uplifts the energy of any place or person, inviting lightness and relaxation.

Rosemary is commonly used in purification rituals because it invites fresh starts. It's the perfect aromatic when embarking on a new path.

Sweetgrass comes braided and, along with sage, cedar, and tobacco, is one of the four sacred Indigenous plants. It's believed to be the hair of Mother Earth, with the three sections of the braid representing mind, body, and soul (or, alternatively, love, kindness, and honesty). The sweet smell is thought to appeal to good spirits, inviting their positivity and goodness into your space. Typically, sage is burned first to cleanse and purify, followed by sweetgrass to attract good energy and spirits.

If sage and sweetgrass aren't your thing, try palo santo. But before you reach for your lighter, it's essential to understand and acknowledge the history and spiritual meaning of palo santo in ceremony, because Indigenous communities were ostracized or persecuted for centuries when they worked openly with this sacred medicine. Marketing and practicing it as a New Age trend without honoring its roots is disrespectful. Palo santo (which translates to "holy wood") comes from the wild *Bursera graveolens* tree in Central and South America. Its use can be traced back to the Inca Empire, where shamans ritualistically burned bundles of palo santo sticks. The essential oil was applied to the skin for protection, healing, spiritual purification, and heightened connection to Spirit—a tradition that continues today in many communities, particularly in Ecuador and Peru.

The *Bursera graveolens* tree be harvested only once it dies naturally—which can take decades—because the wood from living trees doesn't fully develop the signature scent. Unfortunately, many trees are being illegally chopped down so their natural oils can be extracted, chemically enhanced, and infused into random pieces of wood. Although you can buy palo santo anywhere, look for products sold by Indigenous-owned sellers who are transparent about their sources.

Palo santo can be burned on its own, but I find it an incredibly potent follow-up to smudging with sage. With hints of citrus and mint accenting its sweet, woody scent, palo santo is wonderfully intoxicating. It not only introduces positive energy after sage banishes the bad stuff but also makes your space smell less like a dorm room. The most common way to use palo santo is to burn it as you would a smudge stick (I'll provide a thorough how-to in Chapter 3).

Incense

If you can't smudge but need to bring a cleansing calm to your space—like when your toddler is having a meltdown or the in-laws arrive unexpectedly—try lighting some incense. Smell is the only one of our senses wired directly to our brains. The link between scent and brain response is primal and instantaneous, and that's why a whiff of Drakkar Noir instantly transports me back to my grade nine prom. Typically made from resins, dried plants, or essential oils, incense comes in different forms, such as sticks or cones, and releases a wispy stream of ambrosial smoke when lit, instantly shifting your mood and the energy of your space.

Science confirms the potent power of this mystical smoke. In 2008, researchers from Johns Hopkins University and the Hebrew University in Jerusalem determined that burning pure frankincense (resin from the *Boswellia* plant) stimulates parts of the brain to alleviate anxiety and depression, and a 2018 study by the University of Belgrade indicates that both frankincense and myrrh have proven to be as effective as steam for sterilization. Lavender incense has demonstrated sedative effects, while rose increases serotonin levels to help alleviate headaches. These effects are for natural incense that is free from the damaging chemical additives found in synthetic incense (more on that soon), which can aggravate health problems, including allergies and asthma.

Burning incense has played an integral role in rituals for thousands of years. The use of incense can be traced back to early civilizations in China, Mesopotamia, India, Japan, and Egypt, where it was known as the "Fragrance of the Gods." Incense was burned to connect with the spirit world, repel negative energies, and fumigate funky smells (those pharaoh tombs get rank), and not much has changed since then. From Buddhist and Hindu temples to Orthodox and Catholic churches, incense is still a key component of many religious practices. But you don't have to belong to an organized religion (or even leave your home) to bring these scents into your rituals.

Buy incense in stores and online, but be aware that, as with sage and other aromatics, not all incense is created equal. Choose incense that is created from the most natural sources possible; any "fragrance" or "perfume" ingredients are most likely synthetic and will negate (if not worsen) potential health benefits. Look for all-natural incense, made with plant-based ingredients and real essential oils.

Similar to crystals, the energetic properties of incense all serve a different purpose. Nag champa is a fusion of fragrances used in sacred spaces (and almost every yoga studio) and known for cleansing negative energy (so are moldavite and dragon's blood). When it's time to get to business, fire up your focus with amber, bergamot, or lemongrass. And if you're ready to get down to *business* (aka sexy times), spark up some patchouli, jasmine, or copal. Sandalwood, lavender, and vanilla are like somatic lullabies if you can't sleep (ignite as you prepare for bed and extinguish before tucking yourself in). For anxious times, turn to vetiver, frankincense, or myrrh to ease your mind.

Once you've figured out your preferred scent, you'll need to determine how you're going to burn it. Incense (or joss) sticks resemble birthday sparklers, and they're the most popular form of incense to burn because they're so easy to use: simply place the stick (which is coated in incense) into a holder and light the tip of it. Once it catches, gently blow/fan out the flame and the smoldering stick will release a fragrant smoke for about an hour, leaving ash behind.

Incense cones, a combo of essential oils, and combustible ingredients, are also common, but they burn much faster and are *a lot* smokier. You'll need a fireproof base to burn these little smokestacks because they get extremely hot (people often place their holder on a layer of salt or sand to absorb the heat—I personally stick with sticks for this reason). To burn an incense cone, place it pointy side up and light the tip. Similar to the stick, you (gently!) fan or blow out the flame after a few seconds, allowing the remaining ember to smolder down to its base over the next thirty minutes.

Incense powders, coils, and resins can also be burned, but these require charcoal discs or special containers to house them, and I don't recommend any of these methods unless you're an incense pro (or married to a firefighter).

However you choose to burn incense, keep things safe by doing it in a well-ventilated area, away from anything flammable, extinguishing the embers by cutting off the tip or putting it under water (if you won't be using it again), and never leaving it unattended or within reach of kids and critters.

Essential Oils

You can easily tap into the ritual-boosting benefits of aromatherapy with essential oils. These plant-derived compounds are highly concentrated, and they play an important role in our physical, emotional, and spiritual health. One quick sniff of an essential oil can activate your brain to release serotonin (the happy hormone), dopamine (the motivation hormone), or endorphins (the painkiller hormone).

Their emotional and physical effects are proven and profound, but you still have to do your homework when shopping for essential oils. Some of them are harmful to pregnant or nursing women, children, and pets, so be sure to do your own research or check with a health professional before working with these potent aromas. Buy from an established company (like a health food store) that partners with trusted suppliers. Most reputable companies package small quantities of essential oils in dark brown or blue glass bottles to preserve the quality and prevent oxidation. The label should list only a single ingredient, as well as the Latin name of the plant and the source country. Buying organic essential oils is one way to ensure certain protocols have been followed to keep the product as clean and pure as possible.

You can add a few drops of essential oil to water in a diffuser or use an essential oil–infused spray, lotion, or roll-on. Avoid applying essential oil directly to the skin, to minimize the risk of irritation— for that you need a carrier oil, like jojoba, to dilute it. Essential oils are available as a single scent or specific vibe-inducing blends (see Chapter 7 for a more detailed list of oils).

Consider the "why" of your ritual to help you choose an oil to complement it. Are you ready to jumpstart your morning ritual? Check out stimulating citrus oils like lemon, lime, or grapefruit. Does your evening meditation require a cozy comedown? You can't go wrong with ylang-ylang, chamomile, or vetiver. Whether you're mending a broken heart, preparing a huge presentation for work, or just need a good night's sleep, essential oils can support you on your path. And who wouldn't want that?

A CANDLE FOR
EVERY OCCASION

◇◇◇

You can bring the element of Fire into your ritual without sparking up herbs, sticks, or discs of charcoal. Candles have transported us from darkness into light for thousands of years, literally and spiritually. Used for survival and ceremony, candles are an essential tool as we celebrate, connect, grieve, and heal. The soft flickering of a candle can elevate a routine task to a sacred ceremony. Candles carry the energy to ignite your next chapter or transform your current situation. The flame of your candle can release what no longer concerns you or connect you to your dearly departed. They also look pretty and often smell good.

Ritual candles are available on Etsy or at any spirituality store. They're usually sold individually or as part of an intention-based spell kit that includes a crystal or some herbs along with step-by-step instructions. When you buy candles created specifically for rituals, they're about the size of a birthday candle and have a burn time of less than an hour. You can also get them in tealight form, infused with mini crystals and herbs. But if you'd rather use your favorite three-wick candle from Marshall's, that works, too. I buy my double-wooden-wick soy candles from a local seller, and they're not specifically made for rituals. The one I light when I'm writing is an intoxicating blend of myrrh, vanilla, bergamot, and patchouli. It's called Magik, and it lives up to its name.

Wherever you buy your candles, there are some health and safety considerations to keep in mind. Choose a clean-burning soy wax or beeswax candle with a wick that is either 100 percent cotton or wood. Even "premium grade" candles containing paraffin or petroleum release chemicals into the air when burned, so avoid them if possible. You can match a candle's scent to your cosmic intention—like citrus for motivation—but please ensure the scented or essential oils are free from phthalates and paraben (there's no point getting a natural soy candle that's been doused in chemicals). The beeswax candles that I use during my Full Moon ritual emit a deliciously soothing, natural honey fragrance without any additives whatsoever—plus, they keep the bees in business!

To prevent fire or serious injury, always trim the wick to a quarter inch before lighting it and keep debris out of the wax pool. Try not to burn your candle for more than a few hours at a time and be sure to set it on a heat-resistant surface, away from drafts. Never leave your candle unattended, and obviously, keep kids and pets away. Don't extinguish your candle with water (just blow it out gently or use a snuffer), and always let the wax harden before relighting, touching, or moving it.

In the same way the color of your crystals holds significance (for example, green jade invites luck), you can color-coordinate a candle to your ceremony. Aligning your candle's scent or color to a specific intention can boost the potency of any ritual. Use black candles for protection, and green for fertility. Brown candles are grounding, while red incites passion and motivation. Lighting a blue candle can encourage creativity or communication. Pink is great for anything related to love or forgiveness (of self or others). Both white and purple candles invite connection with Spirit and our intuition, while orange and yellow are associated with success, self-confidence, and happiness.

Candles aren't magical on their own, but they are a beautiful way to incorporate the natural elements along with your own energy into a ritual. Use them to bring light to your life lessons and emblazon your manifestations.

WHATEVER FLOATS YOUR METAPHYSICAL BOAT

◇◇◇

The tools I've mentioned are just a starting point for you to assemble your own ritual toolkit. Add anything that compels you, such as feathers and shells or food and drink. Ceremonial items can be pretty much anything—from a piece of yarn to a tube of lipstick—as long as they're meaningful to you. A ritual might feature a specific sculpture or a bowl of salt, a sacred spoon or a witchy broom. You're only limited by your imagination.

TEMPLES & TOYOTAS (DEDICATE YOUR SPACE WITH AN ALTAR)

◇◇◇

Now that you've gathered your ceremonial supplies, it's time to give them a home. An altar is a designated space made sacred by your energy. Altars tell your story and declare your intentions—they reflect who you are and where you're going. Your altar is where you make your magic.

Altars have traditionally been used in religious ceremonies for millennia, and we still create them for rituals without realizing it. A table laden with gifts at a baby shower, your birthday cake ablaze with candles, or the Christmas tree adorned with precious ornaments collected over time—they're all altars. Do you already have an assortment of curated items placed lovingly on a windowsill or bookshelf? Guess what? You've intuitively built an altar without even trying! The modern altar offers a spiritual sanctuary that is as unique as the person creating it. Because an altar is just an outward expression of your inner essence, there is no "right" or "wrong" way to make one, so have some fun with it. You can devote an entire room to carrying out your rituals or use a section of your kitchen counter. It can be a permanent fixture or a temporary altar you tuck away when you're done with it. You don't even need to stay indoors—a tree stump or large raised stone is a natural altar (weather permitting).

If you're starting from scratch, first consider the purpose of your altar. Is it in a quiet space to meditate? Will you carry out rituals? Celebrate the solstice? Manifest through journaling? All of the above? An altar dedicated to manifesting might contain crystals ideal for goal-setting. If your altar is a meditative space, include incense with a calming scent. For an altar used in rituals, arrange your ceremonial tools in a way that incites your senses. An altar is a symbol for self-care; when you assemble an altar, you're honoring yourself. Make it as pleasing as possible by feeding your senses with beautiful colors, textures, smells, and sounds. A beautiful scarf can act as an altar cloth, serving as a sacred decoration and protective layer for the surface it covers. Altar cloths can be any size, texture, or pattern that appeals to you. You can change altar cloths with the ritual or season, use the same one consistently, or not use them at all. A singing bowl (made of metal or crystal, it produces sustained sounds and vibrations when hit or circled with a wooden mallet) or bell can signal the beginning or conclusion of your ritual. Gather any personal objects that you're intuitively guided to add to your altar. A photo, statue, or piece of jewelry can be spiritually significant, but so can a keychain or ticket stub. These items are made sacred by the magical meaning imbued in them by you.

You may feel compelled to incorporate natural objects that honor Mother Earth and also intensify the alchemy of your ritual. Energy is grounded by Earth elements (stones, crystals, or flowers) and flows through a glass of water (or symbolic shell). Fire transforms the energy with candles. And Air (represented by feathers or incense) moves energy while creating a connection with Spirit.

Once you've found your altar objects, clear away any clutter from whatever area you're working with and lay down an altar cloth, if you're using one. Altars are a form of creative self-expression, so make your space as minimal or fancy as you wish. It can be as under-stated as a stone or candle that serves as a focal point during medita-tion or an elaborate crystal grid (see Chapter 9 for more on that). A linear thinker might compose a symmetrical altar with the largest or tallest item in the center and smaller pieces gathered around it in a circle. If your altar is seasonal, try decorating it with fresh flowers in the spring, seashells in the summer, a small pumpkin in autumn, and a fir wreath or bough in winter.

A more elaborate Earth-based altar could work with the four direc-tions, which is common in Indigenous cultures around the world. Think of your altar space as a circle divided into four quadrants rep-resenting north, east, south, and west. Each section corresponds to different elements and aspects of our lives: Earth is physical (stones); Water is emotional (shell), Fire is mental (candle), and Air is spiritual (feather). Assemble your altar within the actual coordinates if that appeals to you, but don't worry too much about aligning your ele-ments with a specific direction (for example, east and Air). Various configurations appear in different cultures, so there isn't a definitive practice or guideline.

An altar can be a permanent space, or it could be something you put together and put away as needed. Setting one up to stay for a while can be helpful, depending on your purpose. For example, dedicating an altar to your grief can bring immense comfort when you're mourning the passing of a person or pet (this is particularly helpful for children trying to process a death). Filling your space with pictures, notes, or mementos helps connect you to your love while grieving your loss. Whether you keep this kind of altar permanently or for a specified time, it becomes a safe space for your sadness to be felt and held.

Altars can infuse any daily activity with spiritual energy. Keep a deck of tarot or oracle cards in the middle of your altar and begin every day by pulling one card to give you a message (your personal "taroscope"). Another daily practice for your altar can focus on gratitude. Set a bowl in the middle of your altar, along with a pen or pencil and some slips of paper. Every evening, write something specific from your day that you're grateful for and place it in the bowl. For example, *I'm grateful to work with someone as funny as Barb* rather than *I'm grateful for my job*. Or *I'm grateful that I bit into the perfect apple for breakfast* instead of *I'm grateful for my health*. This kind of specificity helps your brain create new patterns of optimism. During challenging moments, you can pick some of those slips to remind you of the blessings in your life. You can also dedicate a jar to good news and review your high points at the end of the year. Altars serve as a visual representation of our beliefs and commitments, and focusing on your blessings is an easy way to invite more moments to be grateful for into your life.

If you're constantly on the move or short on space, portable altars are a handy solution. Keep your sacred supplies in a bag, box, or other container to grab on your way out the door. You might fashion a mobile altar out of a tray that can be carried from room to room. Or make a pocket altar by repurposing an empty breath mint tin, filling it with a shell, sprig of thyme, and tealight candle (the candle can symbolize Fire and Air, but you can also add a tiny down feather or piece of incense). I know an Indigenous Elder who leads Full Moon ceremonies, and her altar is a shoebox she keeps in the trunk of her car. As with everything in this book, it doesn't have to be fancy for it to work.

I have a few altars, and none of them were planned out in advance; they all just came together over time until one day I looked around and thought, *Wow . . . I guess these are my altars.* One is on a corner of my bedroom dresser. It has a twig resembling a wand that I found on a forest walk; a wooden box holding drumsticks (musical, not fried) given to me by a dear friend; some tealights infused with essential oils and mini crystals; and my prized crystal pendant necklaces, which are kept in separate velvet pouches (within each pouch are crystals for charging and clearing). I don't use an altar cloth, but the jewelry sits on a disc of birchwood that elevates it (the Latin root of altar, *alt rium,* means "high" and refers to a raised area of worship). In the center of my altar is a big clear quartz point that resembles a tower, guarding everything around it like a spiritual sentry. The only ritualistic action happening at this altar is choosing which necklace to wear in the morning, but every time I look at it, I'm reminded of who I am and how far I've come.

The altar in my office takes up an entire bookcase. Six shelves are full of artfully arranged statues, crystal pyramids and spheres, a fake crystal ball I bought at Target for a dollar, a few witchy books and oracle decks, palo santo sticks, special pieces of art, the abalone shell I use for smudging (filled with crystals), and some rocks from the lakeshore. This altar is in the background when I do tarot readings, and the vibe is witchy elegance. On my desk is another altar that nobody sees but me—it's a storage bin stuffed with my journal, smudging feather, tuning fork and crystal, deerskin rattle, various candles, my tarot deck, more crystals, and a homemade wand that doubles as a talking stick. It may not be as visually appealing as the other two altars, but it does the job of holding the most vital components of my energetic toolkit. It's more than a storage spot because I've deemed it as such: each item serves a ritualistic purpose, allowing me easy access for when I need to create a short-term shrine.

My final altar is a Burn Your Sh*t Kit that I keep in my laundry room (I have no clue why . . . that's just where it always ends up). This portable altar contains a feather, candle, pencil, paper, and crystal all tucked into a tiny bucket (aka cauldron), making it easy to transport for my Full Moon rituals.

Any setup can be a portal to the Divine—*you* sanctify the space with emotion and intention. The box that holds my tarot cards is an altar. The velvet pouch holding my tuning fork is an altar. I am an altar. Your home and your body can become temples if you treat them with reverence. Tend to your altar with loving care, whether it's a light dusting or a complete overhaul. Taking time to clean, clear, or reorganize your altar reinforces your intentions and reminds you of your purpose.

Your altar is a tool for your rituals—it's a place for meditating, visualizing, journaling, praying, grounding, divining, and connecting. Regardless of the gear you bring, remember that rituals begin in your mind. Your intention with any ceremony determines the efficacy of the outcomes—the tools you use simply enhance it. Whether it looks solemn and reverential or fun and quirky—an elaborate room dedicated to spiritual healing or a Tupperware container full of rocks kept in your car—your altar is an emotionally sacred space because it is for you and of you.

CHAPTER 3

CLEAN UP ON AISLE SIX! (CLEANSING WITH SAGE, SOUND, & CRYSTALS)

like to thoroughly clean my kitchen before I mess it up making a meal. And I can't get in a writing flow while my desk is in disarray. In feng shui, energy can't flow freely through the home when it's blocked by clutter, and Marie Kondo is famous for leading people to joyfully declutter their physical space, which in turn enhances their psychological state. There's something about starting with a clean slate that makes tasks easier and more enjoyable. Clearing bad mojo from your space (and yourself) is an important first step in preparing for any ceremony—and this cleansing act is itself a ritual that you can do whenever you want to change the energy around (or within) you.

The effects of intentionally clearing our energetic environment can be just as significant as tidying your room. We all know what bad vibes feel like, even if we can't see them. Sometimes it's blatant, like walking into a room where two people have been arguing ("You could cut the tension with a knife . . . "), or it can feel more subtle yet still undeniable. I stopped doing tarot readings in my home studio after a woman came in with such bad energy that even my husband (who obviously respects what I do but also identifies as woo-woo agnostic) felt it. Although she was smiling when I opened the door, I fought an urge to slam it in her face. The reading was fine, and she seemed pleasant enough, but I needed her *gone*. Her energy was inexplicably bad, and it's the only time I've had that reaction to a client. It didn't help that she stayed in my bathroom for twenty minutes after the reading, leading me to smudge (and Lysol) the entire house.

It's not just people that emit negativity. Years ago, my family visited a country that had recently been at war. The land was beautiful and the people were wonderful, but I was on the verge of tears and my kids barely slept while we were there. The malevolent chill in the air was palpable, which made sense after we left and I found out our accommodations had once been the epicenter of a literal battlefield.

From smudging to sound, cleansing rituals focus your mind and soothe your psyche—they're like a power wash for your soul. When stagnant or toxic energy builds up, it can affect other areas of your life and even manifest physically. I'll elaborate on protecting your energy in Chapter 11, but for now just keep in mind that negative energy breeds more negativity, which can affect your health and happiness if you don't keep it in check. Spiritual hygiene is just as essential as flossing your teeth or cleaning your oven.

When you're ready to smudge, prepare your sage leaves or smudge stick (see Chapter 2 for information about where and how to buy sage). Regardless of the form your sage comes in or what else you burn with it, you'll need a fireproof bowl or abalone shell. Abalone are marine mollusks found all over the world, and they incorporate the element of Water into your smudging ritual. (Pro tip: Smudging kits usually include a shell along with your sage.) Similar to oyster shells, abalone have a beautiful pearlescent interior, and they've been harvested for food and ceremonial purposes by North American Indigenous peoples for centuries. You can also buy a foldable wooden tripod stand made specifically for abalone shells, which I recommend because the shell does get warm, and the stand protects your furniture (plus it's a cute display when your shell isn't in use—mine holds some crystals on one of my altars). Although abalone shells are traditionally used in smudging ceremonies, your smudge bowl can be made of stone, metal, or tempered glass—any vessel that is able to hold loose sage leaves or catch the ashes produced by a smudge stick will suffice (you'll want those ashes for the end of your ritual . . . more on that in a minute). Even if you're holding your smudge stick like a flashlight, always have your shell or bowl handy in case you need to put it down during the ritual and to catch any wayward ashes.

Feathers are another familiar accessory in Indigenous smudging ceremonies, completing the connection with the elements by symbolizing Air. The cleansing smoke is wafted by the feather around a body, an item, or a room, and the stale or adverse energy is swept away. Birds are an integral part of Indigenous culture, and during smudging ceremonies, feathers also symbolically carry messages and intentions to the Creator. The eagle is believed to be in closest contact with the spirit world, and its feathers are revered, often gifted to respected Elders. Messages are also transported to the Creator on the wings of hawks, and hawk feathers are also highly prized. The wild turkey is one of the most prevalent birds in North American Indigenous culture—as a protector and food source—and their feathers are frequently used in smudging rituals. If you're going to use feathers, be aware that—whether you've bought or found them—there are laws in North America regulating the possession of migratory bird feathers without a permit in order to protect native bird species. In Canada, the relevant laws and regulations* include specific exemptions for Indigenous people, who also have the right to give away

---

* The Migratory Birds Convention Act and the Migratory Birds Regulations set out the rules governing the possession and use of migratory bird feathers in Canada.

or sell migratory bird feathers in certain circumstances. As a non-Indigenous person, your safest best to avoid issues is to use feathers of non-native bird species; also, avoid using feathers found in nature because, in addition to legal concerns, they need to be thoroughly sanitized to destroy lice, mites, and other creepy-crawlies. Whatever type of feather you use, make sure that you are allowed to have them and that they have been ethically (and legally!) sourced. Don't let a lack of feathers hold you back from smudging, though. The sacred smoke produced during your ritual can easily be wafted around you and your space with any alternative, including your hand.

Finally, you'll need a lighter or matches. Some people insist on wooden matches, but I just use a barbecue lighter, and I always have a glass of water nearby, just in case.

Now that you have your materials ready, it's time to prepare your space. Prior to smudging, you'll want to get rid of any clutter that might trap nasty energy and make it stagnant. Taking care of clutter will immediately alter how your room feels to you, and many people do this every night so they begin the next day in a calm state. (Note: I am not one of those people, although I do a quick decluttering before I smudge.) Clear countertops, tidy your desk, put away clothes—you get the idea. Before sparking up your sage, give bad mojo an escape route by cracking open windows and doors. If you smudge in an enclosed space, you're just shifting bad energy to another room rather than dispersing it (it's like having a bath in used water from the day before). You may want to disconnect the batteries from your smoke detector (I don't bother), but if you have enough windows and doors open, you probably don't need to. If you do disable it, avoid turning the stove or oven on, and make sure you set a reminder on your phone or write a sticky note (or both!) to put it back together once you've finished.

Ready to start smudging? Not so fast. There's one more step, and it's the most important part of any ritual: setting your intention. Ask yourself, *Why have I chosen to smudge today?* Your answer determines your intention, and your intention empowers your ritual. You might be smudging to clear the air after a difficult conversation or to celebrate the arrival of a new season. You may want to wipe the slate clean before moving into your new home or simply change your energy after a long day at work. Whatever your reason for smudging, make sure you have clarity before you begin—your intention will be reflected in your results.

For example, if you had family stay with you over the holidays and want to (literally and figuratively) clear the air once they leave, you could smudge while saying *I send all harmful energy and tension out to the light, welcoming love, peace, and positivity into my home.* Always include an ideal outcome with every intention because you want to fill the energetic vacuum you're creating with something better.

Close your eyes and take three deep, cleansing breaths, inhaling through your nose and exhaling out your mouth. Place a hand on your belly to feel it expand, making sure your shoulders aren't rising up to your ears. Say your intention aloud or in your head. Tune into your needs and ground yourself in the present moment with each breath to get the most out of your smudging experience. Do you feel calm and relaxed? *Now* you're ready to smudge.

Carefully light your smudge stick or ignite a few loose leaves in your smudge bowl. (Be patient. Sage can be slow to light.) Once the smudge stick or loose leaves catch fire, use your feather or hand to gently fan the sage until the flame goes out (try not to blow it out because that can send ashes flying). The embers will produce the swirling, sacred smoke that anchors your smudging ritual, so take your time with this step.

If you're using a smudge stick, a feather isn't really necessary because you can hold the stick like a wand to waft the smoke in your desired direction. If you're set on using a feather with your smudge stick, have a bowl out in case you need to tap the ashes. Once the lit medicine is producing enough smoke, begin smudging yourself by fanning the smoke toward you.

Start at the top of your head to imbue good thoughts. Move to your eyes, creating clarity of vision and receptivity to sacred insight. Bring the smoke to your mouth for positive discourse. Continue to your heart, inspiring loving kindness and heartwarming emotions. Move down the rest of your body as you impart strength, health, and wisdom upon yourself. Finish with the bottom of each foot before briefly turning around so your back is also touched by the lingering smoke. It's essential that you clear any energetic gunk from yourself before moving on to objects or spaces. If you're doing this ritual with friends or family, you can take turns smudging each other. The recipient stands in front of you with arms and legs extending out. Follow the same format, sweeping the smoke away from you and onto the person, head-to-toe and front-to-back, going down the length of the arms and legs, including soles of the feet.

You can then smudge any objects in need of clearing. I usually waft some smoke over my tarot cards, crystals, and altar items, but you can smudge your computer or car if you get the urge. Paint the air around your items with the smoke from your smudge stick or waft the smoke of loose-leaf sage with your feather (or hand) to cover the objects in smoke. You can also pass each object over the smoldering smudge bowl.

While you want to bathe people, animals, and yourself in the sacred smoke, the opposite is true when smudging an object or room. You need to get that funky mojo away from you. To waft the smoke, hold your dominant hand in front of you like you're about to shake someone else's hand, then move your hand (at the wrist or elbow) in a counterclockwise circle. Continue this circular motion as you reposition your hand so that your palm is facing your body, using the back of your hand to cycle the smoke away from you and onto an object or into a room. (When smudging yourself, you reverse this movement to a clockwise circle, and the palm of your hand carries the smoke in your direction.)

Now that your cell phone and grandma have been cleansed, it's time to purify your space. I was taught to start at the front door (which can be cracked open to help with ventilation) and then walk slowly through each room from left to right, starting with the rooms to the left of the front door (this helps banish the negative energy). Pay extra attention to corners, where energetic gunk can accumulate, and smudge all levels and areas of your home, including the garage. Imagine the smoke collecting all of the static and undesirable energy or entities, and ushering them out the open window. As you carry your vessel of smoking herbs, wafting the smoke away from you, revisit the intentions you set at the beginning of your ritual (for example, *Clear Fred's gross energy from my home and make space for someone better*). You may feel called to recite a mantra or prayer, or to repeat your intention (for example, *I send the oppressive energy that is impacting my thoughts and emotions away to the light, so I may move forward with strength in my heart and spirit*). You might be compelled to pause and even meditate in a particular spot. Allow your intention to expand or evolve as you move through the ritual. The smoke will cleanse and purify everything it touches—let the power of this ceremony guide you. Trust the medicine.

While you're smudging, you may see the sage glow, crackle, or even extinguish itself in high-traffic areas or rooms with an energetic heaviness. If your smoke goes out completely or dwindles to an anemic little wisp, relight your herbs and keep smudging until the energy feels light and clear. End your ritual by smudging your front door, beginning at the bottom left point and working around the door in a clockwise direction, repeating your intention or prayer one final time to close the ceremony. Visualize bright sunlight permeating your entire home as you once again take three deep, cleansing breaths. Say out loud *And so it is.*

Here is the secret to a successful smudging ritual that not many people know: let the sage extinguish itself. You are co-creating this ceremony with Spirit through the medicine, and the herbs will let you know when the ritual is complete. Instead of smothering the leaves or stamping out your smudge stick, place your smudge bowl on your kitchen counter on top of a trivet, hot pad, or other safeguard (that tripod stand I mentioned earlier comes in handy here). This will help you get the most out of your smudging experience. Since you don't want to leave a bowl of smoking embers unattended, use this time to reflect on your experience and how you're feeling. Are you calm or quite emotional? Maybe you had an "aha" moment about an issue or question in your life that was troubling you. You might be exhausted or ready to tackle any obstacle in your way. Acknowledge where you're at and consider journaling about your impressions. (Note: If you're feeling light-headed or nauseous, make sure you've opened enough windows/doors for ventilation, sit down, and drink a big glass of water.)

If you don't have time to let the sage burn out on its own, ensure your herbs are completely snuffed by gently tapping the lit end of your smudge stick into the side of your fireproof container, or smothering the remaining leaves with the back of a stainless steel spoon. Never blow on your sage to extinguish it (that could reignite the flame or cover everything in ash), and avoid dousing it with water, which will make it difficult to relight and may encourage mildew. Once the ashes have cooled completely, take them outside and bury them in soil. Avoid tossing the ashes in the garbage, rinsing them down the sink, or flushing them. You could release them into a lake or stream if that's handy for you, but avoid burying them in potted plants because that little bit of dirt is too contained. Those ashes have worked hard to absorb and transmute the energetic muck, so get them out of your space and return them home to Mother Earth. This also reinforces your ritual's connection to the elements as well as the cycle of life.

Your smudge bowl can be cleaned after every use or as often as needed; be mindful so you don't crack the delicate shell. Unused sage can be saved in a resealable bag or container and stored in a dry, cool place, away from the sun. I've heard of people keeping sage above waist height to honor the sacred medicine and preserve its elevated, purifying properties. Others place it on their altar or carry it with them in a traditional medicine bag. (Confession: Mine is in a freezer bag on a shelf in my closet.) If none of these options resonate with you, that's okay! Make this ritual your own: take what works and leave the rest. Smudging is intended to connect you with ancient magic and spiritual wisdom. Be open to the possibilities you are welcoming through this ritual, and savor the sense of renewal and balance that it encourages (if nothing else, the smell alone has a grounding effect).

You can follow up your smudging ceremony by lighting some palo santo, sweet grass, incense, or even a candle. You could pull an oracle card or have a sea salt–infused bath after smudging (a ritual on a ritual). You'll develop your own smudging style over time. Trust your intuition.

A smudging ceremony can be done in less than fifteen minutes or it can take over an hour. It depends on the size of your space and how deliberately you move through it. Hopefully, you're able to take your time performing this ritual, but a quick smudge is better than none at all. Smudging can be done daily, monthly, or on an as-needed basis. Dealing with a big breakup? Smudge. Moving to a new apartment? Smudge. Looking for a new job? Smudge. Let smudging boost your energy, support your intentions, and foster clarity whenever and wherever you need it.

Even a single session of smudging can have powerful results . . . and unexpected effects. Years ago I worked for a naturopath who specialized in oncology patients, and she wanted the space to be as supportive and healing as possible. I offered to smudge it on a Friday, when the office closed early. I performed the same smudging ceremony I always do when I feel the need to cleanse stagnant energy (thanking the Creator as I move through the space from left to right, asking that negative energy be sent to the light). Her office was on the main floor of a narrow two-story building, and the accountant across the hall poked his head out as I was leaving to see who'd been hotboxing with the naturopath. Even with open windows, the sage made everything smell like a keg party. He rolled his eyes at the smudging explanation and requested I never do it again because the smell had permeated his office.

Two days later, very early on Sunday morning, I got a frantic call from the naturopath. Vandals had broken into the building the night before, forcing their way into one office and sledge-hammering through the shared walls into the neighboring business. The vandals hit every office and destroyed everything in their path—artwork was smashed, computers were hammered, and furniture was ruined—everything *except* the naturopath's and the accountant's offices across the hall. The naturopath had more costly equipment than the other businesses combined (including a six-thousand-dollar microscope), and the accountant's locked door could've been picked open by my kid. And yet, despite being near the main entrance, both of these spaces were untouched. The police couldn't explain why only two offices were left alone. We didn't mention the smudging, but the accountant gave my naturopath a gourmet gift basket and me permission to smudge (with the doors open) any time I pleased.

CLEANING WITH SOUND & CRYSTALS

◇◇◇

If you're sensitive to smells or want to avoid smoke in your space (especially if you have a respiratory or heart condition), don't worry—sound and crystals are great alternatives that are also very effective.

Sound is a universal language. Everything in the Universe is in constant motion, vibrating at a specific energetic frequency. All sounds—whether from a jackhammer, a violin, or a voice—originate from vibrations. The vibrating particles knock into each other, causing a sound wave to move through air, water, or any other type of matter until we sense those vibrations. And just because it isn't heard doesn't mean it isn't experienced. In 2020, cognitive scientists published findings in *Brain Imaging and Behavior* confirming that a deaf person's brain rewires itself to process vibrations in the absence of sound.

We are cosmically connected through sound. Back in the 1940s, Nikola Tesla was telling us that the secrets to the Universe could be found in the frequency and vibration of energy. More recently, a psychologist at the University of California, Santa Barbara, has developed a theory that resonance—or synchronized vibrations (aka vibes)—is the key to understanding human consciousness and the physical reality of all things. When objects (from fireflies to lasers) come together, vibrating at different frequencies, they tend to sync up in ways that can't be explained but can be measured. The researcher refers to this phenomenon as "spontaneous self-organization" (but again: *vibes*).

There are proven physiological and psychological benefits of working with sound because of its impact on the vagus nerve—the main component of the parasympathetic nervous system that regulates your hormones, inflammation, blood pressure, immune system, and digestion. And, in addition to being heard and felt, the vibrations that produce sound directly affect the balance of energy within you and around you because they change the vibration of everything (and everyone) they contact. This is what makes sound such a potent cleansing tool and why—from rattles and drums to bells and bowls—it's been a cornerstone of ceremonies for thousands of years. There is an inherent intelligence found in music that aligns us with all of existence (more on this in Chapter 9). The power of sound is sacred because it connects us to the Divine.

I'll get into the specifics of using each sound tool, but the method I use for all of them is pretty much the same. Similar to smudging, you need a clear intention (what is your "why" for sound clearing at this moment?), and you want to cleanse yourself before moving on to your space. Stand at your front door and allow your mind to quiet as you breathe deeply. Initiate the sound, close your eyes, and let it fill the space. Continue activating the sound until it feels clear and crisp, then move through each room in a clockwise direction, left to right, creating sound as you go and focusing on your intention. Remember to give extra attention to corners, closets, and busier areas. After each room has been cleared, stand in the middle and close your eyes, imagining the space being filled with radiant light. I always draw an infinity symbol (a horizontal figure eight) with any sound tool to seal harmony, healing, and infinite love into the space. I close my ritual standing in the middle of my home (or the closest approximation) and repeat this final step as I envision my intention coming to fruition.

There are tons of sound-clearing tools available, so get curious and try a few to determine what resonates with you. Some people swear by Tibetan singing bowls, holding the bowl and lightly tapping it with the mallet (or circling the mallet around the edge of the bowl to make the note last longer). Balinese bells and wind chimes are also very popular for balancing and clearing energy (in feng shui, the sound is thought to vibrate negative energies into alignment and create positive flow, or chi). Percussion instruments are used in most rituals around the world; beating a drum or shaking a rattle can break up stagnant energy. Specific instruments aren't necessary and rhythm is optional—just make some noise while walking around your home (using the same protocol described earlier). I bought a deerskin rattle from a local Indigenous artisan, and I'll sometimes shake it over any object that feels stagnant or heavy to give it a spot clean (like energetic Windex).

All of these cleansing tools are very powerful, but you don't need pricey singing bowls or bells from Bali to cleanse with sound. A bell from your kid's bike will work. As will tapping a wine glass (gently!) with a spoon. Music also shifts energy, so crank up your favorite tunes to discharge bad mojo. You can also put your voice to work by singing or chanting as you walk from room to room. Even clapping your hands will alter the molecular charge of your space.

My favorite sound-clearing tool is a tuning fork composed of aluminum alloy that produces a frequency over 4,000 hertz. The use of tuning forks for energy work is rooted in Eastern medicine (I was given mine by a traditional Chinese medicine practitioner). The sonic vibrations produced when a tuning fork is struck are thought to invigorate chi (your life force energy) and promote inner healing, but they're also an excellent way to clear the energy surrounding you. Tuning forks come in different sizes (mine is less than five inches), and to use it you simply hold the two-pronged fork by the handle (not near the tines) with your non dominant hand and gently tap one of the prongs near the top. Tuning forks usually come with a small mallet, but I've heard of people using a spoon, ruler, hockey puck, or lipstick (okay, the lipstick was me). Never use your knee (ouch!) and never strike your tuning fork too hard against any surface. I love elevating this ritual by striking my tuning fork with a clear quartz crystal (you can use any crystal, but I like the multipurpose, grounding energy of clear quartz). The effects of the sonorous tone are incredibly soothing, and if you're looking for some grounding energy in a new space or high-pressure situation, it's much easier to tap a tuning fork with a crystal than it is to set a bowl of herbs on fire.

Crystals on their own can be one of the most inconspicuous cleansing techniques, requiring minimal effort and upkeep. Known for their vibrational frequencies, crystals help balance your mind, body, spirit, and space, as we covered in Chapter 2. Think of them as spiritual Roombas: you can just leave them out to do their thing with minimal maintenance on your part. Black obsidian is the Rottweiler of crystals, fiercely guarding you as it absorbs and purifies toxic mojo, so park a couple of them near your front door to keep unwanted energy out of your home. Malachite is known for absorbing negativity and clearing electromagnetic smog, making it a great stone to have in your workspace. Smoky quartz is an all-star cleansing stone, perfect for releasing anxiety while also grounding you. When using crystals in your home, keep in mind that a marble-sized stone won't produce the energetic *oomph* of larger crystals. You can display big stones in clusters or individually on your coffee table, but if the big ones are beyond your budget, grab some smaller stones and tuck them into corners and windowsills. And, when in doubt, follow my lead: stick some rocks in your bra and hope for the best.

CHAPTER 4

MOON MAGIC 101 (LUNAR RHYTHMS)

◇◇◇

The Moon is your emotional compass. It connects you to your sacred feminine, acting as a celestial conduit to your intuition and subconscious. La Luna is your constant companion, illuminated by the reflection of the Sun to guide you through your darkest hours. And while the bold, bright Sun sees your body and nourishes you while you work, it's the cool shimmering of the Moon that sees your soul, offering an opportunity to surrender, heal, and make magic.

Just like the Moon, we pass through phases every month. When we align our rituals to lunar cycles, we're tapping into an ancient energy source that offers an opportunity to pause, reflect, reset, and act. Moon ceremonies are consistently available, easily accessible, and free of charge. When we work with the rhythms of the Moon, they reveal what has been suppressed or hidden from us, providing clarity for next steps. The Moon's phases are like an astral guide for self-care—as you deepen your relationship with La Luna, you strengthen your connection with Self.

Working with lunar energy is nothing new. The Moon has acted as a marker of time and mistress of ceremonies for centuries. Our ancestors were inextricably entwined in nature, relying on the Moon to guide their travel, work the land, and connect with the Creator.

Women's menstrual cycles have long been associated with lunar cycles, and the majority of Moon deities are female. Indigenous people refer to this celestial body as the Grandmother Moon and see her as a powerful teacher, but the Moon symbolizes the Divine Feminine and Goddess of Creation in cultures around the world, guiding spiritual calendars from Bali to Mumbai. Throughout human history, people used the phases of the Moon as their calendar (the word *month* is derived from the Old English word for *moon*), until politicians implemented solar calendars and religious institutions reinforced their use. While only a few countries still rely solely on a lunar calendar in any official capacity, the echo of our ancestors living by the cycles of the Moon persists today.

LUNATICS & LIBIDO
(THE POWER OF THE MOON)

◇◇◇

The strength of the Moon may not be as obvious (or easily measured) as that of the brash, fiery Sun, but its influence is just as significant. As the turner of tides, the Moon's effect on water is indisputable. The difference between low and high tide in Canada's Bay of Fundy can be over sixteen meters (fifty feet) thanks to the gravitational tango between our Moon and Earth.

In addition to stabilizing our planet's wobbly rotation and keeping the tides in check, lunar energy impacts plants and animals across species. The Moon's gravitational pull alters the flow of sap in plants and draws moisture to the soil's surface. In a 2016 study, University of Washington researchers found that the Moon's position changes the Earth's atmosphere, causing a variation in precipitation levels.

And there are many confirmed historical observations from farmers that the health and harvest of crops is maximized when planting occurs during specific lunar phases.

The mating, migration, communication, and foraging of wildlife are all dependent on lunar cycles—even our domesticated fur babies aren't immune to the Moon's powers. A 2011 study at Colorado State University determined that veterinary hospitals report a 20 percent increase in visits during a Full Moon. Dogs tend to howl more when La Luna is peaking (like their wolf ancestors), and cats go into hiding while birds get all aflutter.

It's not just animals acting unhinged during a Full Moon; humans are also influenced by lunar energies. Studies have shown how moonlight alters the way water reacts as it comes into contact with living cells. If other organisms and oceans respond to the Moon, and our bodies are over 60 percent water, it makes sense that we would react, too. The average length of a woman's menstrual cycle lines up with lunation, and many cultures associate the Moon with fertility. The impact of the Moon's celestial circuit on our bodies was disregarded as folklore until multiple studies, including research from Yale and the University of Gothenburg in Sweden, correlated lunar cycles with mood and sleep.

Our understanding of the unique relationship between our world and the Moon is constantly evolving, and scientific proof around the Moon's effect on human behavior is difficult to measure definitively, but there is *plenty* of anecdotal evidence. Nobody is more attuned to the effects of the Moon on the human psyche than parents, teachers, healthcare workers, and police officers. My sister is a nurse, and when she worked at a telehealth call center, she could pinpoint a Full Moon three days before it peaked because the callers got increasingly agitated and their reasons for calling became more extreme. Despite leading Full Moon rituals for decades, I've never tracked them on my calendar, mainly because my quality of sleep is hot garbage in the days leading up to one. In our bustling, tech-driven society, La Luna presents us with consistent opportunities to tune back into nature's rhythms. We simply have to pay attention and take part.

NOT THAT KIND OF WAXING (MOON PHASES)

◇◇◇

The cycles of the Moon reflect the rhythms of life. When you understand the phases, they can anchor you in predictable monthly checkpoints on your journey to self-discovery, awareness, and expansion. By syncing with the cosmic flow, you'll move through life with more focus, greater ease, and compassion for where you're at in the moment.

As the Earth rotates around the Sun, the Moon revolves around the Earth. It takes approximately twenty-eight days for the Moon to complete its orbit, transitioning over two weeks from a seemingly invisible New Moon (when it's positioned between the Earth and Sun) to a radiant Full Moon (when the Earth separates it from the Sun). There are eight distinct phases of a lunar cycle, and each one has its own unique energy to work into your daily, weekly, or monthly rituals:

1. The **New Moon** (also called a Dark Moon) is associated with setting intentions, rejuvenation, and fresh starts.
2. The **Waxing Crescent Moon** relates to deliberating and taking motivated action.
3. The **First Quarter Moon** signifies facing obstacles and pushing forward.

4. The **Waxing Gibbous Moon** represents taking time to reflect and review, adjusting as necessary.
5. The **Full Moon** represents illumination and emotional release.
6. The **Waning Gibbous Moon** is aligned with introspection and gratitude.
7. The **Third (or Last) Quarter Moon** signifies opening and transition.
8. The **Waning Crescent Moon** denotes contemplation and restoration before the cycle begins anew.

The two key lunar phases are the New Moon and Full Moon. The Moon begins its cycle with the New Moon and waxes, or grows larger, for two weeks, until the energy culminates with a Full Moon. From there, it wanes, or grows smaller, until it is new again, and a fresh cycle begins.

You can create a ritual that corresponds with any or all of these phases. Every month the Moon invites you to access the cosmic wisdom of its dynamic energy. I focus my rituals on the New Moon and Full Moon because they're the most powerful moments of the monthly transformation, and their robust energies of commencing and climax make them ripe for rituals.

ECLIPSES:
THE COSMIC WILD CARD

◇◇◇

The Moon shines only because its surface reflects light from the Sun. When the Moon lines up with the Sun and Earth in the same orbit, it forms an eclipse. During a lunar eclipse (which can be full or partial, but takes place only during a Full Moon), the Earth gets in the way and blocks sunlight from illuminating the Moon. When the Moon's light supply is cut off, we see its surface take on a reddish glow (sometimes called a Blood Moon) that lasts a few hours. Conversely, a solar eclipse happens only during a New Moon, when the Moon passes between the Sun and Earth, obscuring the Sun's light for a few minutes. Lunar and Solar eclipses are energetically intense. They show up twice a year in clusters—collectively referred to as eclipse season—that last for about five weeks.

An eclipse can be a catalyst for breakdowns and breakthroughs, heralding significant periods of change and transformation. This turbulent lunation provides a cosmic reset that assists you in connecting more deeply with your purpose and aligning with your fate. During an eclipse, you may feel electrically charged or depleted because you're getting an extra nudge (okay, shove) to have understanding, take action, or pursue healing in areas you've been avoiding. Eclipses simply speed up the inevitable—in ways that can feel erratic and *very* emotional. Traditional astrology suggests taking it easy during these tumultuous periods, so you may choose to skip Moon rituals altogether, but these astral events can also be incredibly powerful portals into a new state of consciousness, leading to massive shifts in your life—you just need to know how to work with this energy (and what to avoid).

Think of a solar eclipse as a supercharged New Moon, ripe with opportunities to manifest your desires. This kind of eclipse can produce big revelations concerning what has kept you from attaining your goals, healing your past, or living your truth. Instead of the usual New Moon manifesting ritual detailed in Chapter 6, you might spend this time journaling or meditating on the internal shifts that need to happen to help you attain your goals. Or you could tap into this heightened energy to magnify your boldest desires, and then buckle up for the results of your mega manifesting. Trust your intuition and listen to your heart during eclipses, working with them to channel this intense energy.

Lunar eclipses amplify the releasing energy of a Full Moon, which can lead to dramatic endings and fraught realizations that seem abrupt or unexpected. But again, they probably need to happen, and the eclipse is simply moving things along at a faster (sometimes frantic) pace. It provokes you to bring light to the shadows and face whatever you've been resisting. Try to accept the sometimes difficult truths that this celestial checkpoint has to offer, because you're breaking through barriers that have been inhibiting your personal evolution. With it occurring during the peak of the Moon's power, a lunar eclipse can ramp up your emotions more than usual, so go easy on yourself and let the Moon support you in letting go of everything (and everyone) that no longer serves you.

Radical self-care is a must during eclipses because eclipses impact you on every level. You're going through an astral growth spurt, and you need to integrate these energetic updates. Drink extra water. Prioritize naps. Feel all the things. If you want to soak in the tub for an hour, go for it—just avoid charging water (or crystals) during a Full Moon eclipse, because that is not energy you want to harness or consume (I'll get into the benefits of Moon water in the next chapter).

You might also hear about supermoons, when a Full Moon is at the closest point to Earth during its orbit, making it appear larger and brighter (this also happens during New Moons; we just can't see them). Supermoons are brilliant to witness, and they boost the energy of your lunar ritual, helping you step into the next chapter of your soul's evolution.

PULLING WEEDS
& PLANTING SEEDS
(HARNESSING LUNAR MOJO)

◇◇◇

Whether a Moon is new or full, eclipsed or super, it will always be moving through the twelve signs of the zodiac. It takes only a couple of days for the Moon to transit through each sign, completing its journey in about a month (the Sun takes a year to travel through the zodiac). Similar to Sun signs, the astrology of each Moon phase delivers a subtle yet distinct undercurrent that adds texture to your ritual. These astrological signs have their own signature vibes and will add a certain flavor to the energy of the Moon (for example, Leo is about bold self-expression, while Cancer focuses on tender feelings). We'll be looking at the celestial symbolism of the Moon in each sign to help you align with this astrological essence.

Lunar energy is always accessible to you, and Moon rituals provide a metaphysical bridge between what was, what is, and what could be. Marking the Moon's rhythms with ceremony helps reinforce your connection with Mother Earth and Grandmother Moon, aligning your goals with the cosmic flow.

New Moons signify new beginnings. Are you ready to launch a business? Start dating after a breakup? Find a new home? New Moons are the perfect opportunity to map out your manifesting by setting your intentions in every area of life (I show you exactly how to do this in Chapter 6). It's a cosmic reset that marks a new cycle of creation in your life. New Moons boost your intuition, inviting you to go within and focus on designing your dreams. This is the most fertile time to plant seeds in the rich soil of the stars. But before you can plant those seeds, you have to pull the weeds—and that's where the Full Moon comes in.

When the Moon is fully illuminated by the Sun, it reaches maximum capacity as its energy peaks (along with our emotions). The energetic release that follows is what we harness to crank up the cosmic current for a Full Moon ritual (aka Burn Your Sh*t). Full Moons are the ideal time to let go of what (or who) no longer serves you, discard the bad habits holding you back, and unload the crap that isn't yours to carry. When you work with the Moon at the peak of its power, you're removing the barriers that keep you from healing your mind, body, and spirit. From crystal charging to Moon bathing, there are plenty of lunar rituals to support you in moving forward unburdened.

The intentions you set during a New Moon are astrologically linked to a corresponding Full Moon six months later. For example, a Taurus New Moon in April–May aligns with the Scorpio Full Moon in October–November. This offers a six-month window to work on your intentions in addition to the shorter time frame between a New Moon and the Full Moon that occurs two weeks later. The personalities of these paired signs can provide subtle direction, but don't feel obligated with work within these intervals—just know that they're available to offer additional insight.

For centuries, farmers have worked with the land in partnership with the Moon, pulling weeds and planting seeds, which is why I suggest doing a Full Moon ritual first and then following it with the New Moon ritual two weeks later. Again, do what works for you. Moon rituals are a monthly opportunity to reaffirm your intentions and release whatever is holding you back. If my New Moon ritual brings to light what needs to be burned under a Full Moon, fantastic! The two rituals go hand-in-hand, and you can do either one whenever you get the urge. The Moon's energy is simply amplifying your intentions and action.

Are you ready for a lunar boost in your own life?

CHAPTER 5

IT'S TIME TO BURN YOUR SH*T (FULL MOON RITUALS)

◇◇◇

I t's finally time. You've gathered your gear. Candles have been lit. Energetic goo has been saged into the ether. You're ready to Burn Your Sh*t.

I've done Full Moon fire rituals for decades, leading groups in person and online as we set fire to the past. I know how powerful and cathartic release ceremonies can be in helping you energetically let go of the beliefs, people, or circumstances that are holding you back. A Full Moon ritual can help release barriers you're not even aware of and allow for the healing of your mind, body, and spirit. Because a Full Moon is a supercharged and powerful time of action—when energy peaks and then releases—it brings things to the surface that need releasing, giving you an opportunity to move forward unburdened.

A Full Moon occurs when the Moon (influencer of your inner world) is positioned exactly opposite the Sun (ruler of your external self), creating a tension between emotion and action. What you cannot see rises to the surface, demanding to be dealt with (or at least acknowledged). Major epiphanies and unprovoked outbursts are common during this lunation because, it turns out, ignorance isn't always bliss.

As the Moon reaches its energetic peak, it reveals what no longer serves you and invites you to leave it behind. When you welcome the gifts of the Full Moon, you invite healing and make room for transformation. La Luna illuminates your shadows to raise your vibration. It lightens your load by excavating unseen burdens from your subconscious. A Full Moon ceremony is the first step to freedom; clearing your path of energetic blocks is a catalyst for quitting habits, leaving situations, and ditching deadweight.

But you can't clean your house in the dark; you have to turn on the light to see the dirt. That's why this ritual is so powerful—it helps you identify what needs to be dumped in order to create space for the good stuff to come. A Full Moon ritual can be a sacred time imbued with solemnity, a joyful celebration with your besties, or frantic scribbling done a few minutes before you start. I've done all three, and they all work.

For thousands of years, different cultures have looked to the skies to guide their lives, using the stars to navigate, the Moon to mark the months, and the Sun to tell time. In many Indigenous traditions, Grandmother Moon was created to teach and watch over us, providing light in the darkness while regulating the waters with her nurturing energy. You may see names associated with Full Moons, such as the Wolf Moon or Cold Moon, that are often attributed to Indigenous traditions, but *The Old Farmer's Almanac* confirms that these names likely have Colonial origins, related to farming or the weather, rather than Indigenous ones. First Nations people *do* have specific names for the Moon that are based on a thirteen-month lunar calendar and apply to the entire month rather than one phase of the Moon. These names also vary depending on the geographical location of the community. For example, March's Full Moon is often referred to as the Worm Moon because the ground is softening with the approaching spring weather and worms start to emerge, but the Anishinaabe know it as Naabidin Giizis (Snow Crust Moon) and the Anishinabek call it Ziissbaakdoke Giizis (Sugar Moon).

FULL MOON FLAVORS

◇◇◇

In astrology, every Full Moon lines up with a different zodiac sign, each one offering distinct attributes and unique opportunities to consider during your lunar ritual. Similar to tarot cards, the zodiac is rooted in archetypes, which are recurring symbols, roles, and patterns of expression that reflect the human experience—examples of archetypes include the Mother, the Explorer, and the Warrior—and they can be found everywhere, from ancient myths to reality television. These astrological archetypes carry different themes to your rituals, acting as a prompt for what you might want to focus on.

Because a Full Moon is positioned on the opposite side of the Sun, it's actually working with *two* astrological signs (the one it's sitting in as well as its counterpart on the opposite side of the zodiac), giving you the chance to experience both sides of the cosmic coin. For example, a Full Moon in Leo always happens in late January or early February, when the Sun is sitting in Aquarius. Anyone who knows a Leo is aware of their playful main-character energy, while quirky Aquarians look for innovative ways to serve the collective. During a Leo Full Moon, you might consider where you're being called to shine bright and express yourself, but also how it could impact your community for the better. You may feel these astro vibes most when they correspond to your Sun, Moon, or Rising sign (which you can easily figure out by plugging your day, time, and place of birth into an online natal birth chart calculator).

It's worth noting for readers south of the equator that the astrology is the same: an Aries Full Moon in Melbourne is also happening in New York; it's just a day or so earlier in Australia. The only difference between the hemispheres is the season in which a sign occurs, but the traits won't change. Capricorn vibes are still cold and unemotional on a scorching day in the desert, while weepy Cancer stays sensitive even during the Southern Hemisphere's winter.

The following is my breakdown of Full Moon astrology for all twelve signs, as well as their relationship to the corresponding Sun signs, to help you gain the greatest impact when you Burn Your Sh*t (I've also included crystal suggestions that align with the energy of each sign). We always begin with Aries because it's been the first sign of the zodiac New Year since ancient Mesopotamian and Roman times (New Year's Day shifted to January 1 only after Julius Caesar decided to reform the Roman calendar).

Aries

Aries has a fiery, courageous, and independent energy—ready to act and get sh*t done (whether you're ready or not). As the Warrior archetype, Aries can bring out the impulsive and emotionally charged ram in all of us. And if you're veering off course, an Aries Full Moon will get you back on track (sometimes rather abruptly). This Full Moon occurs between the end of September and beginning of October, when the Sun sits in Libra, offering you an opportunity to cultivate patience and set boundaries in all of your relationships, while also reminding you to balance your individual needs with those of others—or perhaps release anyone who doesn't support you on your path.

CRYSTAL: RED JASPER

Taurus

The Moon *loves* being in the strong and grounded sign of Taurus. The earthiest of signs, Taurus appreciates comfort and ease, possessions and patterns, stability and sensuality. Taurus is like a farmer, patiently and methodically cultivating its cosmic crops. A Taurus

Full Moon occurs in late October or early November, during Scorpio season. Opposing signs complement and challenge each other, and the bull's soothing self-care vibes are the perfect counterpoint to Scorpio's intense shadow work. A Full Moon in this rock-steady sign invites you to dive deep and uncover any limiting beliefs around financial security, creature comforts, and self-worth.

CRYSTAL: PYRITE

Gemini

Gemini is the chattiest sign of the zodiac—a multitasking, adaptable communicator looking to quickly synthesize, understand, and exchange information. Eager to spread the word, Gemini energy is curious and cerebral, but not the most discerning, which can lead to trustworthy correspondence or fickle gossip (that's the duality of the twin thing). When the Full Moon in Gemini shows up at the end of November or in early December, it will be opposite adventurous and optimistic Sagittarius. This is a time to reflect on the messages you're receiving while refining the ideas you convey, letting go of whatever (or whoever) is holding you back from sharing your feelings and fully expressing yourself.

CRYSTAL: OPAL

Cancer

This sensitive water sign (think: tears) is ruled by the Moon and fueled by love. Cancer feels All. The. Things. As the Mother of the zodiac, Cancer is nurturing and vulnerable, inviting you to connect to yourself and others on a heart and soul level. The crab's protective shell and sideways scamper reminds us that emotional intimacy isn't always easy—and family comes in many forms. Sitting opposite Cancer's Mother archetype is Capricorn, the Father. Where

Cancer is heart and home, Capricorn is career and commitment. Occurring at the end of December or beginning of January, a Cancer Full Moon can amplify feelings of uncertainty or insecurity, but it's also a beautiful opportunity to unclench those pointy pincers and release past hurts, reparenting yourself so you can heal from within. When you listen to your tender heart and prioritize self-care, your outward-facing goals will get the boost they need.
CRYSTAL: ROSE QUARTZ

Leo

Leo's exuberant, confident energy is irresistible and undeniable. The Lion's joyful roar encourages you to tap into your creative expression and step into your higher calling. Leo has the most look-at-me vibes of the zodiac, and its Full Moon wants you to release old narratives, patterns, or beliefs that have kept you playing small, clearing the path to living your best life by being authentically and unapologetically yourself. This playful lunation happens when the Sun is sitting in quirky Aquarius (between late January and early February), providing you with innovative opportunities to let your freak flag fly.
CRYSTAL: CITRINE

Virgo

As the zodiac's most methodical and organized sign, Virgo often gets a bad rap, but its signature perfectionism promotes efficiency, and detailed analysis informs passion projects. Virgo helps you spring-clean your astral closet and set yourself up for success. Coming at the end of February or in early March, when the Sun is in idealistic and intuitive Pisces, a Virgo Full Moon reminds you that boundaries are required to keep your life in flow while bringing your visions to fruition. Virgo may not be the sexiest sign in the zodiac (we'll get to you in a minute, Scorpio), but its qualities are essential for your growth.

CRYSTAL: SAPPHIRE

Libra

Libra craves balance and revels in relationships. It charms and cajoles in an effort to connect, seeking fairness and justice in the world. Your desire for harmony (especially in personal or professional partnerships) is heightened during a Libra Full Moon, making it an opportune time to refine, or release, the relationships in your life. This flirty lunation occurs at the end of March and beginning of April, while the Sun is parked in Aries. The individualistic energy of Aries and peace-seeking Libra may seem at odds (it's the ultimate "me" versus "we" dichotomy), but it's actually a moment to consider how the perspectives of those around you are (or aren't) serving your soul's purpose—and then do something about it.

CRYSTAL: LEPIDOLITE

Scorpio

If you're in the mood for mystery and emotional intensity, Scorpio is your sign. The Full Moon in Scorpio happens between the end of April and beginning of May. It dares you to explore the shadowy depths of your existence, journeying beneath the superficial to confront the unpleasant parts of your psyche and taboo aspects of life (easy stuff like death, sex, greed, and power). A Scorpio Full Moon compels you to dig deep. Resist the urge to resist. See and feel everything that arises. The resulting awareness can ignite massive transformation. Thankfully, the lusty scorpion is balanced by the Sun in steady Taurus. Tend to yourself as you uncover and release what keeps you stagnant.

CRYSTAL: YELLOW TOPAZ

Sagittarius

Sagittarius has an unquenchable thirst for adventure. Equal parts philosopher and cheerleader, the archer is an optimistic seeker and spreader of truth. Occurring at the end of May or beginning of June, a Sagittarius Full Moon invites you to release the fears that are holding you back so you can step out of your comfort zone and discover your authentic self. This is the perfect Full Moon to ditch bad habits and conditioned responses that have kept you playing small. The Sun in Gemini brings focus to the necessary details as you realize your dreams with planning and care.

CRYSTAL: LAPIS LAZULI

Capricorn

Capricorn gets sh*t done. Immersed in the physical world (as opposed to marinating in emotions like its counterpart sign, Cancer), Capricorn has a no-nonsense, practical energy that lends itself to hard work and productivity. If you have daddy issues, they're going to come up during a Full Moon in Capricorn, which is steeped in authority and pragmatism. A Capricorn Full Moon shows up between late June and early July, while the Sun is in Cancer, which makes it an ideal time to remove emotional limitations that are hindering your self-discipline and preventing you from finishing projects or tying up loose ends.

CRYSTAL: BLACK ONYX

Aquarius

Aquarius is too busy being a visionary and healing the collective to worry about your opinion. This smarty-pants sign values radical change over sentimental fairy tales, and the Full Moon in Aquarius, happening in late July or early August, teaches you to honor who you are as well as how your unique gifts can impact your community (globally or within your own home). When you stand strong in your truth, you emit a vibration that elevates the masses, and the Aquarius Full Moon assists in releasing any fears of rejection that may inhibit you. Having the Sun in confident, look-at-me Leo gives you the extra nudge to get going.

CRYSTAL: KYANITE

Pisces

Heart-centered Pisces is the whimsical flower child of the zodiac. This sign is highly empathic (sometimes to a fault), intuitive, and creative. For Pisces, vulnerability is a virtue and sensitivity is a superpower, and this energy encourages cosmic connections with each other—and within. The Pisces Full Moon is a mystical time, ripe with potential for immense healing. A Full Moon in Pisces can be more emotionally charged than usual, taking place between August and September, when it's balanced by pragmatic Virgo's analytical vibes. During this lunation, try to honor your emotions, find the root of what needs to be released, and let it go with intention.

CRYSTAL: AMETHYST

WHERE TO BURN YOUR SH*T

◇◇◇

Now that you have a deeper awareness of your Moon's monthly mood, it's time to assemble your equipment. At the most basic level, you'll need a pen, slips of paper, a fireproof container (no plastic!), matches or a lighter, and a glass of water (because hydration is essential for energy work and represents the element of Water but also: safety).

If you want to spice up your ritual, you can create an altar that includes a candle and any crystals that call to you (or suit the Full Moon's sign), or arrange a collection of shells, rocks, herbs, or flowers. If your altar is outside, ensure that it will be protected from the elements. If it's inside, keep it in a well-ventilated space away from anything flammable and out of reach of kids or pets.

I personally don't create an altar for my Moon rituals because my Burn Your Sh*t Kit acts as a portable altar that I can easily transport. It's a small tin bucket with handles (for when it gets hot) that holds a small notebook, pencil, matches, crystal, tealight candle, and feather. This incorporates the elements of Earth (crystal), Fire (matches/candle), and Air (feather), and then I add Water to the ashes at the end of the ceremony.

You can Burn Your Sh*t on your own or gather some friends to create a little coven. Although it's possible to perform this ritual indoors, I strongly encourage you to head outside. I'm in Canada, and I haul my cookies out to my front porch every month for Burn Your Sh*t regardless of the weather. Although I've been on the cusp of frostbite a couple of times, and I've had to spit out ashes blown at me by the wind, it's been manageable. When I did it inside my home years ago with a friend (*Hi, Cynthia!*), we forgot to open any windows and it was a disaster: the smoke detector went wild; I blew into the cauldron in a panic, which only fanned the flames; and my house smelled like a campsite for weeks afterward.

If your living situation makes fire rituals difficult (for example, a basement apartment) and you don't want to start torching paper in a public park, you can always rip up the paper and bury it.

WHAT TO BURN
(AKA HOW TO WRITE A SH*T LIST)

◇◇◇

The question I get asked most often before a Full Moon ritual is how to figure out what needs to be burned. Before you go digging out your ex's old T-shirt or lugging pieces of furniture into the backyard, be aware that you won't be burning actual objects—you're releasing the limiting beliefs, negative self-talk, and any other funky mojo that's keeping you from reaching your potential and discovering your purpose (which is much more powerful than torching that shirt). You need to make space for the excellent energy coming your way by setting fire to all of the energetic crap that's holding you back.

I'll get into the grounding exercise that can help facilitate this process in a minute, but if you find it's too much pressure to come up with items on the day of a Full Moon, you can get a head start by writing a Sh*t List, which is like a gratitude journal in reverse (cue Oprah giving me major side eye).

Every day you write *I now choose to release. . .* on a slip of paper, following it up with whatever is bugging you in the moment. It can be intense (*I now choose to release fears around changing my career*) or lower stakes (*I now choose to release my rage for the jackass who cut me off in traffic*). You may have one piece of paper or a pile of them, but collect them over the month and store them in a bowl or mug (I keep mine in my sh*t-burning bucket). Before you start burning under the Full Moon, review your Sh*t List. You may realize that many of the items have lost their energetic charge (or you don't even remember what you were writing about) and they no longer affect you. It's like your soul simply needed to be heard at the time, and the act of writing out the release was enough to get the job done.

When it comes to the actual ritual, a lot of people will write out their grievances, spark them up, and then wonder the next day why nothing has changed (I used to be one of those people). Although every declaration starts with the same five words (*I now choose to release. . .*), it's what follows that makes this ritual so profound. You are committing to letting go of obstacles to your growth and healing. You can't banish anxiety or ditch your mother-in-law by lighting a piece of paper on fire. Be open to the revelations that await this energetic excavation. Be willing to dig deep and determine the core wounds or enduring narratives that are holding you back. Be ready to embrace a new way of being in this world. Only then can you begin to shed old patterns and beliefs to move forward. (If this sounds like therapy, that's because it kind of is. I've been told Burn Your Sh*t feels like a year of cosmic counseling.)

People send me stuff to burn on their behalf during Burn Your Sh*t, and it honestly doesn't vary much from month to month. Anxiety, trauma, body shame, health issues, relationship worries, and financial fears always make an appearance (to the point that I end up combining similar requests, otherwise we'd be there until the New Moon). These recurring themes are a big part of why Burn Your Sh*t is so powerful: we're reminded that we are not alone and that we're more alike than we are different.

These repetitive releases still impact us because it's often taken years (sometimes a lifetime) for this crap to be instilled in us, so it could take more than one Full Moon ritual to shift things, and growth often happens in layers. But that's the beauty of La Luna—it shows up every month with an invitation to change your life for the better.

An unexpected benefit of doing Burn Your Sh*t with a group, even when it's online, is inadvertently releasing your sh*t courtesy of someone else. For example, if someone in Finland sends me something to burn and I'm feeling that release almost as if I wrote it, and you're reacting similarly from wherever you're watching, that burn is as much ours as it is the Finnish person's. If it resonates, it's releasing.

I prepare for every Burn Your Sh*t ritual by copying out each release request by hand, and I often reframe them for maximum impact. I wrote this chapter the day before a Full Moon, and here is a sample of what my Instagram followers sent me to burn on their behalf, along with my edits, if required (feel free to use any of these in your own Full Moon ritual):

Original: I now choose to release not being able to make a decision.
Reframe: I now choose to release my definition of indecisiveness, knowing that it's actually rooted in fear, and the wrong decision is still better than no decision, because at least I'm taking action and, if nothing else, learning what *not* to do next time (which is invaluable).

Original: I now choose to release illness.
Reframe: I now choose to release any guilt or shame that I somehow brought this on myself, so I can be tender and patient with my healing.

Original: I now choose to release people-pleasing.
Reframe: I now choose to release the bullsh*t belief that it's my job to fix everyone else's problems (because that only prolongs or enlarges their karmic lessons).

Original: I now choose to release hating how I look.

Reframe: I now choose to release the shame I feel about my external appearance because how I look on the outside doesn't reflect who I am on the inside (and love is an inside job).

Original: I now choose to release my financial scarcity mindset.

Reframe: I now choose to release the lack mentality and scarcity mindset that were instilled in me before I knew what they even meant, so I can begin a new, healthier relationship with my finances.

Original: I now choose to release teeth grinding.

Reframe: I now choose to release blocks that may be preventing me from identifying my stress so I can address it through mindfulness and other techniques.

Original: I now choose to release my past.

Reframe: I now choose to release the fallacy that the past can be erased or released, instead seeing it as growth, learning, and adapting, so I can open myself up to grace and forgiveness (for myself).

Original: I now choose to release sadness, even on a sunny day.

Reframe: I now choose to release fears around feeling my feelings, letting sadness sit alongside joy, acknowledging it, and then putting it aside so that I might experience the full range of my emotions for the moment I'm in . . . because I deserve to feel the good ones, too.

Original: I now choose to release perfectionism.

Reframe: I now choose to release the fear that if things aren't "perfect" I won't be loved, wanted, or accepted (because that's bullsh*t).

Original: I now choose to release my narcissistic mother.

Reframe: I now choose to release the false narrative that I have to keep people in my life who are toxic just because we're related.

Original: I now choose to release self-sabotage.

Reframe: I now choose to release self-sabotage, along with the underlying fears and feelings of unworthiness that fuel it.

Original: I now choose to release bad luck.

Reframe: I now choose to release the false belief that luck is good or bad, and instead look at different seasons of learning and opportunities, so I may shift from a place of "Why not *me?*" to a place of "Why *not* me?"

Original: I now choose to release worrying about the decisions other people make that aren't good for them.

Reframe: I now choose to release the compulsion to control other people's lives (because it's not control, it's anxiety).

Original: I now choose to release the terror of becoming a mother because I was abused by mine.

Reframe: I now choose to release fears around being a mom because I wasn't mothered in a healthy or loving way, knowing that through parenting I will be able to reparent myself and break the cycle that came before me, because I am an adult who is now capable and strong enough to make better decisions for myself, and do better for my own kids.

Original: I now choose to release friends who've betrayed me.

Reframe: I now choose to release those who've shown me who they are so I can make space to surround myself with people who share my values and integrity, and who are worthy of my friendship.

Original: I now choose to release being afraid.
Reframe: I now choose to release the misconception that fear has to be absent before I take action.

Original: I now choose to release procrastination.
Reframe: I now choose to release procrastination, knowing that it's based in fear and I'm not lazy—I'm scared. And I can do things even when they scare me.

Original: I now choose to release doubting my abilities and competency in my business so I can earn a living.
Reframe: I now choose to release doubts and resistance around receiving money for my services, as well as worries that nobody will pay my prices, because the right clients will come if I'm aligned with my worth.

Original: I now choose to release my sixty-year-old husband fantasizing about a twenty-two-year-old coworker.
Reframe: I now choose to release thinking that I have to settle for being second best, regardless of my age, and release the old wounds and negative self-talk preventing me from standing up for myself and seeing that I am worth so much more.

Original: I now choose to release trauma.
Reframe: I now choose to release the lie that I am defined by what happened to me, because it was only one chapter of my story, not the whole book.

Original: I now choose to release caring about what other people think of me.

Reframe: I now choose to release caring about what other people think of me, knowing that their opinions are none of my business, and I am living my one precious, beautiful life for me.

Original: I now choose to release George.

Reframe: (Note: You could just write a person's name down and then torch it, but you can also do a deep dive on what George is here to teach you.) I now choose to release the belief that I can't be whole or validated on my own, or that I can't be alone without being lonely, or that I don't deserve better than settling for whoever shows up.

Original: I now choose to release jealousy of another person's success.

Reframe: I now choose to release the misconception that playing small keeps me safe so I can instead leverage my envy to be aspirational.

You may also benefit from writing a letter (especially for dealing with George, from the example above, along with the husband fantasizing about his coworker, *Love, Actually*–style). The key to writing an effective letter is to be completely raw and unfiltered. Don't hold back. Forget about penmanship, spelling, or political correctness. Just barf your head, heart, and soul onto the page because nobody else will see it and the exercise is for you. Your letter can be written to an ex who lives rent-free in your head, a coworker who infuriates you with every interaction, or even something inanimate (such as an old job where you felt unqualified or the apartment that you hate).

I once wrote a letter to my uterus on the advice of my naturopath because I'd become a fibroid factory, and it definitely provoked a shift in how I viewed my situation. If something has a hold on you, let it know how you're feeling about it by putting everything down on paper. Handwritten is preferred, but if you have mobility issues just type it out or do talk-to-text and print it. Take this exercise to the next level by responding to yourself with a second letter that's written from the recipient's point of view (yes, my uterus wrote back).

Writing a letter to (and then from) a younger version of yourself can also be incredibly therapeutic. Think about an age where things changed for you, or something happened, and write to that younger version of yourself, sharing what you wish you'd known back then. Follow up with a response from younger you, telling yourself what you wish you knew or remembered today. Writing to someone you're estranged from or to a person who has passed away can also be very profound. (If you're still unsure what to write, keep reading.)

HOW TO BURN YOUR SH*T

◇◇◇

Alright, let's do this. Have your pen and paper handy, find a seat with good support, and give yourself time to settle into a position that feels comfortable. You can record the following grounding exercise on your phone and listen to it, or use the QR code on page 303 to hear me talk you through it:

Close your eyes and ground yourself with three deep, cleansing breaths. Inhale through your nose and exhale out your mouth; feel your belly rise and fall with each breath, knowing that you are completely safe and supported in this moment.

Now think about what (or who) is holding you back from step-
ping into your power and discovering your purpose. What is keeping
you from bravely speaking your truth? It can be attitudes, emotions,
illness, debt, grudges, addictions, or habits. Consider what you need
to release in order to reach your potential. Is it a toxic relationship?
Or where you're living?

Are you clinging to expectations about how you thought your
life would look? Do you feel like a disappointment to others—or
yourself? Are limiting beliefs getting in your way? Is it not believ-
ing you're lovable? Or not knowing your worth? Is it a specific job
or how you perceive money? Is it how you look at your body? What
stories are you carrying (that belong to you or someone else) that
need release?

Focus on what comes to mind—what is stopping you from being
unapologetically, authentically you? Notice what's coming up and
trust your intuition. You may have a laundry list of things to release
or one main thing that is blocking you, but trust what is coming to you.

Now, open your eyes, pick up your pen, and write down the following words: *I now choose to release . . .*

Write whatever comes to you on separate slips of paper. Don't do
it all on one page; give each item on your list the respect and ceremony it deserves.

Then read each one aloud and, as you light the piece of paper on
fire, say *And so it is* at the end.

Here are some examples:

I now choose to release fears and anxiety around having difficult
conversations because the anticipation is likely worse than the actu-
ality . . . *light the paper on fire over your bowl* *. . . And so it is.*

I now choose to release the compulsion I feel to live my life for my parents as I try (and fail) to meet their unrealistic expectations . . . *light the paper on fire over your bowl* . . . *And so it is.*

I now choose to release the blocks, either conscious or unconscious, that are keeping me from moving forward with my business idea . . . *light the paper on fire over your bowl* . . . *And so it is.*

If you've written a letter, you can read it aloud or silently, then hold it over your container and say something like *I now choose to release everything contained in this letter. I release our bond in this lifetime, past lifetimes, and future lifetimes. I release the grip you have on my heart and the hold I have on yours. I release you to a life of love, joy, and abundance . . . so I may have the same . . . And so it is.*

Obviously ad-lib whatever you want and just add *And so it is* at the end. Putting ceremony to the end of a relationship is very profound and not done nearly enough (more on this in Chapter 8).

Breathe deeply as you focus on those words burning. Notice how it feels in your body to watch the words disappear before your eyes: you are reclaiming your power and stepping into your story as the author rather than a passive reader. You may find yourself sighing, there might be tears, or your stomach could start gurgling like crazy— these are all signs of energy shifting. If you feel the urge to pause after a particularly potent burn, take a moment. If you're compelled to write out something new in the middle of your ceremony, do that. If you need to crank some death metal and spin under the stars, go for it. Listen to whatever is coming up for you—you have to feel it to heal it.

You might also realize that one issue you've released has collapsed adjacent ones like a house of cards. Some paper may go up in a *whoosh*, while others take more effort to light or stay lit. Ensure that even the stubborn sh*t gets reduced to ash, and if there are little bits of paper that don't burn completely, have a look at what's left behind. You'd be surprised by the words that linger (*my needs, forgive self,* or *I love*) as a final message from the Universe.

Once you've burned all of your releases, you can end your Full Moon ritual. After adding water to the container, place one or both hands over your heart, close your eyes, and take three deep belly breaths, inhaling through your nose and exhaling out your mouth. Be aware of how you're feeling compared to your initial breaths at the start of the ceremony. Read the following words out loud (or record them like you did for the grounding exercise that opened the ritual, leaving space to repeat the words aloud):

I now release those things, thoughts, and people in my life that no longer serve me. I release them without fear or regret. And I replace them with love and healing—knowing that I am whole, I am worthy, I am enough, and I am more loved than I realize. And so it is . . .

Now it's time to dump that sh*t. Empty your container in the garden, on your lawn, in a park . . . You get the idea. By doing this, you've brought the four elements of nature into play: Fire (the most transformative), Water (the most purifying), Air (the engine that makes it go), and Earth (where everything is put to rest).

Check in with yourself. How do you feel physically? Are you exhausted or energized? Lighter or leadened? What about emotionally, spiritually, or energetically? Are you weepy or giddy? Relieved or angsty? Exactly the same? There is no right or wrong way to feel during (or following) a Full Moon ritual, as long as you acknowledge your efforts and honor your healing.

KEEP THE PARTY GOING (AFTERBURN ADD-ONS)

◇✕◇

It's worth taking a moment to journal about your experience. Here are some prompts to get you started:

Before the ritual, I felt _____ and now I feel _____.
A realization I had that I wasn't expecting is _____.
My key takeaway from this burn is _____.
With this release I have now made space for _____.

You might feel like pulling a card from your favorite oracle deck for a message of reflection, or going for a walk around the block, or enjoying a big bowl of ice cream. If nothing else, make sure you drink lots of water to flush any physical or energetic gunk from your system. This is the time to replenish your spirit.

A Full Moon bath is a great way to replenish while making use of La Luna's detoxifying powers. Start by sanctifying your space with candles, music, or incense. Perhaps scatter rose petals in the water to set the mood (or just fill the tub and hop in). Turbocharge your Moon bath with some water-safe crystals to soak in there with you. Rose or clear quartz, amethyst, citrine, and moonstone are always safe bets; stay away from anything that contains copper or iron ore, as well as any stone ending in *ite*, such as celestite (Chapter 2 contains a longer list). If you add herbs, salts, or oils to your bath, keep your crystals out of the water and arrange them around the tub or create an altar in your bathroom instead, just to be safe (Chapter 7 notes which oils are safe for you in baths).

Soaking in a Full Moon bath is a ritual of self-love. Every month you could incorporate your favorite flowers, try different scents, or get creative with your soundtrack. As you run your bath, visualize shimmering moonlight pouring into the tub. Ease yourself into the healing waters, lean back (roll up a towel to place behind your neck or use a bath pillow), close your eyes, and relax. Imagine any remaining negativity being washed away from your mind, body, and spirit. Take three deep breaths—focus on healing with every inhale and releasing with each exhale. Visualize yourself outside under the Full Moon. Ask for any specific guidance you're seeking or simply request *What do I need to know right now?* Pause and listen for a response. Give thanks for the Universal energies and, as the tub empties, visualize the water rinsing away any remaining toxins or negativity.

If you don't have a bathtub (or hate baths), you can still bathe in the moonlight by going outside to bask in the Moon's essence. If you'd rather stay inside (like me), feel free to slip into your coziest jammies, pour a cup of something delicious, and indulge in reading a book, listening to some music, or doing anything else that soothes your soul. It can feel powerful to be near a window where you can see the moon, but the energy will find you wherever you are.

Plan for a good night's sleep, but be prepared for anything because Full Moons are notorious sleep saboteurs—there's a lot of energy at play! You might have the best sleep of your life or the worst. Your dreams may be wildly vivid or you could feel like you've been tranquilized. You may barely sleep at all. I tend to have horrible insomnia in the days leading up to a Full Moon and then sleep like my teenager after the ritual. Keep a journal near your bed to jot down any dreams or insights that reveal themselves around a Full Moon. The veil is thin between the spirit world and the physical realm when we sleep (especially during a Full Moon), so take advantage of this heightened access to Divine energy and your own intuition.

I'll sometimes charge my crystals and tarot deck overnight on a windowsill during a Full Moon, but I'm not obsessive about it. You can also harness lunar energy by making a batch of Moon water. Pay attention to the astrological properties of the month's Full Moon so you know the energies you're working with (for example, a Leo Full Moon exudes confidence, while Virgo imbues order and efficiency). Fill a glass container—Mason jars are great for this—with water from your tap, or use bottled water. You can also collect fresh water from a natural source, like a stream, but only if you're sure you won't be drinking it ("beaver fever" is no joke and no fun . . . trust me). Avoid making this water during eclipses, when the Moon's mojo is too unstable; the water you're working with is like a psychic sponge for La Luna's energy. And skip New Moon water—you want to harness the Moon's energy at the peak of its power, not the start of a cycle. Place your container of water beneath the Full Moon, either outside or on a windowsill indoors, and leave it overnight. The next morning, you can place it at your altar, drink it, use it for cooking, add it to your bath, clean your crystals with it, put some in a spray bottle to spritz around your house, or water your plants—whatever floats your witchy boat.

Gathering on Instagram with strangers around the world every Full Moon has proven the power of this ritual. A woman once wrote asking me to release the cancer (her exact words: *fucking bullshit cancer*) before an upcoming scan that would determine if her tumor had grown. Because Burn Your Sh*t isn't magic (although it *is* very magical), it felt wrong to suggest that an illness could be eradicated. Instead, I spoke about releasing any resistance to feeling all of the emotions surrounding her diagnosis, as well as any blame or shame that she might have brought this disease on herself. I then paused and asked everyone to close their eyes and hold space for this nameless woman, to send her healing energy and unconditional love. I almost fell off my porch from the energy coursing through my body (I have goose bumps just writing about that experience), and I wasn't alone. People commented how intense it felt to envision this woman covered in healing light and how they'd wept in solidarity with her struggle. The woman felt the energy directed at her during the ritual, and a month later she emailed to let me know her scan reported that the tumors had shrunk substantially. I'm not suggesting that Burn Your Sh*t will cure cancer, but it definitely won't make things worse.

Another woman wrote because her nine-year-old son was in the hospital after a horrible ATV accident, and she was waiting to hear if he would lose an eye. She asked me to release both her fear that he wouldn't be okay and her anxiety about being in the hospital. Instead of addressing her worries (which were perfectly understandable and warranted in her situation), I shifted to letting go of the guilt that she and her husband were feeling as parents. I released unhelpful notions of being at fault so they could forgive themselves (because they, like all of us, are only human). Again, I asked everyone on the Instagram Live to close their eyes and send loving support to this boy and his family. Once her son was released from the hospital, she let me know that he was on the mend and his vision had been fully restored. They had watched the Burn Your Sh*t ritual from his hospital bed, and her son was incredibly moved to see so many people focused on his healing and well-being. It didn't change his situation, but it bolstered his faith and courage when facing it.

You don't need thousands of people holding space for you online to benefit from a Full Moon ritual. Years before I did them on Instagram, a man named Ed showed up at my door for a tarot reading looking like a Hells Angel and the last person you'd expect to consult a psychic. His hog was parked in my driveway, he was covered in biker leather, and, despite easily being in his early sixties, his long gray beard was braided to his sternum. Ed may have been the antithesis of my target demographic, but he was also desperate. His marriage was in crisis, and he hadn't slept more than three hours a night for the past few months. A tarot reading with me was his last resort.

It became clear during his reading that Ed's current relationship issues had more to do with his first marriage than his current one. He'd divorced his first wife, Barb, twenty years earlier. Because they didn't have kids together, Ed hadn't spoken to her since the papers were signed. He didn't even know where (or if) Barb was living, but Ed was still energetically attached to his past, and it was preventing him from fully stepping into his future.

It was time for Ed to Burn His Sh*t.

The Full Moon was the following week, and I instructed Ed to do a fire ritual. He was equal parts doubtful and hopeful, and promised to let me know if it helped. The morning after the Full Moon, Ed called me. He'd gone down to the shore of Lake Ontario with a pile of paper concerning his current relationship and job, as well as a photo of him and his ex-wife that he'd printed out. The night was calm and clear. One by one, he read each slip of paper aloud before lighting it on fire and watching the words disappear into ash. Each one caught fire quickly and burned bright, until he got to the picture of him and Barb, which he'd saved for last.

Despite being printed on the same type of paper as the others, this one wouldn't light. Or it would briefly catch before sputtering out. "That final piece of paper," Ed told me later, "was some real stubborn shit."

After a couple of futile minutes, Ed decided that the paper with Barb's picture wasn't burning because it hadn't received a proper send-off. There needed to be more to it. Although he hadn't seen Barb in ages, their marriage was still a major milestone in his life, and Ed instinctively knew this goodbye needed to reflect that, so he tried again: "Barb, I now choose to release you from my life. I release the hold I have on your heart, and the hold you have on mine. I release our sacred bond in this lifetime, past lifetimes, and future lifetimes. I release you to a life of love and happiness, and I release anything holding me back from the same. Our work here is done. And so it is . . ."

Ed lit a match and held it under the paper, which immediately ignited as if he'd soaked it in lighter fluid. The flame was so unexpected and intense that Ed dropped the paper and watched it burn at his feet. Then he went home and slept for seventeen hours straight. I'm not sure if Ed's marriage survived, but I'm certain that the unburdening he experienced through this ritual helped Ed move forward with the confidence and clarity he'd been missing.

We have ceremonies to honor so many turning points in our lives. We acknowledge these defining moments with rituals, whether it's a jubilant wedding or a sorrowful funeral, but there is no generally accepted ritual to mark the end of a relationship, which is essential for closure (I'll expand on this in Chapter 8). We must mourn to move forward.

You have the capacity to adapt and evolve. When you let go of old narratives and beliefs, you allow your past to inform your future rather than define it.

CHAPTER 6

MANIFESTING FOR DUMMIES (NEW MOON MAGIC RITUAL)

◇◇◇

Manifesting is nothing new. It's been a pop-culture staple for decades, thanks to books like *The Secret* or the work of Abraham Hicks. In a nutshell, you manifest by setting clear intentions, identifying internal shifts, and taking inspired action. But the outcome often falls flat because the intentions lack clarity, internal shifts are forgotten, or the inspired action is skipped altogether. I'm going to walk you through my proven techniques for manifesting that have served me (and my clients) *very* well so you can start making your own magic.

My New Moon Magic workshop was inspired by the homework (aka spellwork) assigned to me by my witchy tarot mentor over twenty-five years ago—it's also how I landed my husband. My mentor told me to conjure up a vision of my ideal partner, describe him in writing, and sleep with the paper under my pillow during a New Moon before tucking it away somewhere safe.

To be clear, at this point in my life I was a bit of a dumbass, which was reflected in my very specific list of *Future Husband Nonnegotiables*:

- Must be tall, dark, and handsome (sexy accent preferred)
- Must be a lawyer, doctor, or architect (maybe banker)

- Must be a homeowner (no condos)
- Must drive a Jeep Cherokee (red)
- Must have a dog (ideally a golden retriever)

It went on for another page, but you get the idea. I was trying to manifest a partner like I was ordering a pizza. A week later, after my handsome, home-owning, dog-dadding, Jeep-driving, lawyering husband had failed to materialize, I stuck the list in a drawer and forgot about it.

Fast-forward ten months: I'm dating a broke immigrant who works at a warehouse while attending university, and all of his possessions (including his *bus pass*) fit into two shopping bags. Forget the condo: he rented a room from an alcoholic senior citizen who frequently asked him to cut her toenails in the middle of the night.

I found my love wish list when he and I moved in together, and I realized that while he may not have checked all of my requirements, he exceeded the most important ones: he is kind, funny, smart, cultured and well-traveled, respectful and loyal, and he adores me. He is also over six-feet tall and undeniably handsome, with a Mediterranean complexion and sexy accent. And, in a testament to my manifesting mojo, he was sharing custody of a golden retriever with his ex-girlfriend. To be clear, after writing my list I also took the step of getting therapy for the first time in my life (but Goddess knows not the last), which in turn led to a shift in all of my relationships. That's the inspired action at work.

I honed my method over the years until arriving at the perfect recipe for manifesting in any area of life. I now teach my New Moon Magic workshop every month and have countless testimonials from past participants who've reaped the rewards of this esoteric exercise—like Sasha, who was living in Minnesota while dreaming of a

move to Europe. During New Moon Magic, she was able to identify what was missing in her manifesting so she could transition her
dream into reality (she now lives on a houseboat in Amsterdam).

In many ways, New Moon Magic is a very practical way to
reverse-engineer your life: get clear on your goals, reflect on how to
achieve them, take action to make them happen, and sprinkle a bit of
magic on them to help them grow. We leverage the generative energy
of the New Moon to amplify our intentions. New Moon Magic may
not seem as sexy as setting stuff on fire, but I find it equally (if not
more) powerful than Burn Your Sh*t.

WHAT MAKES A
NEW MOON MAGICAL

◇◇◇

Every month, the New Moon signals the launch of the lunar cycle.
During this phase, the Moon appears to disappear as it comes between
the Sun and Earth, but behind the scenes, the Sun and Moon rise
in the sky together, joining forces to offer a cosmic kick start. The
darkened sky resembles a blank canvas waiting to be embellished
with your astral masterpiece. It's the ideal time to clarify objectives,
launch a project, or initiate collaborations around money, relationships, or health—and we want the energy surrounding these initia-
tives to be as fortified and fertile as possible.

New Moons are a chance to claim what you're ready to manifest
and commit to the desires, ideas, and actions required to get you
there. Although you can manifest on any day of the month, doing
this ritual on or around a New Moon delivers an extra infusion of
lunar energy to your intentions. Putting ceremony to this moment

helps you cultivate clarity about your goals and makes you accountable for the steps you need to take in order to achieve them. It's an extremely powerful time to become the designer of your dreams. Let's make the most of it.

Astrological Flavors

Every New Moon occurs in the same zodiac sign as the Sun (unlike a Full Moon, which sits in the opposite sign). For example, if we're in Scorpio season (late October to mid-November), you'll find the New Moon also sitting in Scorpio. Each sign has its own signature vibe, and a New Moon activates the energy of the sign where it takes place. Your New Moon ritual can be even more potent if you align these energies with the corresponding aspects of your life. Here are some general themes to keep in mind.

Aries (March 21–April 19)

As the first sign of the astrological New Year (occurring on the equinox, in March), Aries ignites your soul's mission and motivates you to step into your purpose with confidence. This is a passionate sign of action—Aries drives you to dream big, explore new options, and take bold moves to make your mark. Aries is the refresh button of the zodiac, heralding eternal renewal and boundless possibilities.

CRYSTAL: CARNELIAN

Taurus (April 20–May 20)

Earthy and comfort-focused Taurus offers insights regarding growth, stability, and the pursuit of pleasure. Abundance in all forms starts by grounding within yourself and connecting to the world around you so you feel supported, secure, and inspired. Embrace a slower pace, indulge in sensual sensations, and anchor into your self-worth—doing so will help you cultivate enduring change on solid and sustainable ground.

CRYSTAL: MALACHITE

Gemini (May 21–June 20)

Gemini season inspires expansion, calling on you to (literally) write a new narrative for your life. Gemini's curious energy is steeped in stories and seeking connection—it can also be a bit scattered as it attempts to gather and synthesize as much information as possible. But its focus on words makes the Gemini New Moon an ideal time to write your intentions, and clarity is the key to making the most of this charged manifesting moment.

CRYSTAL: TIGER'S EYE

Cancer (June 21–July 22)

Cancer is the mother of the zodiac, focused on creating a home with every form of family. Cancer's emotional intensity requires you to nurture your tender heart and keep self-care on speed dial, but make no mistake—a Cancer New Moon is an incredibly potent time. With the Moon ruling Cancer, intuition and imagination are magnified. Intentions are transformed into actuality. Allow yourself to visualize the details and feel the emotions surrounding whatever you plan to manifest (don't worry about the "how"—that's not your business).

CRYSTAL: MOONSTONE

Leo (July 23–August 22)

Courageous in spirit and regal in nature, Leo leads with passion and lives for drama—never shying away from self-expression. Ruled by the Sun, Leo inspires everyone with its playful, joyous energy. A Leo

New Moon is the moment to declare that you are ready to become your truest, most authentically radiant self. Leo energy emboldens you to get creative in how you can stand in your power and claim space on your stage.

CRYSTAL: PERIDOT

Virgo (August 23–September 22)

Virgo is the most misunderstood sign of the zodiac—its perceived faults are actually its best attributes. Hyper-organized perfectionism and obsession with efficiencies? Sure. But Virgo gets sh*t done, and done well. Clutter gets cleared and victory emerges from mayhem. Virgo also *loves* rituals because they infuse habits with meaning, acting as a conduit to clarity. Hard work is like foreplay for this sign, and the effort you put into manifesting during a Virgo New Moon will be rewarded in equal measure.

CRYSTAL: AMAZONITE

Libra (September 23–October 22)

Libra craves balance like bread craves butter. A Libra New Moon invites beauty and justice into your life, while highlighting the power of connection—Libra's fun and flirty charms conceal an insatiable yearning to be in relationship with others, but also with self. When it comes to partnerships—personal or professional—this is the New Moon to manifest them, so define and declare your intentions with gusto.

CRYSTAL: LEPIDOLITE

Scorpio (October 23–November 21)

If Libra's vibe is like a coffee date with your office crush, Scorpio is more of a dominatrix-themed game of Spin the Bottle. Magnetic and provocative, Scorpio's waters run deep. There's a freedom to be found in being fearless, and a Scorpio New Moon bolsters your courage when embarking in a new direction. Lean into your heightened intuition to uncover your deepest desires and focus on how you might bring them to fruition.

CRYSTAL: LABRADORITE

Sagittarius (November 22–December 21)

Sagittarius wants you doing all the things in all the places all at once. The most optimistic, fun-loving sign of the zodiac, Sagittarius imbues every intention with a healthy dose of best-case scenario vibes. A New Moon in Sagittarius asks you to look at life through a lens of exuberance. Have faith in miracles. Dream bigger than you ever thought possible. It's manifesting on steroids.

CRYSTAL: AVENTURINE

Capricorn (December 22–January 19)

Capricorn is committed to building structures that stand the test of time. Nothing turns Capricorn's crank like traditions, boundaries, and hard work—and a New Moon in this disciplined sign is the perfect time to align your intentions with career ambitions. Focus your manifesting on establishing the structures and systems required to set you up for success. Making practical moves in support of your intentions will pay off—big time.

CRYSTAL: RED GARNET

Aquarius (January 20–February 18)

Exceptionally independent and intellectually curious, Aquarius energy inspires you to challenge the status quo. A New Moon in this quirky sign sparks opportunities to think outside the box

and innovate new solutions to problems not visible to many, often in service of the collective. Whatever intentions you're setting, remember to lean into your unique gifts and well-earned wisdom to give you an assist.
CRYSTAL: HEMATITE

Pisces (February 19–March 20)
Being the last sign in the zodiac, Pisces is the most free-flowing sign, steeped in spirituality and marinating in mysticism. Pisces energy fuels your healing by celebrating your sensitivities while honoring your intuition, encouraging you to surrender to Universal flow. Don't hesitate to dream big during a Pisces New Moon—let your imagination lead you to dizzying peaks of possibility.
CRYSTAL: AQUAMARINE

Working with the zodiac can also help you track the progress of your manifesting by providing checkpoints at different moments in the lunar cycle—either two weeks later, at the next Full Moon, or when the Full Moon enters the corresponding astrological sign six months later (for example, intentions set during a Virgo New Moon in August can be revisited during a Virgo Full Moon in March). Just don't let your intentions morph into a self-fulfilling prophecy (like trolling Tinder on the last day of May in order to manifest a relationship by June). These astro cycles are meant to offer moments of reflection, not IBS-inducing dread because you aren't meeting a self-imposed deadline.

You can still perform New Moon rituals during an eclipse, but they introduce intense and unrestrained energy, like a live wire lying on the ground, ready to deliver unexpected jolts of electricity. These highly activated moments can incite abrupt beginnings and endings, so be extra clear and confident about what you're ready to manifest (otherwise, it could be a case of "careful what you wish for . . . ").

MANIFESTING MUST-HAVES

◇◇◇

Dreams become reality with effort. The Universe doesn't indulge our desires just because we've journaled about it or walk around acting like it's already happened. There are a lot of false prophets out there promoting blind faith and fueling broken dreams, which leads to a bunch of ding-dongs sitting in front of vision boards wondering why nothing worked out (I was one of those ding-dongs).

Manifesting isn't about cosmic fairy godmothers granting wishes. It's about taking inspired action toward a clear intention leading to transformation. When you manifest properly, you become your own fairy godmother. It's like goal-setting with a sprinkle of fairy dust.

The first step is figuring out what you want to manifest. Are you ready to find romance? Run a marathon? Get a new job? Whether it's about work, health, relationships, or something else, you have to identify your intention. Any action you take is preceded by intention—from making a sandwich to moving abroad, your objective will determine your outcome. Where focus goes, energy flows. If you're unclear about your goal, you'll get stalled before you start. Setting an intention is like drawing a map, and it becomes the directional force behind your dreams. Without an intention, there is no map. You're just driving down a road with no clue where you're headed.

Believe boldly in your intentions—daydream, journal, create a vision board, or do whatever works for you—then get off your ass and do something. Take inspired action to get the ball rolling; give the Universe something to get behind. You want to run a marathon?

Buy some running shoes, take a learn-to-run clinic, and imagine how you'll feel crossing that finish line. Then forget the rest of the path. Don't try to plan, plot, or visualize every single step, because it diminishes the magic. Instead, be open to the synchronicities and stepping stones that show up (seemingly out of nowhere) to guide you to your goal or lead you somewhere better. Decide to do something or learn something or be something, and make moves in that direction (baby steps are great!). Don't worry about how it will happen once you get started. When you're clear on what you want and take steps to get it, the how will reveal itself.

Now that you're clear on the basics (intention + inspired action + letting life respond), you're ready to start manifesting. You can spice things up by lighting some candles, saging your space, or putting out some crystals, but all you really need for New Moon Magic is some paper and a pen. I prefer doing this ritual during the day, when the Moon and Sun are sharing the sky. If you forget or you aren't home when the New Moon occurs, you can always perform this ritual a few days before or after and still get the benefits.

I'll expand on these concepts and share some real-life stories to help you identify and take ownership for what you want to manifest, and then we'll look at the internal shifts that might be required to help you step into inspired action. But first, let's set the mood and open up energetically.

MAKING MAGIC

◇◇◇

Before you begin, have your pen and paper handy, shut the door, and turn off your phone. Establish a sacred space to work your magic, whether it's setting up an elaborate altar or saging a corner of your closet. Activate your senses by lighting some candles, brewing a cup of tea, or settling into a cozy pile of cushions. Designate the necessary time, space, and energy to perform your ritual—it will help ground you in the moment as you connect with your higher self and Spirit.

Open your New Moon ritual with the following meditation (as with Burn Your Sh*t, you can record it on your phone or use the QR code on page 303 to access a recording of me walking you through it):

Close your eyes and place one hand on your heart and the other on your belly as you take three deep, cleansing breaths. Inhale through your nose and exhale out your mouth, bringing attention to each breath. Feel the rise of your belly as you inhale, and then exhale slowly as you settle gently into a state of relaxation.

Take note of any tension in your shoulders, and release it now. It's okay to let the anxiety go as you soften into your body. Release all of the stress in your neck and jaw. Feel your tongue go heavy in your mouth, letting your mouth open slightly as you ease into a place of complete calm. Feel the muscles around your eyes relax. Let your shoulders drop even farther as you focus on your breath.

Your entire body is relaxed. This moment is for you alone. There is nothing that demands your attention right now. Let go of the to-do list, the "I have to's" and the "I should have's," and sink into this moment of feeling completely safe and totally relaxed.

Visualize yourself beside a beautiful stream. Let the tranquil sound of the water bring you peace and calm as a gentle breeze greets you. Along the edge of the stream is a lush garden. Imagine how the air smells, imbued with the fragrance of nearby plants and flowers. This thriving foliage is a reflection of everything you are growing in your life. This garden represents the energetic seeds that you've been planting. Many of the seeds are just sprouting, while some have bloomed into flowers, and others are still waiting to take root. You nourish them all with ease and love as they grow in abundance. The garden of your life is a beautiful cocreation between yourself, your people, and the Universe. Pause to look around and appreciate everything you have nurtured.

Now, as you look around, notice the setting sun. It is the end of another day. The fading light is dancing on the water. As you continue to softly inhale and exhale, your mind, body, and spirit are perfectly at ease. As the day turns to night, you sit at the water's edge, taking in the glorious nature that surrounds you.

Notice the stars as they shimmer in the darkening sky—the New Moon allowing them to glow even brighter. Your heart smiles at the vast magnificence of the Universe. You are safe and relaxed, enveloped in a beautiful calm. You are open to discovering your potential and stepping into your purpose. Let your spirit soak up this moment of peace and awareness.

When you are ready to return, slowly bring your thoughts back to this moment and your surroundings. Take your time as your body reawakens. Stretch into the space around you, knowing in the deepest parts of your soul that you are ready to discover the fresh start, great joy, and endless possibilities that await.

Write today's month and year along with the word *Intentions* at the top of your paper (for example, *July 2024 Intentions*). Under that heading, write *This or something better.* We always add this phrase to our manifesting because we don't know what we don't know, and we don't want to limit ourselves or put parameters around what is possible.

Take a moment to consider what you are ready to welcome into your life. Do you have one specific goal in mind, or many? Are you ready to show up in the world in a more authentic way? Is there a risk you feel called to take? Are there ways you could be taking better care of yourself spiritually, emotionally, or physically? What do you most desire? Are you craving a career that aligns with your purpose? A new (or improved) romantic relationship? Are you ready to embrace a healthier lifestyle?

Stay still and be quiet—let yourself hear the whispered messages nudging you to connect with the wisdom that lies within you. Be open to receiving intuitive guidance that may be different from what you were expecting. Liberate yourself from expectations so you can discover the direction your soul is leading you.

Write down whatever comes to mind, using positive and affirming statements (I always start with *I am ready to receive . . .*). Avoid *I need* or *I want* in your statements because those words come from a place of lack—you don't want to invite *more* wanting or needing in your life. The words we choose matter, so be intentional with your intentions (it's called *spell-ing* for a reason). Focus on what you want, which sounds simple but can be challenging if you're used to dwelling on what you *don't* want.

For instance, *I don't want to be in debt* becomes *I am ready to be debt-free*. Or even better, *I have a healthy relationship with my money, and it flows easily to me*.

I don't want to be single can be rewritten as *I am ready to be in a loving, respectful, and passionate romantic relationship*.

Even seemingly positive statements can benefit from a reframe. Instead of writing *I am ready to lose weight*, you could write *I am ready to be healthier and stronger*.

Do you see how these goals are specific while still leaving *lots* of room for the Universe to do its thing? Rather than saying you want to work at a particular company doing a certain job for a precise salary, you are declaring that you are ready to find the job that aligns with your skills, experience, and interest, while compensating you generously and allowing you to work from home. It might be the job you thought, or it might be something even better.

You may have one big intention (*I am ready to move into my dream home*) or a bunch of smaller goals (*I am ready to be more organized*). There's always next month, so if you want to save a few for another time, that's fine, too. If you aren't sure what to manifest, your intention can simply be *I am ready to discover my intentions*.

Spend some time visualizing your intentions as if they've already materialized. Imagine yourself one year from today, completely embodied as your future self, living in a state of flow with the Universe and world around you. What kind of foods are you eating? How do you dress? Who are the people around you? Where do you live? How do you spend your free time? Take a moment to pause in this future state and notice what your environment looks like and, more importantly, how it *feels*. Tap into your elevated emotions—feel the rush of gratitude, elation, relief, or whatever else comes up for you. Let it course throughout your body as if you've already attained your goal. Write these impressions as a separate journal entry.

If there is a specific event you're manifesting, like running a marathon, immerse yourself in that moment. Imagine putting on your running shoes . . . feel the surge of butterflies in your stomach at the start line . . . hear the starting pistol. Envision people cheering you on along the way; feel the exhaustion and elation as you cross the finish line hours later. Do this with every item on your list, and focus on the sensations over the specifics (let the Universe handle the logistics).

Now look at this list and ask yourself, *How do I reverse-engineer this? What changes can I make today to be in this future position tomorrow?* Look at each intention and consider the outward actions that need to be taken and the internal shifts that are necessary to help you transition from where you are to where you'd like to be.

If you're looking for a dream job, you can update your resume and buy shoes for the interviews, but you also want to dig deeper. What are your limiting beliefs about money? What is your negative self-talk around the value you'd bring to a company? What bad habits do you have that this future version of you—who's knocking it out of the park at the new job—doesn't have? What kind of morning routine does your future self have that sets a framework for success? Take time to self-reflect in an honest and nonjudgmental way. Get clear on how your perspective and stories need to change along with your habits and actions.

Let's say my intention is to be healthier. Some *external* actions would be eating nutritious foods and exercising regularly. An *internal* shift would be consciously choosing to see my body as worthy of love and respect—because *I* am worthy of love and respect—and trying to honor my body as a beautiful vessel for my soul. Another intention could be discovering your life's purpose. You can take steps toward this goal by doing workshops that pique your interest or setting aside time every day for mindfulness or journaling. More subtle shifts may involve thinking back to your favorite childhood pastimes or getting curious about what makes your soul sing. Give yourself the opportunity for clues to reveal your calling.

Let yourself dream *really* big here. If your inner critic creeps in and starts bad-mouthing your dreams, acknowledge it by writing down whatever resistance shows up. This might appear at any point while you're visualizing. It might even stop you from being able to visualize as you begin, so if it does, pause and write down what's coming up, and then return to visualizing. Repeat as necessary. This can be painful, but it also allows you to dig deep and get to the good stuff. Fear and doubt are normal parts of the manifesting process, especially when you're asking for something major. Gay Hendricks coined the term *upper limit* in his excellent book *The Big Leap*. It describes what happens when our subconscious identifies the changes that come with success as dangerous and activates self-sabotage to keep us "safe" (when it's really just "stuck"). As we ascend to new levels, we can feel more vulnerable than ever because there is so much more to lose. Rather than enjoying our success, we can find ourselves obsessing about what could go wrong.

Think about what you'll gain from achieving your goals, but also what will be lost. For example, losing weight will result in feeling healthier, and clothes may be easier to buy, but it can also bring attention from others that may feel uncomfortable or even threatening. Or your side hustle expands to the point that you can quit your day job, but now you're dealing with high-level executives and magnified financial stakes. Sometimes, we can undermine these moments of personal evolution because our ancestral brains see uncertainty as perilous. Also consider how patterning and beliefs from childhood can thwart future success. Growing up in a family that struggled financially, with parents complaining about how all rich people are corrupt, may result in a subconscious resistance to receiving money.

Be aware of bringing *shoulds* into your manifesting. *Should* is such a shaming word, and we're constantly *shoulding* all over ourselves (*I should be this, he should do that*). Don't ignore these upper-limit problems—they provide insight into potential blocks to reaching your goals. Write them down on a separate piece of paper, and either burn the paper right away or wait for the next Full Moon (or do both!). Once your blocks have been identified and released, continue to let your mind wander. See where your imagination goes when left to roam freely. Go for it. Don't hold back.

By declaring what you are ready to receive and spending time in that future state of success, you'll get more comfortable with the idea of what's possible. When we identify the ways our subconscious is working to keep us safe, even when it's not in our best interest, we can move past these self-imposed ceilings and start taking small steps toward our objectives.

To close your ritual, take a moment to imagine a warm beam of light filling your body and spilling over to infuse your aura with unconditional love. Let it fill those small, dark, hidden places where you don't feel like you're enough. Allow the light to restore and rejuvenate you on a physical, emotional, and energetic level, knowing that it is now embedded in every part of you as you move throughout your day.

THE SECRET SAUCE

◇◇◇

Now it's time to get a little witchy with it. When you're done visualizing and getting introspective, fold up the paper with your intentions written on it, slip it under your pillow, and sleep on it. It's fine if they're written together with the journaling you did about the internal and external shifts, etc., but you may want to copy them onto separate sheets so you're not left with a pillow full of paper. (I usually write all of my intentions on a 5-by-seven inch piece of paper that I then fold and stick in my pillowcase.)

When it's time to do the laundry, don't throw the paper out or burn it. Instead, slide it into your nightstand or tuck it into a book (or pop it back under your pillow to keep cooking). Keep it close and let it percolate. You could also put it on your altar or vision board as a clear reminder. I like tucking mine away to revisit every month because I feel more pressure than motivation when I constantly see my list out in the open.

I've been telling people about this exercise for over a quarter of a century, and it's amazing to see what shows up when you get intentional with your actions (setting goals), do the necessary inner work (turning within), and bring in a little magic (getting witchy).

NEW MOON MISSTEPS & MILESTONES

◇◇◇

I have a tarot client (let's call her Tracy) who was desperate to find a husband. Despite being smart, beautiful, accomplished, and kind, Tracy kept attracting dudes who treated her like garbage. I assigned her the New Moon ritual as homework, and she called me in a panic months later. Her sister's wedding was coming up, and she was determined to bring a date, but—despite writing her list, taking inspired action, and doing the inner work—she was meeting only tall, movie-star-handsome, emotionally unavailable assholes.

Tracy's manifesting mistake was a common one: she was trying to control timelines and micromanage outcomes. Once you figure out what you really want and get the courage to make moves in that direction, it can be difficult to then step back and see what (or who) turns up. If you're not constantly hustling or seeing immediate results, you may feel like you are giving up. But you're not quitting—you're simply surrendering the need to control the outcome. (P.S. As author Elizabeth Gilbert writes, you never really had control . . . you just had anxiety.) Tracy was also expecting her future fella to look a particular way. I told her about my misadventures in manifesting a husband (the broke immigrant student) and instructed her to focus less on what she expected him to *look* like and more on how it would *feel* to be with him. She was seeking a soul connection (not a side piece), and the love of her life might be a short, chubby redhead—but she'd never know if she continued to resist alternative options.

Tracy promised to unclench about finding a certain type of person by an exact day and instead open up to finding her person. A year passed before I heard from Tracy again. She told me her approach to dating had shifted from controlling to curious. She was engaged to a wonderful man she'd met shortly after going on a date with (I promise I'm not making this up) a short, chubby redhead. Once Tracy removed the deadlines from her dreams and consciously let life happen (instead of trying to force it), the Universe delivered.

Getting my agent and publishing deal for this book you're reading was a masterclass in manifesting. I'd already written another book (about tarot) and visualized walking into bookstores to see it on the shelves. Before even typing *The End* on my manuscript, I'd written the acknowledgments that authors include at the back of their books (*I'd like to thank my agent, TBD, for believing in me . . .*). I shifted my intentions from *I just don't want to pay to publish it myself* to *I'm ready for a book deal with a Big Five publisher.*

A woman who worked in publishing reached out to me *the day after I completed my manuscript* to ask if I had any tarot deck or book ideas, which led me to create a proposal and query letter (two must-haves when looking to publish a nonfiction book). Although that conversation didn't lead to an offer, it did jump-start my efforts: I researched agents who were aligned with my category, wrote a query letter that I paid to have critiqued by people in the industry, and created a detailed spreadsheet to track agents as I contacted them. Then I . . . did other stuff unrelated to the book. I focused on growing my Instagram platform, rerecording my online tarot workshop, and researching my next book. I also took longer walks with my dog and spent more time with friends. Having a variety of goals in all areas of my life prevented me from getting hyper-focused (aka clenchy); I was able to avoid my old pattern of getting frustrated and giving up before I'd even started.

Within a couple of months, I had a magnificent agent (*I love you, Alex!*), who secured me a *two-book deal* with HarperCollins! The editors I met with had seen Burn Your Sh*t on Instagram and were very interested in my Woo Woo Without the Cuckoo approach to rituals (which I'd been planning for my second book). That's how I manifested becoming a published author: I was clear on my intention, followed it up with inspired action, and then stepped back, allowing the Universe to bring me that or something better. (Update: It was something better.)

After you've tucked your intentions under your pillow, you can close out your New Moon ritual with a soak in the tub. Water is a conduit for energy and can fortify your intentions (just like it can assist you in amplifying your releases during a Full Moon). A Water-based ritual, such as a bath or shower—or even just washing your hands, feet, or face—is a wonderful way to elevate your manifesting by connecting with lunar power as you relax your body and reset your soul.

Whether you have major goals for massive projects or the itty-bittiest idea that needs to germinate before taking root, you've made moves with this ritual to plant your fresh ideas in the most fertile soil. You can change your life by changing how you live: set powerful intentions, take aligned actions, and trust that you will be supported on your path.

CHAPTER 7

RISE & SHINE (HOW TO START & END YOUR DAY WITH INTENTION)

<figure>◇◇◇</figure>

have a sticky note in my office (I looked at it as I typed this) with four bullet points:

- Words
- Water
- Move
- Breathe

It's my morning ritual: journal when I'm still half asleep (more on that soon), drink a big glass of water, do a few sun salutations along with seated stretches, and sit for a brief (I'm talking six minutes max) guided meditation. I also make my bed, wash my face, and brush my teeth before filming "Card of the Day" for Instagram, but nothing happens before Words, Water, Move, and Breathe. I'll occasionally skip one (or all) of them if I'm sick or have an extra-early start, but I've been doing a variation of this ritual for years, and I still like having that visual reminder to start my day with intention. My evening ritual is a work in progress, fluctuating between: a) hatha yoga followed by an Epsom bath, and b) scrolling Instagram while bingeing Netflix. We're all on our own journey.

Just like holidays or special occasions, daily rituals are an opportunity to align with your values and goals. You likely already have a morning ritual that you call a routine. The difference between the two can be found in the attitude behind the action—routines increase focus and boost productivity, while rituals ground routines in purpose and infuse them with intention. With a shift in perspective, a mundane action like making your bed can become a meaningful practice, but it needs to be internally motivated (in other words, it needs to matter to you), and you need a clear "why" behind your ritual (for example, getting energized versus inviting ease). Your daily rituals play a crucial role in achieving a bigger purpose. If you can engage fully with a task that you've infused with purpose, you'll add enjoyment and efficiency to your day in equal measure—and it has been measured.

Multiple studies published by the U.S. National Library of Medicine have found a link between a consistent nighttime routine and better rest, especially for children (a lot of us parents learned this the hard way). According to the Centers for Disease Control and Prevention, an estimated 50 to 70 million American adults have chronic sleep disorders. Like exercise and eating well, good sleep hygiene can help prevent a variety of health issues, such as depression, obesity, and heart disease.

Many of us start and end the day on our phones, checking emails or scrolling social media. In 2014, Harvard researchers determined that swapping good sleep practices with phone scrolling inhibits the release of melatonin (the hormone that helps us fall asleep, disrupts the circadian rhythm that controls our sleep patterns, and diminishes our alertness the following day).

Dr. David Greenfield, founder of the Center for Internet and Technology Addiction, states that regardless of when you're on your phone, the content you engage with and the act of checking it (as well as the compulsion to do so) can unleash a wave of the stress hormone cortisol into your system that prevents you from drifting off to sleep, or overwhelms you in the morning before your feet even hit the floor.

Researchers also published findings in the National Library of Medicine confirming that cultivating an inviting and consistent sleep environment promotes mental tranquility, improves cognitive functioning, and increases overall happiness. Science is basically telling us that the brain can be kind of stupid sometimes, in need of cues to help it gear up or settle down—and rituals are the medium for the message.

The first and last moments of your day are crucial. Every sunrise offers a fresh start, and how you begin it impacts how you handle stressors throughout the day. Similarly, there is a clearing as the sun sets that wipes the slate clean and significantly impacts your rest (which in turn influences the following day).

Morning rituals are nothing new. Agatha Christie munched on apples in the bath as she plotted her next mystery. Winston Churchill woke up at dawn, enjoyed a cigar with his whiskey, and then worked from his bed until almost noon. Benjamin Franklin started every day with an "air bath" (writing or reading with the window open while completely naked). How you start your morning affects the rest of your day—whether it's enjoying a simple cup of tea while you Wordle or rushing out the door dropping f-bombs on everyone in your path—and you have the power to determine the direction. Cortisol naturally peaks within thirty minutes of waking to prepare us for the day ahead, and a 2017 study by researchers from the University of California and the University of Ottawa showed that jumping right into work or on your phone increases this anxiety-inducing hormone even more, causing it to keep spiking throughout the day. While the repetition of a morning routine definitely helps to mitigate morning stress, a morning *ritual* takes it to the next level by connecting you to your whole self and setting the tone for your entire day.

I was listening to a podcast recently that featured a self-described wellness guru who encouraged people to put aside *three hours* every day for morning rituals, which is an absurd expectation for anyone with a family or job. But determining how you spend the first or last *thirty minutes* of your day? That can be a game changer.

The ideal morning ritual is one that works for you—make it easy to do even when you don't feel like it and flexible enough to modify in the moment. I'll be sharing some common rituals to start and end your day (with a witchy twist, of course), but these are merely suggestions to help you build your daily ritual toolbox. Figure out what works best with your schedule, work or home situation, and internal clock. For example, if you aren't a morning person by nature, or you work erratic hours, you can still have a morning ritual that sets you up for success, even if you do it in the afternoon. While you consider what will work best in your first-thing ritual, remember that nothing kills motivation in the morning and muddies intention (or screws with your sleep) faster than a screen—try to stay away from electronics completely before your morning ritual and after your nightly one so you don't negate the positive effects.

Curate your daily ritual to suit your lifestyle. It doesn't need to be pricey, lengthy, or elaborate; it just has to be yours. If you hate herbal tea, don't drink it. If the thought of doing a spin class before work makes you want to barf, but you want to incorporate movement, do some light stretching in your jammies. Consider your energy, not your time. What's your mood like in the morning? Are you super motivated as soon as you get out of bed or do you hit your stride in the afternoon? I'm more creative in the morning, so I set that time aside for writing. And I don't read tarot cards too late at night because I get so buzzy that it takes me hours to fall asleep.

Choose a few rituals that appeal to you and experiment with different combinations. There may be some overlap or repetition, and that's fine. Your practice may evolve over time as your priorities change or you find something you like better. Simply commit to starting and ending your day in a soulful way—it's not about *having* time for your ritual so much as *creating* time, whether that means fifteen minutes or two hours. Regardless of what your ritual looks like, how long it takes, or when you do it, the goal is to create a daily practice that aligns you with your goals and supports you in your well-being.

EVERY BREATH YOU TAKE (HOW YOU DO IT MATTERS)

◇◇◇

The easiest, most effortless ingredient to any daily ritual is breathwork—it's the foundation of everything we do, even if we don't realize we're doing it. When you bring awareness to your breath, it becomes a sacred practice. Intentional breathwork centers you in the present moment and connects you to the Divine energy in and around you. It also promotes the release of toxins in your body, alleviates pain, and increases happiness. Nothing is as simple and as powerful as breath, but not all breaths are created equal. Babies reflexively fill their bellies with air on their first gasping breath, but as we age our breathing habits change (usually for the worse). Adults tend to live in a state of shallow chest breathing, with most of our 22,000 daily breaths never making it to the belly. (I start every Moon ritual with three deep belly breaths, but the first one is often all in my chest and I can feel my shoulders rising up to my ears.)

Chest breathing inflates your lungs by pulling on the rib cage with your chest muscles, while diaphragmatic (aka belly) breathing pulls down on the abdominal cavity using your diaphragm to fully inflate the lungs. Belly breathing is what we do in a yoga class. Chest breathing is what happens when we hyperventilate. Some people think they're belly breathing when they're really just shifting shallow breath from chest to stomach, so check your ribs to see if you're one of those people. Take a deep breath and pay attention to whether your lungs expand in all directions at once, like a balloon. When your diaphragm is engaged, you'll feel the movement of your rib cage. Place your hands on your lower ribs with the tips of your middle fingers meeting at your belly button. Slide them apart until the heel of your hands are at your sides and then inhale into your belly—if your hands don't move, your lungs aren't expanding. Try doing this as you breathe into your chest to feel the difference . . . if there even is one. This breath check can be repeated along your belly, sides, collarbone, and even back.

When you activate your diaphragm through breath, it stimulates your vagus nerve, which is like a superhighway between the body and brain. The vagus nerve regulates everything from digestion and immunity to blood pressure and skin sensations. It's also the secret to managing your stress, via the parasympathetic nervous system.

Quick Biology 101 refresher: our central nervous system contains the sympathetic nervous system and parasympathetic nervous system. The sympathetic nervous system kicks in when we feel a real or perceived threat, triggering the fight-flight-freeze-fawn response: our heart rate and breathing speed up, nonessential systems (like digestion, immunity, and reproduction) are suppressed, and stress hormones flood our bodies. This stress response is exactly what we need in a moment of high intensity ("A bear is chasing me!") but not great when the threat isn't, in fact, life-threatening ("I got an email!").

Thankfully, our wise bodies bring us into balance through the vagus nerve, which signals the parasympathetic nervous system and initiates our rest-and-digest (aka chill the f*ck out) response. When the parasympathetic nervous system takes over, the stress hormones cortisol and adrenaline are replaced with the feel-good effects of serotonin and dopamine. Breathing slows, the heart rate decreases, and blood pressure lowers as the body is guided into a state of calm and healing. Ideally, we want to spend the majority of our time in a parasympathetic state, but external forces (bills to pay, kids to raise, Instagram) make this nearly impossible.

A lot of us get stuck in this chronic state of panic, with the sympathetic nervous system launching SOS signals nonstop as we try to navigate our relationships, finances, illness, family drama, and insert-your-stress-here. Existing in this space for extended periods of time can lead to serious health issues. My mom was warned by her doctor that if she didn't deal with her stress ASAP, she would likely have a stroke, heart attack, or cancer within the next five years. She left my father three months later and has been thriving ever since. Not everyone can alleviate their anxiety in such an extreme way; sometimes it's simply a matter of getting through a challenging season, such as job loss or a newborn. We can't control our sympathetic nervous system, because its whole job is to automatically shift into high gear in an attempt to keep us safe, which is why tools for stress management (rather than banishment) are essential. And the easiest way to hack into a parasympathetic state is with breath.

Box breathing (also known as sama vritti pranayama) is an ancient yogic breathwork sequence that was made sexy by the United States Navy SEALs years ago and has since been embraced by stressed-out people everywhere. The technique is fairly straightforward: inhale through your nose and into your belly, pause at the top of the inhale, exhale out your mouth, and pause at the bottom of your exhale. You do each step for the same count (for example, in for four, hold for four, out for four, hold for four) and repeat the cycle for a few rounds. Since the mind can only focus on one thing at a time (spoiler: multitasking is a myth), the idea is to direct your focus away from the stressor by bringing your attention to the rhythm of your breath. More importantly, engaging the diaphragm as the belly fills with air activates the vagus nerve to regulate the parasympathetic nervous system. This is why box breathing is used by the SEALs and elite athletes in high-pressure situations—it sharpens concentration and enhances alertness when you need a quick hit of calm. And it's just as effective before job interviews or stepping onto a stage as it is when rescuing hostages or going for a gold medal.

If you find the count of four too long or short, try different combinations to see what works for you. Research suggests that controlled breathing with a longer exhale is optimal because your vagus nerve is activated more quickly and your heart rate is forced to slow down even sooner. Knowing that I can reach a state of calm faster with an exhale that's just a few counts longer than my inhale, I've modified my box breathing from a box into an extended triangle: I inhale for four, hold for four, exhale for eight, and skip the extended pause at the bottom of the exhale (otherwise I end up gasping for the next inhale).

Focused breathing is how I start and end my day, and I definitely feel the effects if I skip it (and so can my family). I'll often assign this breathwork as homework to my tarot clients, and I invite you to try it, too. Do it either sitting or lying down—the key is to do it intentionally (that is, not while you're making breakfast). Find a comfortable position, close your eyes, and take five deep belly breaths, inhaling through your nose for the count of five. Hold for the count of five, and then exhale out your mouth for the count of eight. In for five, hold for five, out for eight—five breaths in the morning, five breaths at night, that's it. This will take less than five minutes of your day and is an excellent foundation for any daily ritual. By breathing with your diaphragm, and exhaling longer than you inhale, you're inducing that parasympathetic state, beginning your day from a place that is strategic, creative, intuitive, and focused. Preparing for sleep with this breathwork recalibrates your emotional state, allowing you to drop the day's worries, wind down, and wipe the slate clean.

You obviously can do this whenever the mood strikes—some people attach intentional moments of mindfulness to daily activities as a reminder (for example, combining bathroom and breathing breaks). When you step away from your busy life, even for a few breaths, you're fortifying your energetic core. And if cyclic breathing is all you can do as a morning and evening ritual, the results can still be life-altering.

HOW TO MEDITATE
WHEN YOU HATE MEDITATING

◇◇◇

You're now breathing like a pro . . . what's next? Countless studies have measured the positive effects of meditation, but starting a meditation practice can be a pain in the ass (sometimes literally), and maintaining one can be difficult, mainly because meditating can be any or all of the following:

Intimidating: If you tell me I have to sit for twenty minutes cross-legged on the floor surrounded by crystals and inhaling incense while a tribal drum is thumped on one side of me and a singing bowl is played on the other, I will say, "No, thank you," and skedaddle away as quickly as possible. I know this will be my reaction because it happened to me when I was backpacking around Australia in my early twenties. It was one of my earliest forays into meditation, and it kept me away for years. People often stop meditating before they start because the options are overwhelming (*When do I do it? How long do I do it? Where do I do it? Do I need a mantra? What's a mantra?*), but it doesn't have to be so complicated.

Boring: Disengaging from the to-do list of life can be incredibly challenging, especially when the alternative is . . . doing nothing. With so many distractions at our fingertips, we rarely have an opportunity to be bored, but the nuggets of wisdom are often buried in the boredom; we just need the time and space to access them.

Uncomfortable: I hated getting pins and needles in my feet from sitting cross-legged as a kid in school, and I hate it even more as an adult. Also, my back, neck, and knees get sore. And don't get me started on the mental misery that comes from being wide awake and completely motionless at the same damn time.

Although meditation is more mainstream than when I was making my way (read: carousing) across Australia thirty years ago, it can still make people leery because they think meditating means emptying your mind, when the goal is actually the complete opposite. Our minds are meant to wander, and meditating doesn't stop thoughts in their tracks. It's an opportunity to flex your ability to focus, whether it's on the breath, a word, a visual, or nothing at all (simply being in the moment). You know when you've tried to meditate in the past and as you sit with your eyes closed, counting your inhales and exhales, you start making a grocery list or wondering if you fed the cat, so you refocus on your breath? *That* is the work and practice of meditation. Emptying your mind is futile; bringing it back to the present moment is magical.

When you go within, you shore up your energetic reserves. And it doesn't need to be a five-hour yoga marathon every morning. Try inviting some form of mindfulness into your daily rituals that allows you to tap into that Zen zone. Whether it's focused breathwork, walking, fishing, or something else—give yourself that gift of solitude, even for a few minutes.

If you're thinking, *Tarot Lori, I have a job and a family and barely have time to wash my face, never mind look for a place to meditate,* I get it. Life can be busy and stressful and messy (did I mention busy?), but meditation doesn't have to be an elaborate or expensive endeavor. Instead of waiting for the perfect time to join a month-long ashram, start by setting the timer on your phone for three minutes, closing your eyes, and taking some deliberate breaths. I used to tell everyone it was mommy's quiet time and the only valid reason to interrupt me was if someone was literally about to die, then I'd go in my closet and inhale as I focused on the word *here* followed by an exhale with the word *now*.

When you bring meditation into your morning or evening ritual, it strengthens your soul and connects you to the Divine. Where intentional breathwork is a powerful stress-management technique, the calming effects of meditation are a secondary benefit. When you understand the underlying objective of meditation—reconnecting with yourself and everyone and everything around you—it becomes a spiritual ritual.

These meditations can be done in the morning or evening, lying down or sitting anywhere that's comfortable (I sit in a chair because I tend to fall asleep if I'm horizontal, and we've already established that I'm not a fan of crisscross-applesauce style of sitting). You may want to play some gentle music or crave complete silence. You can be decked out in your finest yoga gear or pajamas or completely bare-assed. Use the timer on your phone or freestyle for as long as you want. (Tip: Try to schedule a regular time in the beginning to help you stay consistent and also because that's how you get deeper, longer-lasting benefits. Also, when you start, knowing you have a timer going helps quiet the distracting and constant questioning of how long you've been meditating for.) Keep a journal and pen nearby to record any insights or impressions, as well as some tissues in case there are tears, which is more common than you think and always okay.

Crystals & Candles: Your Meditation Besties

Crystals can deepen your meditation ritual, especially when you align them with your intention. Are you looking to make a clear-headed decision, heal an old wound, or just start your day from a place of openness? Do you need to dream big or grieve a loss? Consider the energy of each stone and how it can support your meditation. Let your intuition guide you to the crystal you need in the moment or consider how the vibes of the following gems might be a good match:

Selenite is a mood-brightening must-have. Ideal for removing blockages and raising your vibration, this crystal will balance your energy and invite peace into any meditation.

Black obsidian can ground the most scattered energy, promoting calm as it protects you from negative mojo. If you're doing shadow work or releasing negative patterns with your meditation, this rock has your back.

Rose quartz has a loving and gentle vibe, making it the perfect stone to heal a tender heart. This crystal radiates kindness and invites compassion for those around you and, more importantly, yourself.

Citrine offers an energetic boost in all areas of your life, instilling joy and optimism when you're in a slump. If your meditation is focused on manifesting, especially around financial matters, make this crystal the star attraction.

Labradorite acts as a portal to your higher consciousness, igniting your creativity to take you on an astral adventure. If you're looking for illumination and new ways of thinking, grab this gem and prepare to be transformed.

Clear quartz guides you to your next step when you feel adrift. This healing crystal is the perfect antidote to distracted thinking, encouraging clarity by clearing your cluttered mind, body, and spirit.

Amethyst is the pillar of any meditation practice. Renowned for its ability to ease anxiety as it transports you to a state of bliss, amethyst takes you on a deep dive into the spiritual realm. It's an excellent stone to work with if you're ready to explore your intuition and connect with a higher power.

Once you've chosen your crystal, hold it in your nondominant hand (aka your receiving hand) or place it on your body (or in your bra). Feel free to create a crystal grid if the mood strikes you (more on that in Chapter 9), but simply having it close by is enough for the crystal to do its thing.

I'll sometimes hold a crystal to my heart or put it on a table or shelf at eye level to look at as I soften my gaze to meditate.

If you aren't familiar with a soft gaze, it's basically choosing a point to look at and then opening up your peripheral vision to expand your field of view (kind of like switching the setting of your eyes from zoom to panorama). Try closing your eyes and imagine being on a beach, taking in a beautiful ocean view. Then shift your focus to visualize your kitchen. Your vision automatically narrows as you become more alert and focused, compared to the sigh of contentment you may experience while looking at the ocean. We tend to move through life with tunnel vision, only shifting into panoramic vision with intentional effort. The reason those moments with a softened gaze feel so good is because your parasympathetic nervous system has been activated, flooding your system with feel-good hormones as your body transitions into a place of peace.

Candles can also help your meditation practice in a few different ways: the flickering light creates a tranquil ambience that invites calm; the flame acts as an effective focal point to hold your attention; and the gentle glimmer allows you to soften your gaze as you settle into a peaceful state. Research by S-VYASA University in India shows that candle gazing (also known as trataka or yogic gazing) during meditation can bolster memory, attention, and sleep quality. Concentrating on the flame can also help people who get anxious closing their eyes while meditating or find it difficult to quiet their minds. Additionally, igniting and extinguishing a candle can mark the opening and closing of your ceremony, and I always incorporate candles into my nightly ritual (mainly because: vibes).

A Meditation for Every Mood

Now that you've grabbed a few crystals or sparked a candle and are comfy, it's time to meditate. To get you started, I've included a few variations here. For all of them, either close your eyes or keep them open with a softened gaze.

Body Scan

Begin at the top of your head and slowly move down to your toes. Feel your eyes relax and let your jaw unclench as your tongue rests at the top of your mouth. Allow your shoulders to drop and your limbs to soften as they get heavy. Notice how you're feeling physically (without judgment!) and any emotions that might be tied to your body's sensations. Feel free to hang out in an area that feels tight or blocked, delivering healing with each inhale and releasing stress in every exhale. As you inhale, imagine a beam of white light expanding from the top of your head up into the Universe. On every exhale, visualize roots extending from the bottoms of your feet into the Earth's core.

Doing body scans in the evening can help you identify any tension that needs to be released before bed, while a morning inventory can help you connect to your body and keep you grounded throughout the day. A body scan might mark the end of your meditation, or you can spend a bit more time focusing on your breath, visualizing your ideal future, or opening your heart.

Ho'oponopono

This ancient Hawaiian practice is deceptively simple and incredibly powerful. It's based on the belief that we're all connected, and the purpose of this practice is rooted in reconciliation and forgiveness. Ho'oponopono (pronounced *HO-oh-Po-no-Po-no*) promotes healing for all, allowing you to make amends with your relationship to the Earth, ancestors, community, and self. The word *ho'oponopono* roughly translates as "to make right," and there are four phrases that you repeat out loud:

1. "I'm sorry."
   Repent by taking responsibility for the real or perceived pain you have caused yourself or others, focusing on remorse rather than shame.

2. "Please forgive me."
   Ask for *forgiveness* from those you may have harmed, or from the Universe, releasing any resentment or negativity that you hold so you may move forward.

3. "Thank you."
   Express *gratitude* for what you have and show appreciation for all of the positive aspects of your life.

4. "I love you."
   Offer *love* to others and yourself. Be open to allowing love into your life, knowing that you deserve it.

Repeating these mantras aloud as you focus on a person, yourself, or something else (like our planet) is immensely profound. It may elicit strong emotions because you're unburdening yourself as you simultaneously claim responsibility. Do as many rounds of these affirmations as you feel are necessary, and dedicate it to one person or a multitude, but always end ho'oponopono by focusing on yourself. The magic of this mantra lies in the recognition of our imperfections—it's a meditation for radical compassion and unconditional self-love. As you heal yourself, you heal the collective. And in forgiveness, you find freedom.

Walking Meditation

Some people enjoy a walking meditation as part of their daily ritual, especially in the morning. By combining movement with mindfulness, you'll get an extra dose of happy hormones to fuel your day. Do it anywhere at any time—whether you're traipsing through the woods, strolling in the suburbs, or schlepping around the city—as long as you pay attention to your surroundings and how you move through them. Match your breath count as you inhale and exhale (in through the nose, out through the mouth). Feel the sun, rain, or wind on your skin. Tune in to your body and take note of your arms moving or the stride of your legs (don't change or judge . . . simply notice). See the environment around you—cars passing, dogs barking, kids playing—and just acknowledge it without any internal commentary. When your mind wanders from the moment you're in, gently guide your awareness back to the present. A dog can really help with walking mindfully because they're masters of being in the moment. Focusing on your furry friend and yourself while you walk reinforces staying present and gives you quality time together. And obviously (but maybe not so obvious, so I'm going to say it) your phone has to be left at home or put on airplane mode during your mindful meandering.

Guided Meditations

Letting someone lead your practice is a fantastic option for meditating newbies and seasoned pros, especially if you struggle with quieting your mind. Check out YouTube and Insight Timer (a free app) for meditations to suit any ritual, or subscribe to paid apps (Calm and Headspace are excellent) for a more curated experience.

There are no specific rules for how to meditate. If nothing else, just find a comfortable place to sit or lie down, close your eyes, and breathe. When you get distracted, and you will, simply bring your attention back to your breath. When you incorporate mindfulness into your daily ritual, it's like giving yourself a spiritual hug.

TALK IS CHEAP (BUT EFFECTIVE): THE POWER OF AFFIRMATIONS

◇◇◇

I have a love/hate relationship with affirmations. I grew up watching Al Franken mock the self-help field on *Saturday Night Live* with his Stuart Smalley character ("I'm good enough, I'm smart enough, and doggone it, people like me"). Spouting platitudes of positivity to myself in the mirror seemed like a waste of time, especially when everything was falling apart. I still don't find value in speaking as if something is already true when it clearly is not (for example, repeating *I am a millionaire! Abundance flows to me! Money is everywhere!* when bills can't be paid). A 2009 study from the University of Waterloo has shown that while affirmations can be useful for those with healthy self-esteem, they often backfire and make things worse for the people who need them most (it's called *toxic* positivity for a reason). This is why the law of attraction can be dangerous: people often see it as a shortcut to abundance when it's really just wishful thinking.

Although we can't trick our brains into accepting a fairy tale as true, we can voice our intentions as possibilities (*I am ready to transform my relationship with money so that it flows to me with ease . . .*) as we visualize an ideal future. This, along with taking action and shifting limiting beliefs, can work to bring your dreams to life (it's also the foundation of my New Moon Magic ritual in Chapter 6).

If affirmations make you feel good and you're not expecting them to do all the heavy lifting (manifesting-wise), pick one every day or every week to motivate you in your morning ritual. A 2015 study published by the journal *Social Cognitive and Affective Neuroscience* used magnetic resonance imaging (MRI) to demonstrate that practicing self-affirmations fires up our neural pathways, activating the reward centers of our brain just like winning a prize or eating delicious food would. Reading an inspiring message can boost your confidence and remind you of your strengths, as opposed to the feelings of compare-and-despair that mindless social media scrolling can trigger. Buy a deck of affirmation cards or grab some recipe index cards and make your own. Here are some examples to get you started:

- I am enough.
- Remember to breathe.
- Do no harm and take no sh*t.
- May I be supported by the love that flows to me.
- I will remember my worth, then double it and add tax.
- Mistakes are proof that I'm trying.
- I can do tough stuff.

- Baby steps count.
- May I be held by the confidence the Universe has in me.
- I am f*cking magic, and I'm ready to own it.
- This is my sign.
- My story will be someone else's survival guide.
- My ass looks great today.
- Cupcakes are just muffins that believe in miracles. Be the cupcake.
- I am the author of my story.

As you can see, these simple statements can be silly or spiritual, brash or benevolent. Affirmations don't have to be super serious or intense to have an impact—they're simply a starting point for change.

Take your self-talk to the next level by repeating an affirmation a few times as you look into a mirror. You may find yourself getting emotional while doing this because it's like gazing into your soul. If you're having difficulty talking to yourself this way, consider whether your affirmation needs to be rephrased. *I love you* can be harder to say than you'd think, so it could be modified as *I'm open to the possibility that I am lovable.* You might turn *I am worthy* into *I'm willing to consider that I am worthy, despite what I heard growing up.* (Take note of the affirmations that reveal tender spots, then go back to Chapter 5 and Burn Your Sh*t, or simply sit in that moment of awareness and feel any activation in your body, because that alone can be a great release.)

Research out of the University of Waterloo in 2009 suggested that going even *more* neutral with affirmations, ensuring they're based in reality rather than fantasy (*I'm working on accepting myself as I am*), allows the established neural pathways that support negative thinking to take a back seat as a new path of neutrality develops (one that eventually transitions into something more positive).

WTH IS TAPPING?

◇◇◇

What if there were a practice you could do for free that combines the principles of meditation and affirmations with the science behind cognitive therapy and Chinese medicine? Behold: tapping.

I heard about tapping years ago and was intrigued. Then I tried it and was hooked. During my training, I witnessed a classmate resolve a lifelong phobia of snakes using only tapping. Seriously, she went from hyperventilating at the thought of a snake to reaching in to a cage and touching one in less than twenty minutes.

The emotional freedom technique, or EFT, is more commonly known as tapping because you lightly tap on a set of nine acupressure points with your fingertips while breathing slowly and repeating phrases that name what you're experiencing. It's a fusion of acupuncture, cognitive therapy, and positive reprogramming (without the needles, wait times, and false promises, respectively). Tapping validates your feelings and empowers you while avoiding the denial or spiritual bypassing found in some other healing tools.

If you've never seen tapping in action, it looks absurd. But don't knock it 'til you've tapped it. Multiple studies, including one published in the *Journal of Evidence-Based Integrative Medicine* in 2019, have shown the significant benefits of tapping for people of all ages—from aiding adults dealing with PTSD and depression to helping preschool kids concentrate in class. Emotional energy from stress or trauma can get trapped in the body, and tapping helps to release this long-held tension. It can also assist in high-stress situations, when the critical-thinking part of the brain goes offline. In moments of panic, tapping can guide you to a place of calm by activating the parasympathetic nervous system, similar to meditation and breathwork, while simultaneously (and literally) tapping into and clearing your energetic pathways.

Chinese medicine has focused on balancing the body's energy meridians for thousands of years—it's the basis for acupuncture and acupressure healing—and tapping on these meridian points with your fingertips restores energetic flow by sending calming signals to your brain. But tapping affects more than just your energetic circuitry and biochemistry in the moment—it can also get to the root cause of your stress and support you in releasing old fears, patterns, and beliefs. When you identify stressors (for example, being fired from your job, or the argument you just had with your sister, or even your parents' divorce decades earlier) and speak them aloud while tapping, your brain receives the signal that you are safe despite the emotions you're feeling, allowing you to look at the situation or issue without feeling all of the stress in your body. By addressing the energetic disturbance underneath the emotion, you're able to release the related emotional weight you've been unconsciously lugging around.

Tapping is one of the most powerful elements you can add to your morning or evening ritual (or both!). Don't believe me? Let's try tapping right now. Begin by identifying how you're feeling about a challenging situation (anxious, scared, angry, ashamed, worried, etc.). Rate the intensity of that feeling on a scale of zero to ten, with zero being perfectly at ease and ten being the absolute worst. Be honest with yourself—tapping is most effective with the messier emotions, and you have to acknowledge them.

The sequence for tapping never changes. Begin by creating a setup statement that acknowledges how you honestly feel, giving voice to your deepest thoughts and emotions, followed by a phrase of acceptance. The standard format is *Even though I feel X, I accept myself and how I'm feeling.* You can modify this statement in a way that resonates for you. Just be sure to identify the emotion and follow it up with acceptance. Examples include:

Even though I feel stressed about my performance review, I accept myself.

Even though I'm anxious and don't know why, I accept these feelings.

Even though I feel panicked about my finances, I accept how I'm feeling.

Using a gentle pressure, start tapping the fleshy outer edge (aka the karate-chop point) of your nondominant hand with the fingertips of your dominant hand. Continue doing this as you repeat your setup statement out loud three times. Pause to take a deep breath.

After that, you're going to tap on the acupressure points outlined using either your first two fingers (index and middle) or all four. Since the meridian points are symmetrical on both sides of the body, it doesn't matter which side you tap on (and you can switch from left to right if you like). Tap each point five to seven times at a consistent speed and rhythm that's comfortable for you (there's no need to pause between points). As you're tapping, repeat a reminder phrase that connects to your setup phrase (for example, *All of this anxiety* or *My worries about money*). Your eyes can be open if you're reading a script, or closed if you're freestyling or listening to a recording. If you experience sighing, watering eyes, gurgling stomach, yawning, or sneezing while tapping, those are signs of release that indicate your nervous system is responding and adjusting. It's helpful to sequence through all the tapping points (called a round) a few times during a single session. You can adjust your reminder phrase for each point if you want to, exploring elements that are connected to your setup phrase. I've included examples starting on page 164.

It may seem counterintuitive or scary or just weird to verbalize negative statements while you're tapping (it can almost feel like you're imprinting them even deeper), but it's like pulling the weeds during Burn Your Sh*t before planting seeds with New Moon Magic—you need to identify what's bothering you and bring it to the surface in order to clear it. There is power in acknowledging the bad while telling your body and brain that you are still safe.

Here are the tapping points and the order you do them:

Eyebrow Point (EB)
Between the eyebrows.

Side of Eye (SE)
The bone on the outside of either eye.

Under Eye (UE)
The bone under either eye.
Under Nose (UN)
Between the nose and upper lip.

Chin Point (CP)
The crease between the bottom lip and above the chin.

Collarbone Point (CB)

Just underneath the center point where the collarbones meet.

Under Arm (UA)

Beneath the armpit (where a bra strap would sit).

Top of Head (TH)

On the crown of the head.

Do a few rounds of this sequence before pausing to take a deep, cleansing breath and then rate how you're feeling on a scale of zero to ten. Your intensity of feeling has likely shifted down, but keep tapping if you need to lower it further. If it remains high, try modifying your setup statement to something like *Even though I'm still worried about money, I accept how I feel and know it's safe to relax.*

Once the immediate anxiety has diminished, you can end with a positive round of tapping to fill that void and reprogram limiting beliefs. This is where I love using affirmations—they're truly affirming how you feel now that you've addressed and dealt with the anxiety, rather than trying to mask it with empty platitudes. You've pulled the weeds; now you can plant some seeds. Here are some examples you can repeat as you go through the tapping sequence a few more times:

I believe in my ability to change.
I am ready to relax into my situation.
I have accomplished more than I give myself credit for.

When you're done, take three deep belly breaths and notice the intensity of your emotions. Are they still overwhelming? Do you feel more relaxed? How do you feel now, on a scale of zero to ten? You may need to repeat the tapping sequence several times until the emotional charge dissipates, but even tapping only the karate-chop point without any setup phrase or additional tapping will calm you (my daughter used to do it under her desk at school before tests).

Consistently starting or ending your day with tapping will profoundly amplify your daily ritual, and I've included some morning and evening tapping scripts to get you started. You'll notice that my reminder phrase changes for each point, and they evolve from the most negative to the most positive as I go through multiple rounds. You can do it this way, or you can stick to one reminder phrase per round, especially when you start out, to make it easier to remember. The key is always keeping track of your real emotions and channeling those into the phrases.

Morning Tapping Ritual

Setup statement (karate-chop point): *Even though my day is already overwhelming me, I accept how I'm feeling.* (Repeat three times.)

EB: I'm already stressed about my day.
SE: I have so many responsibilities.
UE: I feel a pit in my stomach.
UN: I can't relax in this moment.
CP: There's too much to do.
CB: If I relax, nothing gets done.
UA: So many people depend on me.
TH: It's too much.

EB: I can't control my day.
SE: I can't relax.

UE: *I never get a break.*

UN: *I could be fired at any moment.*

CP: *If I'm not busy, it means I'm not needed.*

CB: *If I don't do double the work, I won't be noticed.*

UA: *If I'm not worried about deadlines, they won't be met.*

TH: *How do I know this is true?*

EB: *Maybe it's a choice I'm making.*

SE: *To believe these ideas about stress and busyness.*

UE: *I can make a different choice.*

UN: *I can decide to let these beliefs go.*

CP: *These beliefs around what I'm worth.*

CB: *These beliefs about the need for stress and overwhelm.*

UA: *They aren't real, and I can release them.*

TH: *I can make changes, starting now.*

EB: *I can choose how I respond to people around me.*

SE: *I get to choose how my day will unfold.*

UE: *I will be aware of my reaction to the emotions of others.*

UN: *I can disengage from other people's stress.*

CP: *I release my attachment to outcomes.*

CB: *I invite clarity and calm.*

UA: *I am competent and bring value.*

TH: *It doesn't have to be so hard.*

EB: *Every day is a gift.*

SE: *I will not waste this day complaining about what I cannot change.*

UE: *I will focus on what is possible.*

UN: *I am co-creating with the Universe.*

CP: *I will take care of my needs.*

CB: *I honor my body, mind, and spirit.*
UA: *I release stress with every exhale.*
TH: *And I allow all of the amazing possibilities of this day to unfold.*

Inhale deeply through your nose and into your belly, then exhale for slightly longer out your mouth. Close your eyes and place your hands at your heart, knowing you can return to this place of calm at any time throughout your day.

Evening Tapping Ritual

Setup statement (karate-chop point): *Even though my stress has increased throughout the day, I accept myself.* (Repeat three times.)

EB: *I have so much stress.*
SE: *So much tension has built up in my body.*
UE: *How can I let it go when there's so much left to do?*
UN: *I haven't done enough.*
CP: *Tomorrow will be even worse.*
CB: *I'm so worried all the time.*
UA: *I'm carrying so much stress in my body.*
TH: *And I can't let it go just because the day is done.*

EB: *I'm exhausted.*
SE: *I'm too tired to enjoy anything.*
UE: *My anxiety skyrockets at night.*
UN: *I'm so worried about the future.*
CP: *My brain can't slow down.*
CB: *I'm spinning with worry.*
UA: *So much is unfinished.*
TH: *The pressure is too much.*

EB: *What if I stopped trying to control everything?*

SE: *What if I just acknowledge how I feel?*

UE: *I can voice my fears.*

UN: *It's safe to feel my feelings.*

CP: *Knowing that I am safe.*

CB: *I am doing my best.*

UA: *And my best is enough.*

TH: *Because I am enough.*

EB: *I can give myself permission to let this tension go.*

SE: *I can choose to rest.*

UE: *It's safe for me to let go of any stress.*

UN: *I don't have all of the answers and that's fine.*

CP: *I have faith that answers will come.*

CB: *Tonight I can let go and be at ease.*

UA: *I choose to appreciate what I love about my life.*

TH: *My mind is calm and my body is relaxed, so now I can rest.*

Inhale deeply through your nose and into your belly, then exhale for slightly longer out your mouth. Close your eyes and place your hands at your heart, knowing that a deep and restorative sleep awaits you.

I love tapping because it's extremely practical, self-administered, and easy to do. Whether you're ready for some deeper healing or you want to bookend your day with restorative calm, tapping is a secret weapon in your ritual toolbox that can radically shift your mindset and impact your well-being.

ENERGETIC COLONICS
(HOW TO JOURNAL)

◇◇◇

When I journal, I'm usually half awake, drooling on my pillow, and desperately needing to pee, but I don't even get out of bed until I've filled three pages with my illegible scribbling. This practice is known by many as "morning pages." I call it "business planning."

Beginning (or ending) your day with journaling can be really helpful, especially in times of hardship. How many of us poured our innermost hopes and fears into a little lock-and-key diary when we were kids? I did and, over thirty years later, so did my daughter. Unburdening our soul and psyche through the cathartic act of writing is a hallmark of teendom for many young people, but it's even more powerful when done as an adult.

Reaching for a notebook and pen instead of your phone when you wake up is a fabulous habit to get into because scrolling email or social media invites other people (sometimes strangers) to dictate the start of your day. It's also the easiest way to launch your morning ritual when you aren't a morning person. Julia Cameron popularized morning pages in her seminal book, *The Artist's Way*. She instructs readers to commit to three pages of stream-of-consciousness writing as soon as they wake up. I often assign morning pages to my tarot clients (I call it a "dream journal" so it sounds less like homework).

Your actual journal doesn't have to be fancy—a coil notebook and pen from the dollar store will do just fine. When you wake up in the morning, grab your pen before you even open your eyes and barf your brain onto the paper. Write for three pages—no more, no less. Even if the first few lines are *I have to pee. I have to pee. I have to pee.* That's okay. This isn't meant to be a ground-breaking literary endeavor; it's a purge of your worries, fears, expectations, and any other unhelpful burdens swirling around in your head. Write whatever thoughts come through, without censoring them. If they're totally unrelated, write them down anyway. If you're drawing a blank, just write *I don't know what to write* over and over until something else shows up. If you're thinking, *This is stupid and I don't want to do it*, write that down, too.

Forget about punctuation, grammar, and penmanship (that's ego getting in the way). Try not to censor the juicy stuff that wants to be expressed. Don't worry if it's politically incorrect, dull, or irrational. Just let it flow, knowing these pages are for your eyes only and you can always throw them away later. You may find that the words or tone of voice are unusual for you—that's great, too! Write without a filter, nonstop. Don't give up halfway through, because that's when the insights tend to reveal themselves. Clarity will come eventually, and it's often a few days later, which is why consistency is key. By clearing your mind of useless clutter and acknowledging any worries or negative self-talk, stress is reduced and space is made for strategic and innovative thinking. It takes less than ten minutes, but the effects last all day.

If morning pages (or anything morning-related) aren't your thing, journaling can also enhance an evening ritual. Gratitude journals work wonders when done correctly. Being vague or repetitive (for example, writing *I'm grateful for my health and family* every day) won't do much to move the needle on your mood, but focusing on specific moments in your day can result in profound shifts. You won't be graded on this exercise, so be honest with yourself. If your day is a sh*tshow and the only gratitude worth mentioning is that cartoons exist to occupy your kids while you finally shower before dinner, note it. Being realistic helps you to discover and appreciate moments to be grateful for in ways you might normally miss. Also avoid *shoulding* all over yourself in these moments of reflection— you're doing the best you can, and that's enough.

Happiness researcher (yes, it's a thing) Shawn Achor writes about the "happiness advantage" that comes from rewiring the brain to work more optimistically and successfully. When we're in a positive state, our creativity, energy, and intelligence have all been proven to increase far more than if we're feeling stressed, negative, or even neutral. Without happiness, success in any area of life will remain elusive. Luckily for all of us, happiness can be conjured with only a pen and paper in less than five minutes a day. All you do is write three new things you're grateful for at the end of every day. You have to commit for at least a month to get maximum effectiveness because you're training your brain to scan for positive experiences instead of perceived threats (which is often our default setting). Let me show you an example by sharing mine for today:

I'm grateful that I was able to fall (and stay) asleep last night, because I was well-rested and in a good mood today.

I'm grateful that I got to meet a friend today for tea to discuss a common issue we're working through, because it helped both of us feel less alone.

I'm grateful that I wrote 600 words of this book today, despite having a shortened workday (due to my tea date), because it showed me I can be productive and still have fun.

That took two minutes to write and, in that time, I was actively teaching myself optimism. Adding *because* to each example adds a deeper layer of meaning to the experience by specifying why it was important to me. You can also journal about a positive experience from your day, writing in detail about what happened and how it made you feel. This lets your brain relive the moment and deepen the imprint, doubling the meaningful impact of that experience.

As I mentioned in Chapter 5, you can also write a Sh*t List to burn under the light of a Full Moon or whenever you need to release something (ripping it up before burying it also works). Follow this up by listing three things you're grateful for to create a lovely full-circle practice that helps you end your day with a clear mind and open heart.

A CARD A DAY KEEPS
THE QUESTIONS AT BAY

◇◇◇

If you're into oracle or tarot cards (and, if you're reading this book, you're probably at least a *little* card-curious), pulling a card every morning is a really fun and witchy way to get an intuitive nudge/heads up/prompt for the day ahead. It's also a great way to get familiar with your deck if you're new to tarot.

Start by shuffling your deck as you think about yourself (simply envisioning your face in your mind will work, or you can look into a mirror). Cut the deck with your nondominant hand (to access your intuition) and ask out loud *What do I need to know today?* before pulling a card. Take a moment to really look at the card and think about how it makes you feel (happy, sad, scared, wistful, nervous, etc.), and journal these first impressions. I always remind my tarot students that their interpretation of a card is just as important as the traditional definition or my explanation. As you work with your cards, you'll create a specific and unique dialogue with your deck that continues to evolve over time.

Once you've noted your reaction to the card, consult the little how-to booklet that comes with your deck to add additional depth or clarity to your message. Then put your card down—maybe place it on your altar, if you have one—and pick it up again before bed to reflect on how its meaning showed up in your day. Oracle and tarot cards offer validation and act as a conversation starter between you and your intuition. Over time, you'll find yourself getting more proactive rather than reactive about the card's message, letting it support and guide you throughout the day.

WHEN IN DOUBT, DANCE IT OUT

◇◇◇

Just fifteen minutes of fun cardio activity can be as effective as taking an antidepressant, according to a study published by *JAMA Psychiatry* in 2019. Our bodies crave movement, whether it's a Cross-Fit class, dancing in the kitchen, or gentle stretches in the sunlight. Getting physical in your morning or evening ritual will renew your mind, body, and spirit.

Even if your daily schedule is packed, moving intentionally for a few minutes in the morning can make it a little less manic. I'll often go for a walk or swim at some point, but my day doesn't really start until I've done a few sun salutations and seated stretches to signal my body that it's time to wake up. If I don't move, my morning ritual feels incomplete. I may not be burning many (or . . . any?)

calories with this sequence, but that's not the point; I am taking time to honor my body and give thanks for waking up to live another day. When my kids were younger, we would put on classic Motown for a little post-breakfast boogie—it helped them get the zoomies out before school and put a smile on everyone's face. Whatever form of movement makes you feel good, try to incorporate it into your morning ritual to boost your inner peace *and* outward productivity.

Our prone bodies can get stiff as we sleep, but working at jobs that keep us sedentary during the day can be equally detrimental. Even if you aren't stuck at a desk all day, the stress of commuting, relentless meetings, childcare, and life in general can leave you too overloaded or exhausted to consider working out. Similar to your morning ritual, the movement of an evening ritual can be beneficial without being vigorous. Ideally, you want to avoid strenuous workouts within an hour of sleep because your core body temperature won't have time to cool, and sleep quality will be impacted. I love taking my dog for a nightly spin around the block to empty my mind (and her bladder). Gentle yoga is the perfect complement to any nightly ritual (YouTube has millions of free Hatha classes), but any intentional stretching will help you release built-up tension from your day. After that, you aren't allowed to touch your phone or watch a screen until the following day.

NATURE CALLS

◇◇◇

I grew up near the Canadian Rocky Mountains and camped every weekend from May through September, so I'm no stranger to the Great Outdoors. Although my idea of "roughing it" has evolved from no stars to four stars, I still yearn to nurture myself in nature (with a flushing toilet and an actual bed at the end of the day).

Countless studies have proven the physical, cognitive, and mental health benefits of getting outside—in addition to a vitamin D boost courtesy of the Sun, research shows that hanging out with Mother Nature keeps your stress in check, boosts immunity, improves concentration, deepens your relationships with others, and connects you to your purpose. Creating time to savor some sunlight in the morning (even when it's cloudy) will support your productivity during the day and sleep quality at night.

Evolutionary biologist Charles Darwin and prolific artist Georgia O'Keeffe both began their days with a walk in nature, getting their blood pumping and creativity flowing. A 2013 study by UCLA researchers confirms exercise that requires little thought (for example, strolling outside) stimulates the motor and sensory regions of the brain, facilitating the flow of new ideas. Just ten minutes of sitting or walking outside every morning can set the tone for your day, but you have to leave the phone at home or tucked away for optimal effects. I used to blast podcasts at full volume on my morning walk in the woods to help take my mind off the hills I was climbing, but I was also blocking out a symphony of flora and fauna, which I discovered the day my phone died a few minutes into my hike. Instead of suffering through my usual self-imposed forced march, I was able to luxuriate in the spellbinding natural beauty that surrounded me. My pace slowed as my soul soared. A cascade of ideas and inspiration poured into me. I'm now a full-blown hugger of trees, wandering off the beaten path to look for the perfect conifer to cuddle. I bring my phone to note any downloads from my soul, but keep it on airplane mode. I'm incredibly privileged to have an oasis only ten minutes from my house, and I no longer take it for granted. The woods have become my sacred space, a living altar that invites me to connect to every living thing, and myself.

When I was growing up in the seventies, this experience of engaging with the sights, sounds, and smells of nature was referred to as a hike, but it's since been rebranded by TikTokkers and the wellness industry as forest bathing (also known as shinrin-yoku in Japan, where it was introduced in the nineties as an antidote to tech burnout). Another nature-based trend we've actually been doing forever is earthing (or grounding), which is basically standing barefoot or sitting/lying in the grass, dirt, sand, etc., for a few moments. A 2012 study published in the *Journal of Environmental and Public Health* indicated that earthing lessens inflammation and improves overall health, as the body absorbs electronic energy and syncs with the natural frequencies of the Earth.

If you live in an urban jungle with no nature in sight, you could always stare at the sky from your balcony or window, but you can also hack a Rocky Mountain high with the next best thing: visualizing or listening to recordings of the natural world. Imagining yourself in a lush forest or on a beach in the tropics—immersing yourself in the sounds, scents, and other sensations—can reduce depression and physical pain. A 2021 PNAS study by environmental psychologists confirms previous findings that hearing bird sounds lessened stress and annoyance, and the sound of water induced ease and tranquility. (This is also a great option if, like me, you're in a colder climate and have no desire to go earthing in January.) Whether you're digging in a garden, lying on the beach, or imagining an ocean swim, there are many ways to introduce nature into your morning or evening ritual—even if it's just breathing with your eyes closed as you stand barefoot in your yard, waiting for the dog to pee.

GET WET

◇◇◇

When it comes to baths, I find that people are either obsessed with them or loathe them—there isn't much middle ground. I personally love soaking in the tub, but my adult son tells me I'm "marinating in dirt soup" (which, weirdly, is how I feel about hot tubs).

Water has played a pivotal role in ceremonies since the beginning of time. Almost every spiritual tradition uses water in rituals to purify negativity, heal ailments, and bestow blessings. People will travel around the world to immerse themselves in water sources thought to be imbued with special energy, but you can absorb the therapeutic power of water and harness it as a conduit to the Divine in your own home through ritual.

You can create a bathing ritual that connects you with water in simple or elaborate ways, drawing inspiration from spiritual traditions or modern methods. Even if it's only a few minutes long, your morning shower can become a ritualistic experience. Close your eyes and stand under the spray, visualizing any tension or worries being washed away. Focus on the sensation as the rivers run from the crown of your head and down your entire body. Allow yourself to indulge in the purification of your body, mind, and spirit. Incorporating awareness into your shower doesn't take extra time—you're simply connecting to a higher power and yourself simultaneously. (It will also detach any etheric cords that bind you to the energy of other people. More on that in Chapter 11.)

If you want to take your ritual shower to the next level, make it ice cold. Starting your day with a blast of icy water may seem extreme, but data published in the *North American Journal of Medicine & Science* in 2014 suggests that cold showers can boost immunity, improve circulation, lessen depression, speed up metabolism, and increase alertness. A shock of cold water acutely activates the sympathetic nervous system (the fight-or-flight response that, ironically, we've spent most of this chapter trying to suppress). The ensuing influx of adrenaline increases white blood cell production and reduces inflammation. Adrenaline produced for short bursts of time can be beneficial to the body, as opposed to the chronic health issues that arise when psychological anxiety triggers a nonstop flood of adrenaline.

The health benefits of a cold shower are similar to those of the Wim Hof Method, which involves submerging yourself in water that is between 2°C and 16°C (35°F and 60°F) while performing a very specific breathing technique (self-induced hyperventilation followed by breath holding) that causes hypoxia—a form of stress at the cellular level. I've dabbled in Wim Hof breathing and it's not for me, but I've definitely felt the benefits of a cold shower. Although Wim Hof advises building up the intensity and duration of cold water exposure, a 2016 study out of the Netherlands, published by the Public Library of Science, indicates that after fifteen seconds the duration is irrelevant and the water doesn't have to be glacial.

Unless you're stoked to sit in a barrel of freezing, ice cube–filled water, simply end your morning shower with thirty seconds of invigorating cold water. You can also alternate between hot and cold, giving yourself a DIY spa experience. If nothing else, the willpower and endurance required to withstand that icy blast will leave you feeling confident and ready to take on your day, and probably feeling pretty refreshed. (Note: Give the cold shower a miss if you have a heart condition, because it can put extra stress on your ticker.)

A more sensual option that elevates cleaning your body to cleansing your soul is a ritual bath. Although you can take a ritual bath any time of day, it feels more sacred for me—more like a *ritual*—when it's done at night (but the cornerstone of any ritual is intention, and if a spiritual soak in the morning appeals to you, go for it).

Drawing a bath with salts, stones, and botanicals is delightful, but the infusion of meaning is what transforms it into a ritual bath. Are you soothing a broken heart? Releasing the energy of a contentious encounter? Launching your future career? Even if you just need to relax and unwind before bed, that is an *excellent* intention. Bringing clarity to your ritual bath will ramp up its efficacy. As mentioned in the Full Moon and New Moon rituals, La Luna offers extra support at certain times of the month. If your intention is to release negative energy or outdated beliefs, bathing under the Full Moon will add some *oomph* to your ritual. If manifesting is the goal, hopping in the tub on a New Moon is a wonderful way to amplify the fertile energy around you.

Begin by setting the mood with ceremonial touches in and out of the tub to enhance your experience. For me, candles are nonnegotiable. I turn off all artificial lights and light some candles (even if the sun is still out in the summer). I always keep candles on the counter rather than around the tub because I worry I'll somehow catch my hair on fire (which is not baseless, because I managed to set my bedroom wall on fire with a scarf over a lamp as a teen, and my dining room ceiling caught fire when I tried to install a pendant lamp as an adult, so I have a healthy trepidation around any sort of flame). You can also light some incense, but consider what scents you're mixing if you're adding essentials oils or other aromatics to the experience.

Music is a wonderful way to create a mellow and relaxing vibe. The soundtrack for your soul might feature classic Sade or whale sounds—you are your best DJ. If you're looking for some inspiration, check out my curated Ritual Bath playlist on Spotify. If you crave silence, skip the music altogether.

Collect the offerings for your ritual, but before you go dropping random oils and herbs into the tub, confirm that they're suitable for bathing, to avoid irritating your skin, eyes, or other sensitive areas. For the love of Goddess—and your vagina—stay away from the following essential oils in your bath:

- Black pepper
- Camphor
- Cassia
- Cinnamon (and cinnamon bark)
- Clove
- Hyssop
- Oregano
- Peppermint
- Spearmint
- Summer savory
- Thyme
- Wintergreen

Thankfully, the list of essential oils that are great for baths is much longer. Here are some easily sourced options that can be added on their own—a few drops are all you need—or supplemented with a tablespoon of carrier oil (such as coconut, jojoba, or sunflower):

- Bergamot
- Cardamom
- Cedarwood
- Chamomile (roman)
- Clary sage

- Cypress
- Eucalyptus
- Frankincense
- Grapefruit
- Jasmine
- Lavender
- Lemongrass
- Marjoram
- Myrrh
- Patchouli
- Rose
- Rosemary
- Sandalwood
- Wild orange
- Ylang-ylang

A simple salt bath is also an excellent option. Leave the table salt in the kitchen and add two or three cups of Epsom or pink Himalayan salt to the running water. Epsom salts have a high magnesium content that will relax you and draw toxins from your body, while pink Himalayan salt exfoliates your skin and replenishes electrolytes.

Try throwing some flowers or flowering herbs in the tub to benefit from their healing properties. Make sure you secure dried herbs and flowers in a bath bag (it looks like a large tea bag), nylon stocking, or cheesecloth—this lessens the mess and keeps the pipes from clogging. Alternatively, you can brew a bath infusion like you would a pot of tea: boil two cups of water and remove from the heat before adding loose herbs or flowers, letting it steep with a lid on for at least twenty minutes, and then straining the infused water into your bath.

Fresh botanicals such as rose petals, chamomile flowers, and lavender are popular additions. You can use the bath-bag method or let them float loose in the water (just like in the movies!), but always remove loose flowers or herbs before draining your tub (I keep a kitchen strainer in my bathroom to catch the petals, like a pool cleaner). Toss a few crystals in there if you feel the urge—just check if they're water-friendly first. Rose, clear quartz, amethyst, and carnelian are always safe bets.

As the bathtub fills with water, focus on your intention and add any offerings one by one. Whichever spiritual elements you choose to customize your bath, remember that the only requirements for your ritual bath are you, water, and your intention. When you're ready, slowly immerse yourself in the water. If you're short on time—or a tub—soaking only your feet in a small basin also works. Allow yourself to be fully present in the moment as you observe your breath, do a body scan, or focus on an intention. Whether you're meditating, visualizing, or simply taking in your surroundings, this time is for you and you alone. Be aware of how you feel. Notice where healing is needed. Receive any insights that may arise. Allow whatever comes up to move through you without judgment or resistance. Breathe.

Sit for as long as you need and, when it's time, close your ritual with gratitude for the healing and rejuvenation that has taken place. Acknowledge any spiritual connections you worked with and guidance that was delivered. Thank your body for all that it does for you. Honor the nurturing that occurred through this sacred immersion.

LOVE THE SKIN YOU'RE IN

◇◇◇

Prioritizing yourself with a skincare ritual—whether it's splashing soap and water on your face or undertaking a twenty-step process—is about sanity, not vanity. Not only does it revive and protect your skin, but a ritualized skincare regime is also stress-reducing and confidence-boosting.

When you apply a moisturizer (with SPF!) to your skin, you are literally getting in touch with yourself and increasing mindfulness during a moment of intentional self-care. I keep a face roller in the freezer that diminishes puffiness and also wakes me up in the morning. I also apply a serum followed by moisturizer (my friends in the beauty biz keep me stocked with samples, so I'm not loyal to a particular brand).

Your evening skincare ritual is a chance to remove the mental and emotional burdens of your day, along with your makeup. At night you can opt for thicker creams, serums, and masks (doing a mask during a ritual bath is a delightful indulgence). After applying face oil, I use a gua sha stone, which is often made from a crystal such as jade or rose quartz and has rounded edges, to gently scrape across my skin. This encourages circulation and lymphatic drainage, but I mainly do it because it feels good. I follow that up with moisturizer on my face, hands, and feet (covering up with socks to let it soak in) before turning in for the night. The entire process takes under ten minutes, but it signals to my brain that sleep is coming, and I'm usually yawning by the end of it.

Tending to your epidermis can be a transformative experience that is so much more than skin-deep. By undertaking a beauty ritual, you're acknowledging your beauty. Your skincare ritual may open up a part of you that has been looking to be loved and needing to be nourished. By caring for yourself so explicitly and intentionally, you're opening up to receiving care from others.

EAT, DRINK, & BE WITCHY

◇◇◇

Now that we've covered what you're putting *on* your body, it's time to consider what you're putting *in* there. From doing tequila shots with salt and lime to taking Communion with wafers and wine, rituals around food and hydration have been around for centuries. Most spiritual traditions include rituals for preparing and consuming meals and beverages, and many of us develop our own personal rituals to show gratitude, invite comfort, or celebrate community.

Beginning each day with a glass of water kick-starts your metabolism and digestion, while preventing your cognition from plummeting. We all wake up slightly dehydrated and need liquid replenishment (I keep water by my bedside at night so my morning glass isn't bracingly cold). Drinking water becomes ritualistic when you take time to respect the water you drink: use a glass or pitcher that is pleasing to the eye and try adding fresh citrus, basil, mint, or cucumber to your water for a light flavoring. Taking time to nourish yourself with a glass of water as you start the day is a simple yet foundational act of self-care.

If water isn't your thing, try a smoothie or kombucha in addition to morning MVPs like coffee or tea to get going. Whatever you're drinking, how you make and consume it can be an integral part of your ritual. Japanese tea ceremonies elevate preparation to an art form, and the underlying elements (harmony, respect, purity, and tranquility) can be applied to a chai latte or protein shake. A tea ceremony involves specific tools and actions, such as using a particular bowl or removing your shoes, and you can adapt this by savoring your beverage of choice in a special cup while sitting in your favorite chair. Once your drink is ready, try not to gulp it. Take a few seconds to center yourself with a couple of breaths. Notice how the cup feels in your hands. Close your eyes and smell the aroma before taking a sip. Concentrate on how it feels and tastes in your mouth. Does it evoke a specific memory? Bring all of your senses into the experience. This ritual takes only a few minutes, but it can alter your outlook for the rest of the day.

I've never been a coffee drinker, but I end each day with a warm cup of Calm (a magnesium citrate drink that helps with sleep). The same guidelines apply: sip, savor, and sense. A warm drink can feel like a liquid cuddle before bed, and I highly recommend it.

The same ritualistic guidelines apply to the food you eat. Moms may be on to something when they say the main ingredient of a favorite meal is love. A 2012 University of Maryland study confirmed that food prepared with loving intention really does taste better. Creating a nutritious lunch at home to eat at work can become an act of self-love, so point that love laser at every meal you make, even (especially!) if it's just for you.

Nourishing yourself and others through the preparation of a meal is a sacred act, and your kitchen is a temple. If you feel the urge, celebrate this sanctity by dancing or singing as you cook. Chop and measure your ingredients mindfully. Treat your table as the altar for your meal, decorating it with natural elements such as pine cones in a bowl, flowers in a vase, or stones as a centerpiece. A beautifully set table, minimal or extravagant, connects you to your meal and honors the natural world that provided you with this nourishment. Light a candle to soothe your senses, invoke gratitude, and signal the start and end of your meal. Immerse yourself in every aspect of any meal—experience the tastes and smells as well as the texture and temperature. Chewing and swallowing with intention aids digestion, keeping you better attuned to your hunger and satisfaction cues.

Ritual mealtimes are definitely geared toward adults. Even if your kids are older, this kind of focus can be unrealistic (my family can polish off a sushi meal—with appetizers!—in fifteen minutes or less). Ritualistic elements can be incorporated into family meals simply by sharing the high and low points of your day (sometimes called "roses and thorns"). This offers a chance to practice gratitude, empathy, and active listening while connecting you to your loved ones.

If it's a challenge to turn *any* daily meal into a ritual, you can still give your taste buds a bit of bliss with a ritual snack time. Indulge in a piece of chocolate, closing your eyes for a full minute as it dissolves in your mouth. Bite into a warm piece of freshly baked bread slathered in homemade jam, taking in the fusion of flavors. Appreciate the sweetness of a sumptuously ripe strawberry. Noticing the fullness of the flavors, textures, and smells can take the smallest bites to another level.

CLEAN YOUR MESS
TO CLEAR YOUR STRESS

◇◇◇

Imagine walking into your kitchen in the morning to find the counters wiped clean, dishes put away, and garbage emptied. Now repeat this visualization, but instead imagine that the sink is filled with dirty dinner dishes, there are crumbs on the counter, and there's a funky smell in the air. Are you having a mild panic attack?

In 2019, researchers from UCLA found that clutter contributes to stress, anxiety, and even anger. Taking a few minutes to straighten up your space every night will leave you with a final sense of accomplishment as you drift off to sleep and, more importantly, will set you up for success the next day. As wonderful as morning rituals are, their success depends on what's done the night before.

Fill your bedside glass with water at bedtime so there's no excuse to not drink it in the morning. Pick out tomorrow's outfit and assemble your gym gear if you plan to work out the next day (preparation can shift an intention into action). Wash your favorite mug (along with the pan you put in the sink to "soak"). Pack lunch for you and the kids so you can grab and go. Get the coffeemaker ready and tidy up any mess (it doesn't have to be a deep-clean—putting scattered papers in a pile counts). Preparation alleviates anxiety and overwhelm because you have less to think about first thing in the morning. Plus, waking up to a mess is demoralizing. Instead, you'll be free to focus on easy stuff (like making your bed) when you get up.

Multiple surveys have shown that when adults make their beds in the morning, three-quarters of them still feel productive and successful at the end of the day. This small yet productive chore activates your brain's reward center, which encourages you to seek out more feel-good hits by doing additional tasks. Even if the rest of your day is a disaster, you're coming home to a bed that you made—and that will feel good physically and emotionally. The little things add up, and smaller, more mundane tasks can become meditative, giving your brain a much-needed break (that's how you can solve the world's problems while folding laundry). When you honor your home, you honor yourself. Your space is your sanctuary. So hang up your jacket and load the damn dishwasher. Your future self will thank you.

PUTTING IT ALL TOGETHER

◇◇◇

Daily rituals are moments to ground, nourish, and soothe—they should never be burdensome to-do items. Sitting at your kitchen table for two minutes, holding your favorite crystal with your eyes closed, breathing deeply? That's a ritual. Doing an hour of naked yoga in your yurt at the break of dawn? Also a ritual. Curate how you begin and end your day in a way that makes sense for your likes and your lifestyle, and allow it to grow and evolve as you do. Here are examples of different combinations (it goes without saying—but I'm still going to say it—your phone isn't involved in any of these options):

Morning

1. Make your bed. Drink a glass of water. Do five yoga sun salutations. Go for a mindful walk or run it (could be ten miles, around the block, or anything in between). Shower with intention and end it with twenty seconds of cold water.

2. Make your bed. Brew a cup of tea/coffee and pull a tarot or oracle card to think about as you sit with your eyes closed for five slow, deep belly breaths.

3. Journal for three pages before you're fully awake. Make your bed. Do a few minutes of light stretching (reach up to the sky, bend down to touch your toes, sit with the soles of your feet touching in front of you and your knees out to the side). Drink a glass of water.

Evening

1. Choose tomorrow's outfit and wash your favorite coffee mug for tomorrow. Light a candle and do three rounds of tapping.

2. Draw an Epsom salt bath and dim the lights or light a candle. Apply a face mask and soak in the tub for twenty minutes.

3. Revisit the tarot or oracle card you pulled that morning and think about how the message or lesson showed up in your day (journal about it if you feel the urge). Read a book for pleasure as you sip on a cup of your favorite herbal tea.

To develop a consistent morning and evening ritual, keep track of the different combinations you try and note the most appealing variations. Or mix it up and do a different ritual every day. This is your time and you get to decide what to do with it.

Carving out time for yourself with daily rituals will reset your inner compass and help you recover from the demands of daily living. By bookending your days with ritual, you're creating boundaries that empower you to have agency over your time and attention. Many of us are glued to our phones and tethered to our jobs, and rituals can mark the start and end of work mode, which is an important distinction to make, especially if you work from home (learn more about energetic upkeep in Chapter 11).

At its core, your daily ritual is an energetic love letter to yourself. Regardless of how your ritual looks—making a meal, climbing a mountain, or washing your face—it's the dedication of time for you and you alone that is the gift. Through morning and evening rituals, you're making a choice to show up for yourself. You're also showing the people in your life and the Universe that you are worthy of being tended to and prioritized. The choices you make every day can have a greater impact on your physical, emotional, and spiritual well-being than your biology, genetics, or environment.

Choose wisely.

CHAPTER 8

BIRTHDAYS AND NEW YEAR'S AND DIVORCE, OH MY! (EASY RITUALS FOR ANY OCCASION)

ecember 24, 1979. I'm nine years old and in the back seat of the family station wagon as my parents figure out where to get dinner after a day of shopping. Everything is closed and everyone is hangry. The holy trinity of last-minute meals—McDonald's, A&W, and Kentucky Fried Chicken—aren't an option. My mom is making Christmas dinner tomorrow and has no interest in cooking at this hour. We head to Chinatown and strike gold: Silver Dragon is open, and it is packed. The mood is festive, the food is delicious, and we return every Christmas Eve until my sister and I leave home years later. It remains one of my happiest childhood memories and is the tradition I associate most with Christmas, despite being born out of necessity and having nothing to do with Santa, presents, turkey, or baby Jesus.

When I got married and moved across the country, my husband and I modified this seasonal ritual (swapping Silver Dragon for sushi), and it's now a holiday highlight for our kids (to the point that they declined a Christmas beach vacation because we'd miss sushi at our special place).

Rituals weave depth and dimension into our lives, allowing us to transform our perspective and process our emotions during times of transition. Marking significant occasions with ritual brings families, communities, cultures, and countries together in crucial ways. Rituals are the spiritual safety net we've inherited from our ancestors to keep us safe, cohesive, and connected to the Divine. Regardless of religion, culture, or ethnicity, ceremonial markers unify us, creating a sense of shared emotion that nourishes our souls. An event becomes a special, often sacred, experience when we imbue it with ceremony. We crave ritual to ground ourselves in times of change or challenge, such as childbirth, marriage, or death. The urge to gather during these transformational moments is embedded in our DNA—they mark the passage of time and give us a sense of meaning.

This universal truth was proven beyond any doubt during the COVID-19 pandemic, when the global quarantine forced the cancellation of countless shared rituals. From graduations and weddings to births and funerals, our collective well-being suffered when these occasions were abruptly called off. Interestingly, that vacuum inspired the creation of new innovative rituals, further demonstrating how vital they are. Both of my kids had drive-thru graduations, which may not have seemed fun in the moment when compared to a traditional ceremony, but were definitely memorable.

Your ritual can be done solo as long as you assign meaning to it (particularly when it comes to grieving). Yes, rituals are essential for joining us with others, but they also connect us to ourselves and a higher power. You don't need other people or religious leaders to celebrate important life events. Look at your own unique life path and come up with a personal ritual based on your needs. Trust that you know what is best for you.

BABY LOVE

◇◇◇

Many of us are celebrated with ceremonies before we're even born. Rituals for pregnancy and childbirth have been around since women started having babies. Because pregnancy and childbirth have been a historically dangerous time for women, many ancient rituals focused on protection. Ancient Anglo-Saxons considered it good luck for a pregnant woman to walk on a dead man's grave and then step over her husband (who was lying on the ground) while repeating an incantation. During medieval times, women were expected to confess their sins to priests *during labor* (I'd rather give birth at a cemetery).

Baby Showers and Mother Blessings

We can thank the Boomers for introducing baby showers after the Second World War as a way to "shower" the expectant mother with practical newborn essentials. Today's baby showers often focus on the mother's wants (baby-wipe warmer) rather than basic needs (diapers), and some baby showers have evolved into Real-Housewives-consumer-driven-gender-reveal extravaganzas, but the desire to help prepare soon-to-be parents and celebrate a new life remains strong. Most people opt for a traditional afternoon baby shower hosted at the home of a grandma-to-be or close family friend, featuring lots of presents and silly games (anyone else traumatized from licking a diaper full of melted chocolate?), but you can supplement the typical baby shower with a ritualistic twist, ditch the baby shower altogether, or do both!

I love pregnancy rituals that nurture the mom-to-be, because you know she'll go from being the star of the show to a recurring character as soon as that baby arrives. Some pregnant or adoptive women gather their friends for a day of indulgence at the spa or enjoy a beautiful meal. Others will do a preggo-friendly activity, like a painting or belly dancing class. (Fun fact: Belly dancing is actually a labor dance—the undulating movements assist the baby's journey down the birth canal.) To heighten the ceremonial vibes of your pre-birth ritual, you might consider a Mother Blessing.

Inspired by the Navajo's Blessingway, this ritual focuses positive energy on the woman and her birthing partner as they transition into parenthood. A Mother Blessing can be as massive or intimate as you'd like—it depends on whether the woman prefers the support of a few close friends and family or a larger crowd. You can include the birth partner or keep it to friends and honored elders. It's a participatory ritual, so you'll want the guest list to be manageable (you can always have a bigger reception following the Mother Blessing or once the baby arrives). Have everyone bring food to share or a meal that can be frozen until the baby arrives (or schedule meals to be dropped off following the birth). If possible, everyone sits in a circle (more on circles in Chapter 12) facing one another with phones put away. You may choose to light a candle to open the ritual, creating an atmosphere of reverence. It's also nice to begin by saying a few words acknowledging the female ancestors who came before you, as well as the inherent strength found in every woman. Although gift registries are usually saved for traditional baby showers, there is no set agenda for a Mother Blessing, and you can customize it to be meaningful for the mother. Here are a few suggestions to get you started.

Birthing Crystals
Guests bring a crystal for the mama-to-be that was chosen for its specific properties (such as protection, calm, or love . . . you can

provide a "Crystals 101" explainer with the invite). During the event, each person presents their crystal to the mother and explains why they chose it. Use a decorative bowl or container to collect the crystals—they can be kept in the baby's room or used as a focal point during labor.

Bead Ceremony

This is a wonderful option for including people who can't attend the Mother Blessing. Everyone sends a bead and a note of encouragement in advance of the event. The beads are used to create a bracelet or necklace worn during labor (or used like mala beads if jewelry during labor is a no-go). It's a tangible reminder of the mother's strength and an amulet of encouragement.

Pampering

Place a bowl of warm water infused with flower petals, salts, or crystals at the mother's feet for her to soak them. Give everyone a chance to spend a few minutes massaging her hands, feet, or shoulders. Brush her hair as you whisper words of encouragement in her ear. The mama's only job is to relax and receive. This is a powerful opportunity for her to practice surrendering to the moment she is in.

Meditation Stones

These are created during the Mother Blessing. Get some palm-sized, flat stones from a craft store, along with some paint supplies (you can use Sharpie pens if nobody likes getting crafty).

Have guests decorate their stone with words, symbols, or other imagery that conveys their wish for the mother while she is laboring. For adoptive moms, it can be a wish for their transformation into being a parent. After the stones dry, have everyone hold their stone in both hands with their eyes closed, infusing it with their wish. The stones can be given to the mom-to-be along with an explanation of the wish, or you can gather them in a container for her to examine at a later time. During labor, she can hold or rub the stones as a reminder of the love and support surrounding her. (Confession: If I'd been handed rocks while in the throes of labor, I would've thrown them at someone, so it's important to consider the woman being honored for what ritual feels right.)

Wrist Binding

This ritual is less kinky than it sounds and incredibly powerful, especially when it's done to end the Mother Blessing. You'll need a large ball of yarn or string and a sharp pair of scissors. Everyone stands shoulder-to-shoulder in a circle, passing the yarn and tying a bracelet around her wrist. Once everyone has a bracelet, hold hands and close your eyes in a sacred pause that acknowledges this moment of sisterhood. Wear your bracelets as a reminder to hold the mama in your heart and envision a peaceful birth. When you learn she is in labor, everyone cuts their bracelet and sends loving energy her way.

Post-Birth Rituals, Naming Ceremonies, & Placenta Placements

Some cultures wait until after the birth to celebrate a new life. Take, for example, the Aztecs, who ensured baby boys would grow into strong warriors by burying their placentas in enemy territory. Or ancient Europeans, who placed the placenta of a newborn over his or her own head to prevent sore eyes (which may seem bizarre, but placentas have their place within modern rituals, too—plenty of parents have placentas in their freezer right now, ready to be nibbled on or used for other ceremonial purposes).

If a baptism or bris isn't your thing (or it is, but you feel called to add your own spin), plenty of post-birth rituals commemorate a baby, and they're an important reminder to the new parents that they aren't alone in raising their child. Naming ceremonies or blessing rituals are a chance for families and their communities to honor and welcome a new child. Create your own itinerary that includes a structured ceremony or an informal gathering where everyone can hang out and get to know the newest member of your family.

In lieu of a religious officiant, you could ask a celebrant, close friend, or family elder to perform the ritual. You may wish to place a symbolic wreath of botanicals and foliage around the baby during the ceremony. Small gifts or offerings can be placed on a table for the child or family, similar to a baby shower, and guests could be invited to use a guest book or recipe index card to write their hopes for the baby, which will be given to the parents following the ceremony. Open the ritual by lighting a candle (guests can participate, too), smudging, or lighting incense. Invite loved ones to read poems or quotes, sing a song, or play music. The celebrant may anoint the child with water or essential oils (jojoba or coconut oil infused with a drop of lavender or peppermint) and call upon ancestral spirits or the four elements to provide love, guidance, and protection. Or the blessing might focus on the community your baby is joining. For example:

Thank you for joining (parent name[s]) on this beautiful day as we welcome (baby name) to our community. (Parent name[s]), we honor and love you with all of our hearts. We give you our love, knowledge, and support as you embark on the path of parenthood. We are here for you.

(Baby name), we are thrilled to meet you. We promise to always support, teach, and protect you as you grow into your truest self. Most importantly, we promise to love you unconditionally and forever, because we are your family. Today we celebrate everything about you. We love you for who you are and who you will become. Our wish for you is a life filled with peace, guidance, abundance, laughter, wisdom, strength, and love. Let's take a moment to bless (baby name) by closing our eyes and sending all of our love to this magnificent new life.

Thank you all for coming to bless this beautiful family.

The transition to parenthood can be rocky, especially for new moms. Bringing loved ones together to offer their love, support, and wisdom can help ease the way.

HAVE YOUR CAKE AND EAT IT (WITH A RITUAL)

◇◇◇

I have a friend who takes an entire week to celebrate her day of birth (she would like it to be an official holiday), while another friend refuses to acknowledge, let alone celebrate, her own birthday. However you feel about getting older, birthdays are auspicious occasions that are ripe for rituals. I advise my tarot clients to do readings and rituals around their birthday because it marks the start of their personal New Year—the Sun adds energetic *oomph* when it enters the placement of your birth. The goal of a birthday ritual is to immerse yourself in love of self. This sacred moment is your solar return. Make the most of it by embracing your body and empowering your soul as it launches on another trip around the Sun.

These birthday rituals are meant to be done on your own (I'm so *over* putting expectations on other people to make my special day special). Aside from that, let your imagination run wild. Curate a day (or an hour on the day) filled with authentic indulgence, joyful simplicity, and quiet contemplation. Here is a birthday ritual that you can adapt to suit your situation and desires. Most important: let it be a time of closure, creation, and celebration.

Start by creating a space that is open and inviting to you, smudging it as you focus on your intention (appreciating yourself!). Set up a birthday altar (this can be a kitchen counter or nightstand) with your favorite crystals, fresh flowers, and anything else that appeals to your senses (you may want to add a picture of yourself as a child). Pour yourself a glass of water or a cup of tea (perhaps buy yourself a cup that's only used on your birthday). Put on some music that makes your heart smile. Dim the lights or shut the blinds. Close your eyes and ground yourself with three deep breaths. When you're ready, light one votive or tealight candle for every year of your life. As they burn, reflect on your journey up until this moment. Journal, meditate, or just stare at the flames as you consider the obstacles you've overcome, the lessons you've learned, and the people you've loved. If you feel compelled to, revisit old journals or photographs. Give thanks for everything you have achieved and the wisdom you've gained over the years (and especially this past year). Get bold about what you're ready to call into your life, and write it down. Pull a card from your preferred deck to get a message for the upcoming year. Open the beautifully wrapped gift you bought yourself in advance (it doesn't have to be expensive, but ideally it's something you *want* and don't necessarily *need*). Finally, close your eyes for one final moment of gratitude before gently blowing out or extinguishing your candles.

You can supplement this birthday ritual with a leisurely bath (adding whatever offerings you love most), a scrumptious treat, or spending time in nature—remember, this is *your* day. If your birthday is a heavy time of year for you, it's time to flip the script. Be your own best friend and write yourself a birthday love letter. Share your favorite things about yourself and how proud you are of your accomplishments—don't be afraid to brag!—and then read the letter aloud to yourself (while looking in the mirror, if you can handle it).

I always pick a power word for the coming year, and it's one of the most inspiring acts I do on my birthday. Choose a word that encompasses your goals and desires. Look back on the past year for themes, challenges, or areas of improvement to help you identify your word (examples include *freedom, bliss, power, sass, vitality, ease, surrender, unity, presence, worthiness, self-care, hope, forgiveness, love,* and *strength*). Write your word down, put it where you'll see it often, like a sticky note on your bathroom mirror, and commit to saying it out loud three times every day.

Whether your birthday ritual is a few minutes or an all-day affair, creating a sacred moment for yourself is the best birthday gift you can receive and will magnify your intentions for the year ahead. Happy birthday, gorgeous!

POTENT MOMENTS MADE FOR RITUALS

◇◇◇

Some birthdays or stages of life are more significant than others, and these milestones call for a ritual to mark their importance. Many cultures ritualize the threshold from childhood into adolescence because this shift inevitably changes who we are and how we're perceived by our community. Bat mitzvahs and confirmations are coming-of-age rituals rooted in religion, whereas high-school proms are culturally based rituals (they originally served the same purpose as a debutante ball—introducing young women to eligible young men, like a cross between Tinder and a livestock auction). Quinceañeras are a combination of religious ceremony and coming-out party that can be traced back to Aztec times.

The Kids Are Alright (Coming-of-Age Rituals)

Many cultures initiate children into adulthood with feats of strength, like the Inuit, who send their young sons to hunt with their fathers in the harsh Arctic wilderness to prove their endurance. Vision quests are a more supernatural rite of passage that have been used by people around the world for centuries. Traditionally, a vision quest will involve fasting and solitude in nature as a way to build survival skills, gain spiritual enlightenment, and connect with the natural and spirit worlds. Participants return to their communities with confidence, knowledge, and purpose.

The summer before each of my children entered high school, we sent them on a three-week backcountry canoe trip in Northern Ontario that was designed by the organizers to be a modern rite of passage. My kids were transformed. They returned to us with a maturity that was slightly intimidating. During this time isolated in the wild with their group, they learned how to take risks, overcome challenges, and communicate effectively. But this experience wasn't just about knowing how to paddle a canoe or survive the elements— the gift was found in understanding themselves. They realized what they are capable of away from the expectations and distractions of life at home. They literally and figuratively disconnected from the outside world and, in doing so, they left judgment and self-doubt behind. They entered high school knowing they could handle anything because of everything they'd handled in the wild.

These rite-of-passage rituals are crucial because they incite the shift in consciousness we need when entering a new phase of life. Many of these practices have been lost to us because they were often undertaken by the community, usually within a religious framework, but you can create your own—and you don't have to disappear into the woods or be a tween to do it.

In My "DGAF Crone Era" (Celebrating Menopause)

There's a theory that menopause evolved in women for the same reason it exists in female elephants and orcas: once the ability and obligation to reproduce ends, women are free to lead. This, dear reader, is cause for celebration.

Menopause has been cloaked in mystery and derision for decades, but it wasn't always that way. Female elders enjoyed an elevated status in ancient societies around the world, revered as leaders for their wisdom and healing abilities. The word *crone,* from Kronos (Cronus), the ancient Greek god of time, reflects the knowledge women gain over the years, but it mutated from compliment to insult—from wise woman to witch—during the medieval period (because: patriarchy). Rituals surrounding menopause help make sense of the discomfort or grieving that can accompany this transition—and they can give women an opportunity (and motivation!) to recognize and revel in this majestic stage of womanhood.

As the focus on exterior beauty and reproduction diminishes during menopause, women enter the peak of their power. We stop getting our worth from the admiration or judgments of others, as the pressure to be pretty—or at least presentable—is lifted. And that freedom is often terrifying. Thresholds are inherently scary because a part of us must be left behind so that we can evolve into a new version of ourselves. Beauty is in the eye of the beholder, and the beholder becomes us. When everyone stops valuing how we look on the outside, an opportunity arises to discover the beauty that lies within—a beauty forged in crushing disappointment, heartbreaking joy, and lessons learned the hard way. As our attention turns from the shiny shell to the incandescent core, we realize that we're f*cking gorgeous. And powerful beyond measure.

I spent my fifty-second birthday in my birthday suit. I invested in professional hair, makeup, and photography to have a boudoir (aka nudie) photo shoot. It took all day, and although the result had more of a draped-fabric art vibe versus centerfold (and I have yet to print a single photo), that experience changed my life.

When I committed to stepping into the spotlight with nothing to hide behind, I signaled to the Universe (and myself) that I was ready to be seen—and that caused a shift that manifested immediately. During the photo shoot, I received an email from a publisher about the book I had finished writing (literally!) the day before. That email didn't result in a book deal, but it sparked the chain of events that led to my agent and this book (as part of a *two-book* deal).

On that birthday, I birthed a new me—the real me. In baring my ass, I bared my soul. I stepped out of my clothes and into myself. When I said *yes* to that experience, the Universe responded with more opportunities for YES: YES to showing up and speaking out, YES to adventure and ambition, YES to life. I encourage you (or the wise women in your life) to celebrate this milestone with an initiation of some kind. Go on a trip, get a tattoo, give fewer f*cks what anyone thinks of your choices. Or, if you're really stuck for ideas, grab a camera and get naked.

YOU (DON'T) COMPLETE ME (RITUALS FOR DIVORCE)

◇◇◇

The global wedding industry is worth over twenty *billion* dollars, and there are countless resources to find unique wedding rituals, from oathing stones to rope warming (it's a thing . . . google it), but nobody wants to talk about rituals for divorce. It can be devastating when a relationship ends—whether it's romantic, platonic, or familial—which is why a ceremony to mark its completion is a crucial step to moving forward.

Divorce (like marriage) is a massive rite of passage that is worthy of honor and recognition, and a divorce ritual is the key to closure. It offers a finality that transcends legal proceedings, allowing you to reflect on the past and grieve unmet expectations for the future. This marriage-ending marker invites you to release what could have been as you embrace what is to come. This ritual declares that divorce is not a failure: it's an initiation into your next chapter.

Create a divorce or separation ritual that resonates with you. Gather a few close friends or make it a solo affair. Plan it in advance or let it be a spontaneous event. You can even include your ex for an uncoupling ceremony, which is a dissolution service centered on love over hate, and healing rather than revenge. The couple recommit (often in front of loved ones) to being caring co-parents and friends, reframing divorce as a reflection of growth without blame. It's a beautiful testament to your relationship if you and your ex can pull this off—kudos to you and your enlightenment. For everyone else, there are other options.

If you aren't sure where to begin, write a letter. It may be a letter that's never sent, or you and your ex could write each other goodbye letters that share what can't be said in person. If you're searching for closure when a relationship ends without warning, or there's a lot of animosity, a letter can be very therapeutic. Write it by hand, if possible (rather than typing it out), and definitely don't save it on your phone or computer. This is something you'll want to release or dispose of in a ritualistic manner. Similar to Burn Your Sh*t, this is a chance to unburden yourself, so ditch the filter and don't hold back—write without worrying about spelling, penmanship, or political correctness. You can write one letter to your ex or an entire series of letters that includes your in-laws, lawyers, so-called friends, or anyone else living rent-free in your head.

In addition to a letter, think about any objects that symbolize your marriage that can be incorporated into your ritual, like a wedding ring, photos, or marriage license. Look at how the natural elements align with your emotions, and bring them into your ritual in any way that resonates.

Fire is a powerful and transformative energy often associated with intense emotions like anger. Burn your letter, wedding pictures, or marriage license in a ritual fire (do it under a Full Moon to add extra fuel to your ritual). If you've written a letter, you may want to read it out loud or to yourself before lighting it. Before you set fire to your letter, picture, or document, say these words, or something like them:

I now choose to release everything contained in this letter. I release the hold you have on my heart and the grip I have on yours. I release our bond in this lifetime, past lifetimes, and future life-times. I release my expectations about things I cannot control. I release the dream of what could have been to create capacity for the adventure that awaits me. I release you to a life of love, joy, and prosperity—and I release myself to this abundance as well.

Then, as you light the paper on fire and watch it burn, say *And so it is.*

This will release negativity, transform your rage, and create space for resignation and, ultimately, acceptance. You can also have your ring melted (if it's a gold band) or repurposed into a new piece of jewelry (if there are gems), but don't attempt to melt jewelry at home—leave that to a professional. You may also have an urge to torch all of your ex's belongings in a bonfire (à la Angela Bassett in *Waiting to Exhale*), but that could release toxic fumes in the air. Keep your burn to some paper or a few select photos, like Ed the biker in Chapter 5, who burned his sh*t and realized that the picture of his ex wasn't burning because he needed to deepen his release of their relationship.

Water is the element of love and emotion. It purifies as it energetically honors your tears and supports your grieving. You could scatter the ashes of burned photos or other paper into a lake, or throw a mini Viking funeral for your marriage by making a little paper boat from a letter or marriage license and lighting it on fire before setting it adrift on a body of water. You may feel compelled to toss your ring in a lake or ocean, but give that some serious thought before warming up your pitching arm—a better option might be selling the ring and going on a beach vacation with the proceeds. You could always write the name of your ex (or your married name, if you're changing it back) on a rock and, after taking a moment to imbue it with all of your pain or anger, throw *that* in the water.

Soaking in a ritual bath ushers the release of emotions connected to divorce or separation. Infuse forgiveness and heart-healing energy into the water by adding a rose quartz crystal, or ground and protect yourself with some tiger's eye. As always, setting your intention for the bath is a key step.

Earth is the ultimate grounding energy that keeps us rooted and secure. Burying a symbol of your married life in the soil puts your relationship to rest. There is a finality to this act that evokes the mourning we do when someone dies, and it can help you accept that your marriage is truly over. Consider planting some seeds along with your offering to signify how the end of your marriage echoes the cycle of life as well as signaling the start of your new season of growth. You could go to a place that was special for you as a couple and spend some time reflecting before burying a rose quartz crystal that symbolizes your love story, or another meaningful memento from your relationship (but again, maybe not the ring; I want you to treat yourself with the money you make from selling it!).

Air is the breath of life that connects us to the Divine. Candles incorporate the element of Fire as well as Air, and you can perform a reverse unity candle ritual by extinguishing a symbolic shared candle and then lighting an individual candle to represent your independence. Scatter the ashes of burned letters or photos into the wind like you would the cremated ashes of a loved one. Yelling into the wind is also extremely cathartic, and if you've never screamed at a wave when nobody's around, I highly recommend it. If your divorce was particularly contentious, light a small candle (like a tealight or birthday candle) to represent that person and talk to it—be completely honest and uncensored as you speak, yell, curse, or sob everything you've been holding back. Unleash until the candle goes out, or snuff it out yourself, and then dispose of any remnants outside of your home immediately. End your ritual with some breathwork to ground you into your body, and with each breath remind yourself that you are capable, resilient, and loved.

Even with the most amicable splits, a divorce ritual brings intense emotions to the surface. Dose yourself with extreme self-care before, during, and after your ritual. Book a pedicure in advance. End your ritual with a soothing bath. Plan dinner with friends at your favorite restaurant (their treat!). With a divorce ritual, you forge a path to forgiveness and freedom. By witnessing your pain, you transform it into wisdom. Honor yourself and your experience—it is a gift . . . and so are you.

RITUALS FOR GRIEF

◇◇◇

Death is the final rite of passage we will encounter—and also the most overlooked, feared, and resisted, especially in North America. Although death is unavoidable, how we handle loss varies wildly. In many ways, we've cauterized ourselves from the most natural and inevitable rite of passage we'll ever face. Medicine is now valued over mysticism, and dying has been outsourced to hospitals, leaving little room for the ritualized touchstones we've relied on in the past. We've lost our connection to loss.

Even when we belong to a religion or culture that marks the end of life, the traditions often aren't personal enough, or they're too far removed from everyday life to support our healing in the ways we need. Grief requires an outlet—it is an energy that demands to be acknowledged and expressed—yet it's often repressed because it scares the crap out of us, and often makes the people around us profoundly uncomfortable. Nobody escapes grief—whether it's the loss of a person, pet, relationship, or circumstance—and rituals are the bridge that leads us from shock and despair to comfort and peace. Ceremonies around saying goodbye also offer a template for how we can show up for and support other people who are grieving.

In every ritual there is a visible action that articulates an invisible intention, which is why ancient death rituals persist—we need them to survive the unimaginable and process the unknown.

Funerals assist us in facing the reality of mortality. Rather than a shortcut to closure, they offer a pathway to feeling our pain. Traditionally, the funerals of different cultures have focused on easing the transition of the deceased to the afterlife. Many Indigenous communities believe we come from the stars and view death as a natural transition from the physical plane to the Great Spirit in the sky. Tibetan Buddhists facilitate reincarnation by ritually dissecting a corpse before leaving it for vultures. After a somber procession to the cemetery, exuberant jazz funerals take over the streets of New Orleans to celebrate someone's passing. Funeral rituals may vary widely, but they all serve to honor our loved one while providing an outlet for our anguish. Grief brings intense, sometimes conflicting emotions—such as rage, yearning, fear, sorrow, and relief—and rituals can help us process these intense feelings. You can carry out a modern version of time-honored rituals that is supportive for everyone.

Ask a few close friends or family members if they would like to participate in advance of the funeral or celebration of life. On the day of the service, set up a container filled with water (aka the "spirit bowl"). Give participants a pen and piece of rice paper cut to the size of a sticky note. Ask them to write down a burden that was carried in this lifetime by the person who passed, such as illness, loneliness, physical pain, lack of confidence, or self-doubt. During the service, explain how various cultures throughout history have rituals that unburden the soul of the traveler who has been called home, transforming these burdens into gifts. Invite the participants to join you at the spirit bowl, telling attendees that these people have written a burden that they would like to release from the spirit of the departed. Ask them to take turns submerging their rice paper into the water, where it will dissolve as if by magic, releasing the burden with it. During the unburdening, play a meaningful or beautiful piece of music and allow the participants to read the burden out loud or keep it to themselves. This is particularly powerful when death has come way too early or as the result of a long illness.

Once the burdens have been released, it's time to celebrate the gifts. As each guest arrives at the service, have a basket of polished white stones set on a table with gold or silver Sharpie pens. Display a sign instructing guests to write one word on the stone that describes the gifts or essence of the person who passed (examples include *funny, brilliant, friend, artist, genuine, soulful, inspiring,* or *strong*). Ask guests to keep their stones until the end of the service, and following the unburdening give people a moment to close their eyes and focus on their chosen word as they hold their stone. Encourage them to imbue the stone with healing and love—for the soul of the departed as well as the friends and family who remain. Invite guests to take turns bringing their stones to the family members, placing them in a basket. Explain that these stones will be set in a garden, on a mantlepiece, or in another area of significance as an enduring reminder of the impact their loved one had on the world and the people around them.

These kinds of personalized rituals can soothe the ache that comes with loss, and they aren't limited to humans. The loss of a pet can be traumatic—especially for children or when euthanasia was required to end the animal's suffering. A ritualized farewell offers healing for all. Invite people to your pet's service who will respect the sacredness of this ceremony, whether it's one individual or a group of people.

If there is a grave, people can gather to create or decorate a marker. Even without a grave, you could choose a garden or special tree in a park to place your memorial (piling rocks into a cairn is also an option). You may wish to sit in a circle and pass around your pet's collar or favorite toy, taking turns speaking about a special memory or how the animal impacted your lives. Share the love story of you and your pet—how you came together, milestone moments, and how your life was forever changed. End the ritual by thanking your furry (or scaly, or feathery, or prickly) BFF for the unconditional love and joy they provided. Incorporate music, poems, prayers, or anything else that resonates with you and reflects the bond you shared.

Rituals surrounding loss help pave the way to peace, and an altar can provide psychological comfort and spiritual solace as you mourn. When the pain is too much to manage, an altar dedicated to your person or pet can help you manage the energetic overwhelm that comes with loss.

Clear a dedicated space—such as a table, mantle, bookcase, or other flat surface—and smudge the area with sage, palo santo, or incense. If you'd like, arrange an altar cloth that is either purple (like amethyst, it symbolizes spirituality and the transition from life to death) or white (a color long associated with purification and mourning). Alternatively, use a piece of fabric that holds significance, like a dog blanket for a pet's altar. Or skip the altar cloth altogether.

Build your altar using any or all of the following elements.

Incense or Essential Oils
Burn or diffuse your scent of choice to create a calming atmosphere. Frankincense has been used to mark rites of passage for centuries, while myrrh connects you to your courage, and myrtle heals your soul. Lavender and sandalwood are also wonderful all-purpose aromatics.

Herbs

Herbs can also be burned (see Chapter 3 for smudging instructions) or artfully arranged on your altar. Rosemary is an ancient symbol of friendship and remembrance, thought to help guide spirits to the afterlife. Hawthorn is a healer of heartbreak and grief and is used medicinally in teas and honey. Thyme is associated with caring and courage for mourners, but is also placed in coffins to ensure safe passage for the deceased.

Crystals

The healing vibrations of crystals offer a soft source of comfort as you grieve. You can place them on your altar or hold them during your ritual. Dolomite provides relief from sorrow, rose quartz is the gentlest heart healer, and Apache tears activate emotional healing while promoting forgiveness. Amethyst, smoky quartz, and amazonite are also useful in times of grief.

Candles

Place a candle on your altar (purple or white, like the altar cloth, or any other color that speaks to you), ensuring it's safely away from flammable objects. Use a plate or other fireproof surface on altar cloths and, for safety, only keep candles lit when someone is present).

Mementos

Elevate your sacred space with natural elements (such as pine cones or fresh flowers), photos, or other keepsakes (jewelry or letters for people, collars or toys for pets) that are meaningful reminders of your loved one.

Once your altar has been set, light the candle and take a moment to close your eyes (or stare softly at the flame), and breathe. Use this time to connect with your person or pet. Cry, talk, sing, meditate—express whatever is in your heart. During this time, you are in communion with the soul of your dearly departed and there is no wrong way to do it.

Tending to your altar can be a daily or weekly ritual—tidy, dust, or smudge the space before lighting the candle and speaking from your heart. Add crystals such as rose quartz (to represent your love) or angelite (to encourage peaceful acceptance), taking care to clear them whenever necessary. You can also drop by your altar and light the candle whenever you feel the urge to connect with or pay tribute to those who've passed. Whenever you decide to commune with your altar, make sure you're giving this time the reverence it requires by getting quiet. Ask for guidance. Request protection. Appeal for healing. Or just sit in solitude and remember what this soul meant to you in this lifetime.

Keep your altar for a specific period of mourning (a month or year, for example) or until you feel its purpose has been served. The goal of your altar is to make you feel loved, supported, and connected to your loved one as you grieve. Only you can decide the duration.

If you'd like a more permanent monument of remembrance, create an ancestor altar. Include any of the above-mentioned items and pay tribute to all of the lives that have led to yours. Commemorate your lineage with an open invitation to connect with the wisdom of your past. Earth altars are another option and can be assembled spontaneously while you walk in nature. Gather twigs, stones, branches, berries, or any other component that catches your eye. Clear a patch of ground and arrange each piece of your altar in a pleasing manner. Sit in a moment of remembrance for your loved one. Earth altars are a beautiful way to honor the cycle of life while reinforcing the singular beauty and impermanence of all living things.

Death Day

Every year, Día de los Muertos (or Day of the Dead) gives families an opportunity to fortify their relationships with departed souls. The veil between the living and dead is thought to be at its thinnest, allowing for stronger connections with the afterlife. It's a joyful celebration dedicated to remembering people who came before us. Jewish traditions also mark death with Yahrzeit, when a candle is lit on the anniversary of a loved one's passing in accordance with the Jewish calendar. Rituals—religious or personal—can help you stay connected with your loved one long after they are gone.

We've been lighting candles to honor the dead since fire was first discovered, and lighting a candle to signify the day you lost a special person or pet is a powerful testament of your love. Additional ways to honor a birthday or death day with ritual include writing a tribute (or even just their name and a word to describe them) on a stone to place along a riverbank or in a park. Compose a letter to the person or pet who died, and then burn the letter as you envision the smoke carrying your message to them. Perform a random act of kindness anonymously and dedicate it to your loved one's memory. Treat everyone to a drink or dessert at your loved one's favorite restaurant in their honor. You could also take your loved one's spirit on a date, which sounds a little woo-woo even for me, but I have a story that proves its power.

To mark the first anniversary of her mom's death, my friend Kim went for lunch at her mom's favorite café. She asked that the extra place setting remain and even ordered her mom's signature drink in addition to her own. Kim enjoyed her lunch as she read a book in the near-empty restaurant, finishing with a decadent dessert. As she waited for the bill, Kim raised her glass to clink it against her mom's drink and said, "I love you, Mom. And I miss you so much." At that moment, the sound system's volume was cranked up and the song "Whatever Lola Wants" blared across the restaurant. Lola is the name of Kim's mom—not a nickname and definitely not common for a woman of her generation. It was, in fact, the song most associated with her in life, and it didn't match the style of music that had been playing in the café up until that moment. Kim's body was jolted with a million volts of goose bumps, and she just knew that her mom was celebrating with her in her favorite café with her preferred drink and signature song. Although she hasn't experienced anything quite as blatant since then, Kim returns every year to take her mom for a birthday lunch date, their bond as strong as ever.

Rituals for Dying

What about when death is imminent but hasn't yet arrived? For a person who is actively dying, spiritual support is as crucial as conventional healthcare—and rituals infuse palliative assistance with ethereal meaning. Although the focus is on bringing comfort, calm, and closure to the person nearing death, friends and family also benefit from end-of-life rituals. Simple acts of caring can be sacred rituals. Sitting with the dying person and reading aloud. Holding hands or gently stroking an arm. Tucking them in with a blanket. Brushing the person's hair and offering small sips of water. Giving a manicure or rubbing lotion on the person's feet. These expressions of love are rituals of reverence. They ease spiritual suffering for everyone by offering sacred moments of understanding, acceptance, healing, and pure love.

We can honor our dying loved ones by celebrating them while they're still able to understand the impact they've had on others.

Whether it's a huge party or an intimate gathering, a celebration of life before death allows everyone to give (and receive) their love. A deeply meaningful end-of-life ritual is creating space for the dying person to tell their story, share their wishes for you, voice their fears and regrets, or bask in all of the love that surrounds them. Being there for that person is a ritual. Ask people to join you in holding the emotions of the person facing death. Light a candle to signify the beginning of the ritual, and settle into silence. Invite anyone to speak aloud any feelings that arise. When people share, offer simple statements (*I hear you* or *I am with you*) and don't try to make anyone feel better. You are bearing witness to each other and that is enough—it's actually an incredibly powerful intention. When you are ready to close the ritual, blow out the candle or let it extinguish on its own.

Music and singing are often present when a person passes away. In a 2020 study, researchers from the University of British Columbia reported that a dying brain can respond to sound even if the person is unconscious. The Gregorian chants of French Benedictine monks brought comfort to the dying in the Middle Ages, and singing hymns or chanting as people take their last breath is still common in many cultures. Today, threshold choirs (or deathbed singers) are available in some hospices; they administer love in audible form, imbuing an often fraught time of transition with transcendence.

Music can soothe our souls and also ease one's passing. My mom's friend Garry was dying of cancer and not ready to leave. His exuberant life force diminished rapidly near the end, and he lay unresponsive in a hospital bed for weeks—barely hanging on and refusing to give up—as his friends took turns at his bedside. Everyone gathered on the day Garry died, somehow knowing, without knowing how, that his time was limited. They shared stories about Garry while playing his favorite music. Just as his go-to karaoke song ("My Way") ended, Garry took his last breath. A fitting finale for a quintessential performer.

Death is unavoidable and sometimes scary, but there are opportunities for awe and beauty (and even humor) to be found. Through grief we discover new ways to love. Rituals before and after death help you honor the past as you acclimate to a different future.

SHAKE YOUR MERRY-MAKER (SEASONAL RITUALS)

◇◇◇

I firmly believe that New Year's resolutions are a yearly bet we make with ourselves that sets us up to fail. They are the ultimate con. Don't get me wrong: I appreciate a good end-of-season celebration. I just think they can be a bit more potent (not to mention attainable) when they're infused with intention and informed by the wisdom of the natural world. When we sync our rituals to the rhythms of nature, it amplifies their power. Seasonal rituals are auspicious opportunities to release and replenish; they invite healing and hope.

If a ritual to mark the New Year floats your boat, go for it (remember, your ritual needs to speak to you), but don't add unnecessary pressure by expecting your life to change the minute the clock strikes twelve. Instead, bump up the date of your end-of-year ritual by a couple of weeks to give it an astral boost.

Yule Is Cool (Solstice Celebrations)

Solstice rituals aren't tied to culture, religion, or location—they're written in the stars. The word *solstice* combines the Latin words *sol*

(Sun) with *sistere* (to stand still), and humans have been celebrating it for thousands of years. Many of our modern Christmas traditions are rooted in the Pagan festival of Yule. The solstices occur on the longest and shortest days of the year, in June and December, when the light of the Sun begins to increase or decrease. In the Northern Hemisphere, the Winter Solstice, on December 21, marks the shortest and darkest day of the year, while the Summer Solstice, on June 21, is when we have more daylight than any other day. It's the opposite for people living in the Southern Hemisphere, but regardless of where you live or what season you're in, this celestial turning point is always worth celebrating.

Our lives cycle through different seasons, similar to the natural environment that surrounds us. There's the lush and bountiful garden of summer, when the fruits of our labor are flourishing in full bloom. Conversely, winter is a desolate frozen tundra that feels completely barren. It may seem counterintuitive, but the most inhospitable months are usually the most robust and productive time of all. This is when the Earth regenerates, nurturing the soil with natural cycles that repair and replenish. Without winter, there is no spring.

Winter

The literal darkness that pervades the Winter Solstice asks us to get quiet and go within. This dark night of the soul is an opportunity to heal. It is a time of rest and reflection as you confront your shadows to identify what (or who) no longer serves you—this sacred pause is preparing you for a symbolic reawakening. Ancient cultures revered this time as a threshold for the Sun's return, bringing focus to the cultivation of new crops. The Winter Solstice signals rebirth and renewal—as you relinquish outdated narratives and unhelpful habits, you create space for transformation.

Think about the past year. How have your circumstances changed? What did you lose? What was gained? How are you wiser? Where do you still need to grow? What (or who) are you ready to release? What challenges did you overcome? What were the lessons found in loss? Where are you at . . . physically, spiritually, emotionally, financially? Write down your impressions and look for patterns or connections. Burn (or bury) what's ready to go.

The Winter Solstice is also a time of illumination. Maximize this moment by setting bold intentions. Where would you like to be a year from now? What lights you up? Can you identify your deepest desires? What are your strengths and where can you improve? Think about your goals and how you might achieve them. Write down what you're ready to receive. Anchor your aspirations in reality by writing a letter from your future self to the current you—dated one year from now—that details your dreams as if they've already come true (forget about the "how"). Slip these notes under your pillow to sleep on for a few days before tucking them away or sticking them where you can see them (for example, on a bathroom mirror).

Solstice rituals set the tone for your upcoming year in a way that is more empowering than New Year's resolutions (and far less daunting . . . kind of like a Burn Your Sh*t/New Moon Magic sandwich). You're taking an honest look at where you've been, where you're at now, and where you want to go—along with the steps needed to get you there. For me, the Winter Solstice is the most auspicious day to release and renew. Even if you don't do the rituals above, there are opportunities to recognize this seasonal shift: salute the Sun with yoga at dawn, go for a walk outside, or simply take a moment to acknowledge and honor your growth over the past six months. Set up an altar that includes seasonal touches, such as pine cones and boughs or mistletoe and holly (keep them away from curious kids and pets). Burn incense made from frankincense or myrrh. Decorate your space with fairy lights to bring in the light and set a festive tone. Keep a candle or lantern on a gold or yellow altar cloth to celebrate the Sun's return. Your altar is a visual reminder that even in the darkest times, the light will eventually reappear.

Summer

The Summer Solstice celebrates the longest day of the year and a shift in seasons. Also known as Midsummer (or Litha), this is when the Sun is at the peak of its powers, radiating light to nourish all living things. It's a lush, fertile time of abundance, and your Summer Solstice ritual helps you absorb this invigorating energy.

Honor the Sun's bounty by spending time outdoors. Feel the Sun's warmth on your skin, listen for the sounds of nature, and appreciate the beauty that surrounds you. Collect any flowers, sticks, water, sand, or soil to bring home with you and place on your seasonal altar. You may want to set up your altar outside, but inside near a window facing the Sun also works. Buy (or make!) a beeswax candle and set it atop a gold or yellow cloth. Add any other items that symbolize the ripe, sunny vibes of summer: crystals (citrine, carnelian, or yellow calcite); fresh sunflowers or marigolds; a small dish of honey to symbolize the sweetness of the season; or any freshly harvested fruit. Revel in this period of plenty by gathering with friends for a feast (make it a potluck), a bonfire, or both. Take turns speaking your intentions aloud (to give them energetic heft) and invite the Sun's fire to fuel your ambitions.

For solo celebrations, wake up early and perform your ritual during the day when you can embrace the light. Welcome the Sun into your space by opening blinds and windows, honoring this vibrant energy with twelve Sun salutations (representing the months of the year and average hours of sunlight in a day). Sit at your altar and light a candle, staring softly at the flame or closing your eyes, and sit for a few moments of silent contemplation or with a guided meditation to work with the energies of the season.

Now think about what you've been cultivating since the Winter Solstice and how things are coming to fruition. Journal about the internal and external growth you've experienced. Read your reflections aloud and pause to close your eyes, place your hands over your heart, and bask in the bounty you have created. Give yourself a literal hug and pat yourself on the back for all of your accomplishments. Tell yourself (out loud!) that you are doing a great job and how proud you are of your continued evolution. Let the full force of the Sun embolden you. You've earned this moment—enjoy it.

Sexy Times & Pumpkin Spice (Equinox Rituals)

An equinox brings balance when we need it most. It occurs when day and night are equal in length (the word *equinox* comes from the Latin *aequus nox*, or "equal night"). Equinoxes occur in March and September, serving as midpoints between the Winter and Summer Solstices, and they mark the start of spring or autumn (depending on your hemisphere). These are moments of perfect harmony between light and dark—a time of reawakening and recalibration as a new cycle launches. Explore the unique character of each equinox to help you benefit from its gifts.

Spring

The Spring (or Vernal) Equinox ushers in a surge of new life—trees are budding, plants poke through the soil, and wildlife is multiplying.

Also known as Ostara, this is a verdant time of year. It is the energy of creation.

Spring Equinox rituals are rooted in the feeling of fresh starts, so give your space a thorough tidying (aka spring-cleaning—the urge doesn't come from nowhere!) by organizing your closets and clearing clutter from your home. Open windows and steam-clean your carpets. This is an active time of cultivation and renewal—it's time to create space for what's to come.

If you're building an altar for the Spring Equinox (and remember, you don't need one to perform a ritual), choose a windowsill or shelf with access to sunlight, if possible, and give the area a quick cleanse with sage or sandalwood. A green altar cloth represents the season, but it's up to you if you want to use one (I rarely do). Go outside to gather grass clippings, twigs, rocks, or other natural objects. If you have limited access to nature—or, like me, you live where the ground is still frozen solid and trees are bare in March—get some fresh-cut sunflowers or marigolds at your local florist, or grab a few lemons from the grocery store. A Spring Equinox altar also benefits from vibrantly colored crystals, like citrine, peridot, or sunstone. Additional seasonal touches include eggs, seeds, and honey—let your intuition guide you in the creation of your sanctified space.

Begin by lighting a candle or incense. Sit or lie down comfortably, settling into your surroundings. The equinox prioritizes balance in all forms, and you can sync with the rhythm of this season by opening your ritual with a meditation that honors equilibrium (aligning your chakras, for example). Have this meditation be the foundation for your Spring *and* Fall Equinox rituals.

The Spring Equinox brings attention to beginnings and encourages you to focus on what's to come. Let your ritual reflect this generative energy by first sitting in gratitude for what you have now (appreciating what is already true helps elevate you to a vibration of abundance). You can note any insights in your journal or simply acknowledge your blessings internally. Now think about a project or relationship you're ready to begin, or a dormant endeavor that requires a reboot, and write them down (you don't have to go into great detail—phrases like "certified yoga instructor" or "begin dating" will suffice). Pull a tarot or oracle card for a message to help you along your path, or sit in solitude and allow the guidance to emerge. Keep your intentions on your altar and take a moment over the coming days or weeks to pause and recommit to what you are manifesting. Visualize yourself achieving your goal—live in that moment in your mind—and speak your intention out loud. You could plant your written intentions with some literal seeds by placing the paper at the bottom of a container before covering it with soil and seeds. As you nurture your plant and pursue your project over the coming weeks, repeat your intention as you imagine it being fully realized. Full disclosure: I kill every plant I meet, and it would bum me out to watch my intention plant die, so I skip the literal planting of seeds and my manifesting still kicks ass. But if you have a green thumb or the idea sparks something in your belly, give it a try.

This is a potent ritual, so be prepared for big shifts and unexpected opportunities. Growth is never easy—sometimes it's terrifying—but it's always necessary. Be open to embracing change because the Universe often has better plans for you than you have for yourself.

Autumn/Fall

With the Fall (or Autumnal) Equinox comes a time of harvest, feasting, and reflection. Also called Mabon, the Fall Equinox is an opportunity to appreciate all that you've accomplished while taking stock of where you're out of balance. It is a call to recalibrate.

Honor the season with an Autumnal Equinox altar. If possible, go for a walk in the woods and gather leaves, acorns, flowers, or other items from nature. Because the Fall Equinox is a time of looking back, you might include family heirlooms or pictures of your ancestors. Pumpkins, root vegetables, and apples also add a symbolic touch. Choose an orange or brown altar cloth (if you're using one), and work with crystals that support the season, such as tiger's eye, carnelian, or red jasper.

Emphasize the balancing nature of the equinox by lighting two candles: one black and one white. After taking a few minutes to bring yourself into equilibrium through your breath, it's time to get introspective. Be honest with yourself as you consider the intentions/seeds that you planted in the spring. Be curious about what worked, what didn't, and how you might do things differently next time. Are there any insights you can harvest? Some revelations that can assist you in upcoming seasons? Grieve the plans that didn't pan out or any relationships that fizzled, possibly with a special Burn Your Sh*t (Equinox Edition) if you feel called to do so. Look for wisdom in these wounds so you might forge maturity from misfortune. Learn from your mistakes, knowing that people fail their way to success every single day.

Now shift your focus to gratitude. Sit in an extended moment of appreciation for the abundance you've received and the desires you were able to indulge. Which gifts were the most unexpected? The most delightful? Acknowledge where your efforts paid off. Write down any wins you earned or windfalls that blessed you. Revel in your good fortune (even if it boils down to: "Omigod, I survived"). Let the proof of past success give you faith moving forward that it could happen again. Marvel at the mysteries of the Divine.

When we root our rituals in the cycles of nature, it brings awareness to how these seasons mirror our inner journey. For example, manifesting can be done on any day of the month, but my workshop is always on the New Moon in order to take full advantage of that fertile energy. Taking a further step back, you can see how my teaching lines up with the seasonal cycles:

Step 1: Set a clear intention. (Winter Solstice)

Step 2: Take inspired action. (Spring Equinox)

Step 3: Step back and let the Universe respond. (Summer Solstice)

Step 4: Reflect on learnings in preparation for a new cycle. (Autumnal Equinox)

There are cycles to be found around and within all of us. They each have gifts, lessons, and opportunities for those of us willing to explore them.

Getting Witchy with It

If this all sounds a bit witchy, that's because it is—pagans traditionally worshipped the natural world, but they certainly don't have a monopoly on deifying nature (see also: Hinduism, Taoism, and Indigenous peoples around the world). Many cultures recognize Earth-based wisdom, and the rituals of their holidays are both informed by and intertwined with Mother Earth. "Paganism" is an umbrella term applied to a number of different faiths, including Wicca, but not all pagans are Wiccan. Although my tarot mentor was a legit broom-toting, spell-casting witch—and I've been known to write "Wiccan" on official government forms requiring a declaration of religion for ease of reference—I'm not a practicing witch. There are plenty of excellent resources if you're interested in exploring this topic further, but since we've already covered half of them with solstices and equinoxes (the remaining festivals are points in between), it's worth mentioning all of the key Wiccan holidays and their associated rituals here.

Wiccan celebrations (also known as "sabbats") are synced to the rhythms of nature as the Earth travels around the Sun. This calendar is called the "Wheel of the Year," and it consists of eight sabbats that correspond to seasonal shifts.

1. **Yule** marks the Winter Solstice and the longest night of the year, which we covered earlier in the chapter, starting on page 218, with ritual ideas and the significance of the day. Think: going within, illumination, and daydreaming your ideal future.

2. **Imbolc**, also known as Brigid, falls between the Winter Solstice and Spring Equinox. This is a time to stoke inspiration and creativity in preparation for the coming spring. *Imbolc* translates to "in the belly" and symbolizes the seeds being planted—literally and metaphorically. Honor this moment with a ritual bath or light a candle and meditate on the intentions you are growing.

3. **Ostara** is the Spring Equinox, a fertile time that is ripe for cultivating your intentions; ritual ideas were covered starting on page 221. Think: renewal, beginnings, and possibility.

4. **Beltane**, also known as May Day, marks the midpoint between the Spring Equinox and Summer Solstice. Honoring the union of the masculine and feminine, this is a frisky day of peak prosperity and fertility (that maypole everyone dances around represents a big ol' penis). It's also a fiery holiday: light a bonfire and have a make-out session with your sweetie (or some intimate time with yourself).

5. **Litha** pays homage to the Summer Solstice. Also called Midsummer, this is the longest day of the year and an incredibly potent moment. See the earlier section starting on page 220 for specific ritual ideas, but think invigoration, abundance, and making magic.

6. **Lammas**, or Lughnasadh, marks the halfway point between the Summer Solstice and Autumn Equinox. It celebrates the first harvest of the season and venerates Mother Earth and all her bounty. Honor this festival of grains by baking bread to commemorate the occasion (it's a ritual of carbs, what's not to love?).

7. **Mabon** marks the Fall Equinox and the final harvest of the season. It's a time of balance and contemplation that can be celebrated with the rituals mentioned starting on page 223. Think: gathering, gratitude, and preparation.

8. **Samhain**, also known as Halloween, is the one you've probably heard about or associate with witches and Wicca. It marks the New Year and is the Wheel of the Year's most sacred sabbat. Occurring between the Fall Equinox and Winter Solstice, when the veil between worlds is at its thinnest, Samhain is a time to remember and connect with the ancestors. It's also a time to journey within and descend into a spiritual underworld, confronting the parts of you that often remain hidden in the shadows. Seek awareness of what you must release in order for you to heal—when we excavate and bring those parts of us to the light, their power diminishes. Any release ritual—like burning you sh*t with a bonfire—can assist you in this process, along with some good old-fashioned therapy.

Don't feel you have to wait for a particular day of the year, or time of month, to engage in ritual. During the COVID-19 pandemic, my daughter and I started a weekly ritual of getting Dairy Queen Blizzards and driving around town singing Taylor Swift at the top of our lungs—something we're still doing long after lockdown (although it's become more of a monthly ritual because my pants stopped fitting). Watching the sunrise every morning with intention is a ritual. Family game night every Friday is a ritual. A particular weekend you feel called to mark a personal transition can be a ritual. Every day can be a special occasion that is worthy of ceremony. You are worthy, and the alchemy comes from you.

CHAPTER 9

A MERKA-*WHAT*? (THE POTENCY OF SACRED GEOMETRY)

◇◇◇

The Universe (and our place in it) seems unpredictable and chaotic, but it's actually a highly structured realm that is rooted in the infinite beauty of . . . math. From a cresting ocean wave to the curl of a chameleon's tail, geometric shapes and patterns are repeated throughout every aspect of our reality, including nature, sound, and space. The rhythms and patterns of nature reside in every living cell—the tiniest known particle of the human body is a microcosm for the entire cosmos. Geometry is the basis of everything that is—it is the foundation of creation.

Although scientists refer to fractal geometry as a revolutionary new way of looking at the world—a new field in science that unifies mathematics, art, theoretical physics, and computer science—humans have been fascinated and guided by these cosmic equations since ancient Mesopotamia. Throughout history, certain geometric forms appear across cultures in art and architecture, from Egyptian pyramids and Greek temples to da Vinci's sketches and Indigenous teepees. Archaeologists still can't explain why or how these shapes have figured so prominently (and precisely) in these disparate civilizations—and that's where the "sacred" part comes in.

There is an inexplicable logic and undeniable mystery to these geometric shapes; they're literally woven into the fabric of humanity.

Snowflakes share a hexagonal symmetry, and even though they are all formed the same way (when water vapor freezes), each one features a beautifully delicate and intricate pattern that is wholly unique (kind of like . . . humans). These geometric shapes are sacred because they're fundamental templates for all life in the Universe. They reveal the creative intelligence of the Divine.

Every pattern of movement or growth can be traced back to a set of geometric shapes that transcends race, religion, time, or location. The infinite and inherent wisdom of sacred geometry exists beyond what we can see. Similar to archetypes that convey the innate knowledge of our collective unconscious, geometric shapes and patterns are programmed into our souls, connecting us to something greater than ourselves.

Every sacred shape is thought to carry a particular spiritual significance that provides a unique energetic effect. Just like organized religions have been doing for centuries, incorporating sacred geometry into your rituals can amplify their potency. Despite all the math, it's easy to add sacred geometry to your rituals. You're likely already doing it. Whether you're looking to magnify manifesting, align with your purpose, or elevate your vibration—there's a shape for that.

SPIRITUAL SHAPES

◇◇◇

To understand sacred geometry, you need to know about Platonic solids, which are a set of five shapes described by ancient Greek philosopher Plato (seriously, sacred geometry has been around *forever*). These are the only perfectly symmetrical three-dimensional forms possible, and they are the building blocks of the Universe—from atomic structures to planetary orbits. The Platonic solids include the tetrahedron (four-sided pyramid), hexahedron (six-sided cube), octahedron (eight-sided shape), dodecahedron (twelve-sided shape), and icosahedron (twenty-sided shape). These shapes are the foundation for all of the symbols and patterns found in nature (the veins of a leaf), religion (the Sri Yantra, a 12,000-year-old Hindu diagram), and architecture (the Parthenon). But Plato didn't stop there—he associated certain properties to each shape and connected them to the five elements.

- The *tetrahedron* is associated with Fire. Fire transforms. It connects you to your passion. Pyramids direct energy—the square base anchoring its foundation while the apex points up to the Divine. The tetrahedron supports as it elevates, unleashing energies of awakening and manifestation.
- The *hexahedron*, or cube, is the most stable shape and reflects the element of Earth. When we're in need of grounding, we call upon the Earth, and the hexahedron provides a connection to our physical realm. There is inherent support and security. It offers a sense of protection and dependability—it is your foundation.
- The *octahedron* resembles two five-sided pyramids meeting at the base and represents Air, or life force. It unifies your inner and outer worlds, offering a path to forgiveness, healing, and acceptance. The octahedron brings mental clarity and focus, while also helping you access unconditional love for all, especially yourself.
- The *dodecahedron* resembles a twelve-sided die, with each side being a pentagon. It correlates with ether (also known as Spirit or heaven) and fosters your ascension to Divine

energy. Ideal for meditation, the dodecahedron raises your frequency to higher dimensions, allowing you to access Universal truths and your own higher wisdom.

- The *icosahedron* is made up of twenty equilateral triangles. It is associated with the element of Water, enabling you to balance your mind and heart as you go with the flow. The icosahedron invites transformation, facilitates freedom of expression, and removes creative blocks—making it the perfect partner for artistic endeavors.

The combination of these five geometric shapes is the foundation of all form and matter. Sacred geometry suggests that they provide structural equilibrium and spiritual balance in equal measure. Just like seasonal cycles reflect our individual journeys, the patterns found in nature are inextricably linked to our personal development and spiritual evolution—in fact, they guide them. From honeycombs and crystals to human DNA, nature is our greatest teacher and also the most vast, exquisite work of art in existence.

Energetically, these geometric shapes are thought to have distinct vibrations that support balance and growth. When combined to create symbols, grids, or patterns, their energy is activated (like flipping on a switch) and can be used to heighten your connection to the Universe. Metaphysicians believe you can elevate consciousness and self-awareness when you observe and meditate with sacred shapes.

Circles and spheres are not Platonic solids, but their symbolism throughout history and prevalence in nature are just as irrefutable. Circles are associated with eternity, oneness, and the cycle of life. Another example of geometry that is sacred but not Platonic is the Flower of Life: a set of nineteen overlapping circles that can be traced back almost 6,000 years, making it one of the most ancient geometric symbols used for, among other things, marking time—from seconds to seasons. Both the spiral of a snail's shell and the Earth's orbit around the Sun follow a mathematical pattern known as the Fibonacci sequence.

Sacred symbols and shapes span civilizations, religions, and philosophies. You can access these cosmic connections whenever you need them because they are everywhere, all the time.

MEET YOUR MERKABA

◇◇◇

One of the most well-known and mystical shapes in sacred geometry—and the one I work with the most—is the Merkaba (or Merkabah). *Merkaba* comes from the Hebrew word for "chariot," and its name breaks down phonetically from an Egyptian translation to be *Mer* (light), *Ka* (spirit), and *Ba* (body). The Merkaba transports us to unite in light, body, and spirit.

Two tetrahedrons (four-sided pyramids) come together to form a Merkaba—one pointing up and the other pointing down—with their bases overlapping about halfway down. It looks like a three-dimensional Star of David, with the upward point (male) bringing us closer to the Divine, while the downward point (female) connects us to the Earth. The tetrahedrons spin in opposite directions, creating harmony from their opposing forces and bringing balance between masculine and feminine, yin and yang, light and dark.

When you work with a Merkaba in meditation (which we'll do in a minute), it raises your vibration to activate a field of energy that can be programmed with possibility. This grid is within and around you at all times, and the Merkaba helps you plug into these cosmic connections. Like crystals, your Merkaba is programmable. As with any ritual, it starts with intention. A Merkaba meditation can hone your intuition, balance your chakras, uplevel your life, ground you, expand your awareness, connect you with your purpose, or actualize your deepest desires. Think of your Merkaba as an open line to Source energy, and make sure you're clear on what you want to cultivate.

As with the Moon rituals, you can record yourself reciting this meditation or access my recording using the QR code on page 303. There is a very intricate breathwork sequence commonly used in Merkaba meditations that involves hand gestures and visualizations, which you can find online. I personally don't bother with all of that and just focus on diaphragmatic (belly) breathing while the recording guides me through the imagery. Do what works for you. Here's the meditation:

Find a quiet spot and get into a comfortable position. Take a few breaths as you settle into your body. Close your eyes and let your mind know that you are ready to program your Merkaba. Visualize the tetrahedrons surrounding your body, male pointing upward, beginning at your knees and extending several feet above your head, and female extending down from your shoulders to below your feet. Activate each pyramid so they each spin in a different direction—male spinning left to right as it points to the sky, and female spinning right to left toward the Earth. (Don't worry about the details here. Everyone's Merkaba will look a little different.) Notice if you feel energized as they activate and spin. Through the spinning of your Merkaba, you are creating new coordinates of consciousness. Now envision yourself being lit up by rays of luminous energy. See a light field around your body, expanding in a saucer-like shape. Feel your vibration rising as the Merkaba spins and the light expands. Breathe in deeply and slowly exhale.

Notice the pulsing energy coursing through your body—surrender to it and see where it takes you. (PAUSE FOR 30 SECONDS TO ONE MINUTE.)

As the Merkaba continues to spin, focus your attention on what you desire. Set your intentions, and your Merkaba will work on your vision without any deviation. (PAUSE FOR AT LEAST TWO MINUTES.)

When you are clear on your visualization, give thanks and say "And so it is." In your mind's eye, see your aura glowing around you. Imagine each of your chakras all in tune, spinning in each color: red at the base of your spine; orange at your lower abdomen, just below your navel; yellow at your upper abdomen; green at your heart; light blue at your throat; dark-blue indigo between your eyes; and violet at the top of your head. Believe that your entire body, down to the smallest strand of DNA, is fully charged—you are energized and your energy is conspiring with the matrix to call forth all that you desire. Ground yourself back in your body. Give thanks and have faith that your vision is being actualized. Expect magic and miracles to materialize—as you have willed it, so shall it be. Take your focus off your Merkaba and see your aura. Bask in the healthy, vibrant glow that surrounds you. Your chakras are perfectly in tune, and your cells are turned on to their fullest potential. You are energized, and you are well. Return fully into your body, into this space, and be ready for life to happen. And so it is.

Take a moment to journal any sensations or inspiration. Or simply sit in the afterglow of this experience for a few minutes. If possible, go for a quick walk outside and observe the sacred geometry of your surroundings, wherever that may be. The Merkaba meditation is one of many ways you can actively introduce this principle into your life.

WITCHY BIDNIZ
(GRIDS, SIGILS, & SOUND)

◇◇◇

If you thought crystals on their own packed a cosmic punch, try using them in a grid—it's like birthday sparklers versus rocket ships. A crystal grid is the arrangement of several crystals that are energetically aligned in geometric patterns. For those of you thinking, *OMG, Tarot Lori, are you kidding me with all the math?*, hear me out. Aside from a few guidelines, this is a very intuitive process (for *decades* I was placing my rocks in patterns that appealed to me without realizing they were actually sacred symbols). Just like you can do a tarot reading with only a few cards, you really only need a few stones to make an incredibly potent crystal grid, as long as you're clear on your goal.

As detailed in Chapter 2, every crystal carries its own vibration and offers a distinct attribute. Decide what you're wanting more of in your life, because a crystal grid will act like a power station, amplifying the character of each stone. Are you looking for protection? Love? Financial abundance? Inspiration? Motivation? Courage? Choose stones that align with your intention. This can be done with the type of crystal (rhodochrosite for self-love), the stone's shape (a cube for grounding), astrology (red jasper to honor the energy of Aries), or the season (orange calcite to celebrate summer).

The amount of crystals you use is up to you, and both tumbled and raw stones will work great (even four or five crystals make a powerful grid). If you aren't sure where to start, grab some citrine for abundance, rose quartz for love, smoky quartz to clear negativity, kyanite to improve communication, black onyx for protection, angelite to contact ancestral spirits, labradorite to enhance your intuition, or amethyst to connect with the Divine. You may want to include a piece of clear quartz to further boost the power of the surrounding stones. If needed, give your crystals a cleanse with sage or palo santo before you begin.

To build your grid, you can draw or print out the image of a sacred pattern (for example, the Flower of Life) to help you recreate it or place the stone directly on top of the paper. Crystal grid boards are another option if you want to build or buy something that appeals to you for your altar (Etsy is a great resource). Try forming your crystals in the flat shape of a Platonic solid to further affect how your crystal's energy is channeled. For a birthday ritual, you might place the stones in the point positions of your astrological constellation. If you're looking for a multipurpose grid, create a Sun shape, with each ray representing a different objective. Or tap into the power of the elements to support your grid: Water grids bring healing and release through their circular shape; a Fire grid looks like a star and aligns with courage or leadership; an Earth grid will ground and project you with its square or angular form; while the spiral shape of an Air grid attunes you to love, peace, and ascension.

As with your altar, you can mark the four directions (north, west, south, and east) on your grid using natural elements: a stick, leaf, or bowl of dirt to symbolize Earth; a candle or incense to represent Fire; a feather for Air; and a small dish of water or a shell to represent Water. Note that I've seen multiple sources attribute the elements to different directions, so stick with what resonates for you. I use the four sacred directions taught by many Ojibwe Elders based on the Indigenous medicine wheel: east (yellow) is Fire, south (red) is Earth, west (black) is Water, and north (white) is Air. You can invoke these elements out loud as you place them on the grid:

I call upon the energies of the east to energize our spirit and ignite our passion with your fiery power.

I call upon the energies of the south to protect and strengthen us with your Earthly offerings.

I call upon the energies of the west to honor our magic and bring us into flow with the gift of water.

I call upon the energies of the north to imbue our words with power in every breath as we connect to Divine magnificence through the air we breathe.

Don't worry about creating exact shapes, words, or directions—perfection is never the goal. Shift the crystals around the grid until they feel "right" to you. They're directing this process as much as you are—probably more.

If you have a crystal generator (which looks like a silo, with a flat base and pointed top), a sphere (think: crystal ball), or a wand (self-explanatory), put it in the center of your grid—it will pull in Universal energy and distribute it evenly throughout the rest of the grid. Add flowers, pine cones, leaves, or any other natural elements that appeal to you. As with every ritual, your crystal grid can be super fancy or deceptively simple—it will work either way. Making a circle or heart shape with your favorite stones is a fabulous crystal grid. Creating a random formation that you think is pretty will be perfect.

Let your intuition guide you. Declare your intention out loud as you build your grid (for example, *I am creating this crystal grid to call more joy into my life.*).

When you feel your crystal grid is complete, sit quietly for a few minutes and focus on your breath as you gaze softly at the creation before you. Close your eyes and be open to any thoughts, sensations, or epiphanies that arise within you.

Crystal grids can be part of your regular ritual habits or used for an occasional boost. I generally use gridge only on special occasions and gatherings, so don't feel obligated to make a crystal grid every time you use crystals. There are plenty of other ways to bring sacred shapes into your ritual. Different patterns or symbols, such as mandalas, can be used as focal points as you meditate (or grab a mandala coloring book and some pencil crayons for a more active meditation). Carve a triangle, sphere, or any other shape into a candle with a knife or even a toothpick before any ritual to help you affirm your intention and access any astral flow.

If you're feeling really creative (and extra witchy), try creating your own sacred symbol. Known as a "sigil" by contemporary Wiccans, this personal talisman can be carved into a candle or written on a piece of paper to burn or tuck away (depending on your ritual). Begin by writing your intention in a positive, affirming statement (for example, *I am confident*). Now cross out any vowels and consonants (so in my example, we are left with MCNFDT). Now get creative! Combine these letters—laying them on top or overlapping each other—until you have a symbol that resonates with you (like a logo for your ritual). Some people envision their intention already fully realized as they burn their sigil. Others place it on their altar or under their pillow (like a New Moon ritual). This is your amulet, and you can do whatever you want with it.

You are, by your very existence, Divine—and your symbol, which you created, is sacred.

If sigils and grids and rotating pyramids aren't your thing, you can still leverage the magic of sacred geometry simply by being aware of it. Pay attention when you walk in a forest. Trace the spin of a spider's web. Stand at a shoreline and observe geese flying above you in formation. Stare deeply at a floret of cauliflower at the market. Take in all of the shapes around you and see the beauty in their symmetry.

Music that moves you is sacred geometry—it's why certain notes blend together in heavenly harmony, while others make us cringe. Through music, the laws of vibration aurally convey the Universal mathematical patterns found throughout everything in existence. The intrinsic intelligence of music explains why it has been such an essential part of our rituals and healing modalities since ancient times. Sacred geometry can easily be added to any ritual, from listening to music during your evening bath to making a mini crystal grid before your morning meditation to keeping a personal symbol tucked in a special spot.

There are layers to sacred geometry that we aren't even aware of because it exists in dimensions we barely comprehend. Scientists focus on quantifiable formulas like the Fibonacci sequence, while we feel the energetic effects of a Merkaba meditation—but we're all drawn to these shapes and patterns in some way because they exist within us all. Through these sacred principles, nature teaches us how to be cocreators of our lives, how to be in a loving relationship with ourselves and the world around us.

From cells to solar systems, sacred shapes show you who you are and what you might become. They are the geometric blueprint for your soul.

CHAPTER 10

ANGELS & DEVILS (CONNECTING WITH SPIRIT & DITCHING YOUR DEMONS)

◇◇◇

W e all have an open invitation to collaborate with angelic energy that is eager to offer Divine guidance and spiritual support. We also have unlimited access to a bottomless pit of shame and insecurity. With the right rituals in your energetic toolbox, you're able to be your own medium and to slay your own dragons.

GRANDMA SAYS HI (CONNECTING WITH YOUR SPIRIT SQUAD)

◇◇◇

My friend is an extremely smart, very serious, fancy-shmancy divorce lawyer who deals with combative people in contentious situations all day long. But when she gets home, she'll often swap out her designer outfit for the coziest jammies, go into her walk-in closet, and talk to her dead dad. She pours her heart out to him, sometimes out loud but usually in her mind, and asks for his advice, validation, or comfort. And he answers her. His reply comes in the form of a flickering closet light—a light that, over the years, has been checked for faulty wiring and had numerous bulbs replaced. She can't explain how it happens (or why that particular closet), but my friend always leaves these dad-and-daughter chats feeling reassured.

In life, we are never truly alone. We each have a team of light supporting and guiding us, even when we can't see or feel it. Whatever you call this realm of energy—Buddha, Archangel Michael, the Universe, or Grandma—it's there for you, like indulgent parents ready to spoil you rotten. But engaging with your spirit squad isn't like in the movies where ghosts show up and start meddling in your business—you have to invite this energy in and work with it (always with the intention of receiving celestial guidance for your highest good).

Over the years I've developed an approach to connect with our spirit guides and ancestors that I call the "Three As of Angels." I share this method with many of my tarot clients, and it has three steps: ask, acknowledge, and allow.

Ask

The first thing you have to do is ask for what you want in a way that works for you. That might mean dancing naked under a Full Moon, talking to Grandpa while brushing your teeth, or praying on your knees at an altar. Ask for guidance on next steps, healing for your body, help getting out of a sticky situation, or a good price on a dishwasher because yours just broke. The asking can be deep and soulful or easy and superficial. Just put it out there.

Speak it out loud, keep it in your thoughts, or write it down. Be clear in what you want, but don't get bogged down with timelines or outcomes. Ask for help finding your ideal partner or support for an upcoming job interview, but if it takes a while to find that person or you don't get the job, it doesn't mean your angels weren't listening. Have faith that your spirit squad is working to get you what you need—and that's not necessarily what you want (or when you want it). Rejection is often redirection or protection in disguise.

Your spirit guides may have names, but don't worry if they're more of a faceless, nameless energy. A name may come to you during a meditation, but it's not a requirement. You may refer to this energy as God, Universe, or the Divine. My spirit squad feels more like a vast galaxy of constellations than an entity named Morpheus or Walter.

Your deceased relatives might be important members of your spiritual team even if you didn't know them well (or like them much) when they were alive. I've been told by psychics and energy workers all my life that my mom's mother is always with me. She parks herself at my left side and doesn't budge (one reiki healer said the energy was so thick that she had to work around it). I even feel my grandmother's spirit sometimes, like an energetic squeeze on my left forearm, but here's the wild part: she died when my mom was only nine years old, so I never met the woman. And, by all accounts, that was a blessing because she was a terrible person (and a victim of horrific circumstances). The first time I was told my grandmother was hanging around, I told her to piss off because I had no interest in having her nasty ghost lingering in my business. I've since learned that our souls transform back to an energy of pure love once we die, and who they were in life doesn't carry over to the other side. We've now come to an understanding—she can stick around and I refer to her as "Grandmother" (not "Grandma")—and she remains one of the clearest, loudest, and most fiercely protective members of my spirit squad.

Regardless of who or what you call this energy, it's ready and waiting to be called into action. Ask for a sign that holds significance for the person who passed (like a certain song), or something specific (a flamingo or a waffle). You can also keep it vague (*I need a sign!*) as long as you're alert for what shows up, because something *will* show up, which brings us to the next step . . .

Acknowledge

When you put out the call, there's always a response, but celestial energy communicates in signs rather than words or touch, and you have to acknowledge these signs to keep the channel of communication open. The signs are everywhere, and they present themselves in a multitude of ways—you simply have to ask and then be open to seeing them.

Imagine asking for validation about a big decision you need to make (I will literally think *If this is the right choice, I need a clear sign . . . now*), and then turning on the radio only to hear the song that was played at your brother's funeral. Or the lyrics of the song that comes on are like therapy, giving you the advice you need to hear. Or the car in front of you has a bumper sticker that says "If You're Waiting for a Sign . . . This Is It!" Or you look up at the sky and see clouds that look like snow angels. Or dimes start randomly showing up in unusual places. I once asked for a sign, opened a sliding closet door, and found ten dimes in the track of the door.

When I go walking in my fairly new suburban subdivision, I'll sometimes ask for confirmation and return home to find a feather on the hood of my car that looks like it was plucked from a pterodactyl. I once asked for a sign while walking in the woods and came across a tree with the word *yes* carved into it. Ladybugs, dragonflies, butterflies, and birds (especially cardinals, blue jays, hummingbirds, and hawks) are also common signs. I attended an outdoor gathering a few years ago, and we all sat with our eyes closed as the facilitator led us on a meditation to connect with our guides. Suddenly, we all heard (and felt) a huge *WHOOSH* (like a mini sonic boom), and a woman who'd been peeking during the meditation reported that a massive hawk had swooped down, flying straight through our circle like a missile. My grandpa used to wear a hat with a red feather in it, and after he died I would sometimes be followed on my walks by a very curious red cardinal. It would flutter from tree to tree, keeping an eye on me the entire time. Speaking of my grandpa, he also makes his presence known with the smell of cigarettes when I'm home alone. Unique scents in unusual places—such as cigarette smoke in a library or perfume in your car—are another common sign.

If an undeniable sign shows up unexpectedly (like me minding my own business and suddenly smelling cigarettes), take a minute to consider what you were just thinking about. Are you worried about something specific? Is there a tough conversation you're avoiding? Do you have an important test coming up? A sign doesn't always come with massive messages; sometimes it's just a reminder that your angels are there, cheering you on. Although I hate the smell of smoking at any other time, my grandpa's sign always makes me smile, and I think of it as an unexpected hug.

People also report number sequences (11:11 on the clock is a popular one), dream visitations, sweet synchronicities coming out of nowhere, or things suddenly falling into place. Keep a journal or even just a note on your phone to track these seemingly small or unrelated signs when they show up—like the tiny feather that floated out of nowhere in the Starbucks I was in when I wrote this and landed on my laptop!

Regardless of what your sign is, when you encounter it, you'll likely experience goose bumps, butterflies, or some other bodily reaction (or you'll just *know*). This meaningful coincidence is your spirit squad's way of saying "Got the message. We're on the case!" Your acknowledgment keeps things flowing between you.

Our spirit squad often shows up just as we're falling asleep or waking up, when the veil between worlds is thinner, and it's a great time to try reaching out. The first time I tried talking directly to my team of light, the results were shocking, even for me (it takes a lot to shock me because I've seen some wild stuff . . .). I was lying in bed, wide awake on a random Tuesday night while my husband slept. I'd recently attended a "How to Communicate with Your Angels and Guides" workshop and was desperate for validation about a big decision I'd made, so I decided to give it a shot. Almost immediately, I felt energy (which I now call my "goosies") above and below the surface of my skin, like the tingles you feel after standing up too fast combined with pins and needles. My initial reaction (*This is so weird and cool!*) was quickly followed by suspicion (*This is too weird to be real . . .*).

We'd been instructed in the workshop to ask for signs as confirmation that we were plugged into this energy. *Listen up, angels,* I thought, *If this is real, I need a clear sign and I need it NOW.* The words were barely formed in my mind, still lingering like a cartoon thought bubble over my head, when my bathroom light turned on. I acknowledged the sign, thanked them for showing up, and told them they could leave now. (*Wow. Okay, that's great and it's enough for tonight . . . Byeeee!*) The light went out.

The next day, my husband dismissed my story, telling me that he'd meant to change the shower light bulb because it had been flickering. I hadn't witnessed it flickering any other time, but his explanation made sense. A few weeks later, I couldn't sleep and decided to try the angel thing one more time. I breathed deeply . . . focused inward . . . felt the goosies . . . asked for a sign . . . and the bathroom light turned on again. It felt like they were saying, "Listen, we can do this all night . . ."

It's easy for spirits to influence electricity because it's all high-frequency energy. Pay attention to flickering lights or other electrical disturbances when you've been asking for spiritual support. While these signs may seem insignificant at first, they'll often increase in frequency and size when you acknowledge them.

Allow

This is the most important step, and the one we tend to screw up. Once our prayers are being answered and dreams start coming true, we often hit the energetic brakes (*What's going on? How's this possible? When's the other shoe going to drop?*). Momentum that was building fizzles and everything stagnates. You may be thinking, *What gives, spirit squad?* You have free will, so you can make choices and take actions that propel you forward, or you can do nothing and stay stuck. Even when the new opportunity or direction is obviously amazing, change can be scary, and it's often simpler to stick with what's easy or familiar, even when it's not better. It might be the upper limit problem I mentioned in Chapter 6, where we inadvertently sabotage our efforts, to (supposedly) keep ourselves safe, or there's an underlying sense of unworthiness that prevents us from thinking we deserve the good stuff (that's just your little devil, which we'll get to in a minute).

When you feel resistance to the miracles taking place, you have to breathe through that discomfort. Remember that you are worthy of these blessings and that receiving them doesn't take from anyone else—there's enough for everybody. Also, and this is crucial, be sure to thank your angels and guides so you can move to the next thing on your list. (You've made a list by now, right?)

Despite being a professional tarot reader and generally immersed in a world of witchy, magical things, I sometimes still need to be clunked over the head with the signiest sign that ever signed. I was recently waffling about booking a trip to Los Angeles with my daughter for her birthday because hotels were filling up and flights were pricey in the summer (plus, I'd just missed a big seat sale). I asked my spirit squad to let me know if this trip was a good idea—I've learned that if something doesn't go my way, it wasn't meant for me, so I was resigning myself to the idea that the trip wouldn't happen. Later that day, my friend responded to a text I'd sent days earlier with an offer to stay at her place in L.A. *Hmmm*, I thought. *Pretty good sign, but I need something more obvious.* I opened Instagram minutes later, and the first post that came up had the caption "Book the ticket." *Wow*, I thought, closing Instagram. *If I get another sign like this one, I think I'll book the trip.* I then checked my email and the top message was from my favorite airline offering a flash seat sale with flights 30 percent cheaper than they'd been the day before. Needless to say, we went to Los Angeles.

This angelic energy is always available and already working for you. When times are tough or you're feeling at a loss, call Grandpa in for an assist (it won't make things worse, so you might as well try). You can still have a very close, intimate relationship with people after they die—it sucks because you can't have a regular conversation or feel their touch, but you can still connect with their energy by keeping them in your thoughts and even reach out when you're in need of validation or reassurance. It requires learning a new language—one that's based on signs and symbols, tingles and feathers, dimes and dreams—and it can initially feel like trying to translate Japanese to Spanish when you only speak Greek, but you'll get there if you're patient and open.

These signs are pure love, and there is nothing stronger than that.

There is, however, something much, much louder . . . which brings us to the devil.

FIND YOUR LITTLE F*CKER (HOW TO EXTERMINATE LIMITING BELIEFS)

◇◇◇

When I talk about the devil, I don't mean it in a satanic or Biblical sense. This devil isn't evil—he's just an asshole. The devil is the shadow side we all have; the dark part of ourselves that stays hidden from the world (whether we realize it or not) because it doesn't line up with the image we want to convey or who we want to be. We try to disown these unsavory parts of who we are, pushing them as far down as possible, but repressing the shadow only serves to feed it, until it inevitably undermines and sabotages every area of our life.

The devil is the gremlin on your shoulder telling you something won't work because you suck. It's the voice in your head saying things will never change because you don't deserve any better. It's the impostor syndrome confirming you don't belong and the self-sabotage that reaffirms your inadequacy. Whether it's a persistent whisper or a piercing shriek, you need to understand that this voice isn't real; it just feels that way because you accepted it as true when you were very young, before you had the ability to discern that it was utter bullsh*t. The harmful patterns of your past don't dictate your destiny—they inform the potential of your future. But before you can break a toxic pattern, you have to see it. Usually, that pattern is created by a parent, coach, teacher, or other formative influence you interacted with as a child. These people may have been doing their best with what they had at that time, but that doesn't make it right (or fair). The underlying damage that you experienced as a child gets packed away in your subconscious, like boxes of trauma getting shoved in the back of a dark closet on the highest shelf. But it's not a shelf, it's the self . . . the shadow self.

Although the closet is closed, the door has cracks and those boxes are made of flimsy cardboard that allow the shame and pain to escape—often under the guise of depression, rage, or panic. It's a slow and insidious ooze that you often don't realize is there until you find yourself attempting to use food, shopping, sex, drugs, or whatever other panacea is on hand to fill those cracks in the door.

What if there were an alternative? Instead of hiding from the shadow self, maybe you engage with it. You could open that closet door to carefully remove just one of those boxes and then, with an incredible amount of patience and tenderness (perhaps with another person bearing witness, or a therapist), you take a peek inside. You no longer deny, reject, or ignore the experiences and very real hurt that are bursting from that box—now you're naming, claiming, and reframing the contents of that container.

But how do you evict a voice in your head that's been living rent-free for so long? The logical part of you knows that limiting beliefs and negative self-talk are getting in the way. They're preventing you from stepping into your power and living your best life. But how can you possibly undo years (sometimes decades) of negative self-programming?

I have a ritual for that.

It was developed by a friend who is a life coach (*I love you, Lisa!*) over thirty years ago, and I've been assigning it to my tarot clients for over twenty-five years. It might sound a bit goofy, but it works.

Prepare your space by smudging it (cedar is a good protective herb), and then light a candle (white for serenity, black for protection . . . or whatever you have on hand). You may want to incorporate protective crystals, such as malachite, black tourmaline, or clear quartz. Have a pen and some paper nearby to make note of any impressions, and tissues in case you get teary (tears are always welcome!).

Close your eyes and ground yourself with some breathing. Imagine what your devil looks like. Is your demonic inner critic a big monster or a teeny little bug? Is it a she, he, or it? Is there a voice? A smell? A name? Give your devil a full character sketch—the more detailed the better. I always tell people that my devil looks a bit like Dobby (the house elf from Harry Potter, but not too cute), smells like dirty diapers, has a voice like my father, and his name is F*cker. Your job is to find your inner F*cker. Do you have a clear visual of what your devil looks like? Good. Now murder it.

Throw your devil off a bridge, flick it off your shoulder, put dynamite down its pants. Be as creative as you want, as long as you get rid of it. This is why you probably don't want your devil to be a cute little bunny. In this murderous moment, you may feel lighter, almost giddy. You might realize you can breathe a little easier, a bit deeper. Or you could feel teary—from the emotions stirred up, but also because you've just executed a piece of your identity that may not have been welcome but was definitely familiar (maybe even comfortable). Perhaps your devil kept you playing small and pointed out your faults before anyone else could, under the guise of protecting you from potential pain inflicted by others, and now you feel exposed. But once this insidious lie is debunked, you realize that you weren't afraid of being hurt. You were actually terrified that other people might see all of the reasons you don't love yourself. Take a moment to journal any insights. Perhaps write your devil's origin story or make a sketch of it to burn (or rip up and bury). To close your ritual, consider taking a bath or shower to help you release any evil remnants.

Your pesky devil always comes back, but now you see it for what it is. This awareness is your energetic arsenal moving forward. Be on the lookout for intrusive thoughts: *Things won't change . . . I'll screw it all up . . . I can't do that . . . I'll never get there . . .* When they show up, take a minute to visualize your devil doing the talking, and then grab your murder method of choice and assassinate that little f*cker all over again. Squish it, shoot it, steamroll it, vaporize it. I use the dynamite from Road Runner cartoons, and it's *very* effective (guts everywhere!). It may seem silly, but there will be a shift. You'll think, *Nobody's going to die if this doesn't work . . . I don't know how to do that—yet . . . I've been through this kind of thing before and survived . . .*

You will feel a sense of ease, and the stakes won't seem as high once you put things in perspective. More importantly, you've taken that voice in your head, the one you've accepted as true without ever questioning it, and you've turned it into a separate entity—one that's not even part of you. By creating this distance, you won't identify with it as strongly. Once you've annihilated your devil a few (dozen) times, you'll notice the volume of those negative thoughts has lessened just a bit. And when those thoughts start to creep in, you'll find yourself adding "yet" or "until now" at the end of them: *I can't do that . . . yet. That never works . . . until now.*

The good news about your devil? It's all in your head. The bad news? It's all in your head. Even if you only do this ritual once, you'll still diminish your devil's power. When you meet your shadow this way—identifying (rather than denying) the most disturbing parts of yourself and bringing them to the surface—transformational shifts can occur. By stepping into the darkness, you discover your light. In fact, the light gets that much stronger. Your soul wants to be seen and your heart needs to be heard. When this happens, the boxes you shoved in that closet (and the devil who gave them a voice) disintegrate to dust.

You can bring your angels and your devil into your rituals sporadically or on a regular basis. The ceremony itself might be as simple as holding a protective crystal while you imagine demolishing your devil or lighting a single candle to connect with a deceased loved one. A ritual can reveal the shadows of your psyche to heal your deepest wounds, or work with the loving light of Spirit to reach your highest potential. It's all ready when you are. What are you waiting for?

CHAPTER 11

WRITING WILD & CUTTING CORDS (TAPPING INTO & PROTECTING YOUR ENERGY)

$\diamond\diamond\diamond$

When my daughter was a toddler, our family went on vacation with some friends. Early flight times, connections, and traveling with kids meant that we arrived absolutely exhausted. Our little villa had access to a pool that was a ten-minute walk down the road and, aside from some maintenance workers, our street was deserted. While everyone took off for the pool, I stayed behind with my daughter to unpack some essentials . . . and promptly passed out like I'd taken a double dose of melatonin. Down at the pool, my husband popped up from his lounge chair like a meerkat. "Be right back!" he hollered over his shoulder as he sprinted barefoot up the gravel road. Outside our villa, he found our baby girl toddling toward the main road. She'd managed to open the front door by herself while I drooled on the couch.

We hear stories all the time about people who pay attention to a feeling that ends up saving the day or who ignore a hunch about someone who ends up doing them dirty. *Intuition* comes from the Latin word *intueri* (meaning "to look within"), and that's exactly what it is: an inner well of wisdom that can be accessed at any time if you know how. Some of the most intuitive people I know claim to be psychic turnips, while others are desperate to be clairvoyant but couldn't find their intuition with a map. We sometimes recognize it and often ignore it; we're eager to use it, but don't know where to start.

Guess what? We all have psychic abilities—some of us just have the volume turned up a little higher than others. Thankfully, intuition is like any other muscle: the more you use it, the stronger it gets—and the rituals I include here will help you listen to (and, more importantly, *trust*) your inner wisdom. We need to protect ourselves once we've opened up energetically, so we'll also look at ways to safeguard your energy (psychic and otherwise).

PLUGGING INTO YOUR INTERNAL GPS (INTUITION HACKS)

◇◇◇

We all have a little voice—call it a hunch, sixth sense, gut instinct, or something else—that we often ignore but then in retrospect end up thinking, *Why didn't I listen to the little voice?* When we hone our intuition, we can intentionally become more proactive, rather than reactive, with that little voice.

You may be thinking, *Sounds easy for a professional, Tarot Lori, but what if my little voice is on mute?* Intuition can be challenging for anyone to recognize because it's such so personal and is easily confused with ego. When our ego speaks, it's usually critical, rigid, or fearful, while intuition comes from a place of quiet clarity. The easiest way to know if you're hooking into your intuition is understanding what validation (aka an intuitive hit) feels like for you. It could show up physically as a wave of goose bumps, every hair standing on end, or as an inexplicable knowing. Unfortunately, it's difficult to hear our intuition when our ego won't shut up.

The easiest way to bypass the ego and tap into intuition is through mindfulness (yep, more meditating; see Chapter 7 for details). Your breath is the bridge between emotion, ego, and intuition—get still and let the best option reveal itself. Taking even a few minutes to step away from the screens and disengage from your to-do list can help you connect with your inner knowing. Think about those times you've driven somewhere and arrived with no clue how you got there because your mind was wandering the entire drive, solving all of the world's problems. That's the kind of zone you want to be in to access your intuition (just not while driving, because that's dangerous). You don't have to sit and meditate for hours unless you want to—it can be as simple as going for a walk, doing yoga, or sitting in your car for a few minutes with your eyes closed, listening to yourself breathe.

Consider holding a crystal or creating a grid during these meditative moments to enhance your intuition. Lapis lazuli, amethyst, celestite, and moonstone are all psychic superstars. Pull a card from your favorite oracle or tarot deck and meditate on its meaning in relation to your question (even if your question is simply *WTF is going on?*). However you choose to crank the volume on your higher knowing, remember that this isn't making predictions or fortune-telling party tricks; it's looking within for empowered guidance to make the best decision for yourself rather than abdicating responsibility of your life to some rando with a crystal ball.

Listening to your gut doesn't mean ignoring your head and heart—let your intuition, intellect, and emotion all have a seat at the decision-making table. This is often easier said than done. Here's a great exercise to help you balance thinking, feeling, and knowing when there's a big choice to be made.

Sit where nobody will bug you, ground yourself with some deep breaths, and close your eyes. Imagine your dilemma and the options you have, and then visualize the first path, using all of your senses to make it as vivid as possible. What are you wearing? Is there a dog barking in the distance? What's that smell? Once you have a clear picture in your mind, immerse yourself in the second path. When you're on each path, ask yourself, *How does this make me feel?* Notice how your body responds. Is there a tightness in your neck? A heaviness in your chest? Are you feeling butterflies in your stomach? Do you have a smile on your lips? Do you want to poop your pants? Your body always gives you clues, so pay attention.

One path will always feel better or less yucky than the other. It's not always a case of one feeling great while the other feels horrible: the first path might give you immediate acid reflux or a pit in your stomach, but the second feels even worse. Conversely, one option may feel fantastic, while the other one is even more incredible.

I've been telling tarot clients about this exercise for years, and I do it myself because it never lets me down. In fact, it's now such a natural reaction that I don't have to do the visualizing. I just pay close attention to my body's reaction.

You don't have to act on these intuitive nudges at first. Simply acknowledge them. If you meet someone and feel strongly one way or another, pay attention to that. If you feel compelled to go one way versus another, notice it. I was walking alone to my car after meeting friends for dinner in Toronto one night. I'd parked on a quiet side street, which didn't seem like a big deal when I arrived in the light of day. But now, late at night in the eerie quiet, the flickering streetlamp did little to cut through the blanket of darkness that enveloped me. I decided to walk in the middle of the street, rather than the sidewalks that were buffered by hedges on one side and blocked by cars on the other. I could see my car a block away. Almost there.

Suddenly, I felt a wave of dread as every hair on my body stood on end. I was instantly covered in sweat, my pulse racing. Without thinking, I pulled out my phone and pretended to take a call. "Hi, babe! Yep, I'm almost there . . . " As I spoke in a clear, loud voice that verged on a yell, a group of male figures emerged from the shadows ahead of me. I picked up my pace, taking no notice of them. "Oh, you're waiting at the car? Yes, I see you. Did you bring the dog?" I continued having a fake conversation with my husband about our fake Doberman as the men veered in the opposite direction, silently and in formation. Nobody spoke or made eye contact.

I didn't stop talking until I was in my car, shaking so violently that it took me a few tries to get the key in the ignition. I couldn't tell you how many men were there or what any of them looked like, but I know for certain that my intuition saved me from evil intentions that night. The more you start to trust your intuition, the more often it will show up. The answers you're seeking are within you—your job is to honor them.

Swinging Stones (How to Use a Pendulum)

Pendulum work—sometimes referred to as "dowsing"—is an extension of your intuition. Usually it's a crystal attached to a chain, but a pendulum can be any weighted object that hangs from a thread or cord of some sort. I was taught by a legendary dowser who once used a shoelace tied around a wine cork. Pendulums act as a receiver and transmitter for your higher wisdom (they're also a really cool party trick). They've been used to keep time since Galileo in the 1600s, but people were looking to pendulums for guidance in ancient China and Egypt.

Whether you're using a rare stone or a ring wrapped in twine, all pendulums work the same way: they cut through the clutter of your conscious mind to tap into signals from your subconscious. Once you program your pendulum (we'll get to that), the tiny nerve endings in your fingers will react subconsciously to the questions you're asking, causing the pendulum to move in a particular direction. In other words, your body and intuition are able to connect and communicate through your pendulum. On a more spiritual level, some people view pendulums as a tool to interact with our angels, guides, or ancestors. This may be true, but I believe the magic of pendulums can be found in the conversations they facilitate with your soul.

Using a pendulum is fairly easy: you program it, ask it a question, and hold it steady to observe the movements. Once you have your object on a string (seriously, I've used a piece of ribbon with a paper clip), you're ready to program your pendulum, which is how you get to know each other. Sit with it in your hand for a few minutes to establish an energetic bond (don't think of any questions yet; just take a couple of breaths as you hold it). Now that you're ready to have a conversation, you need to establish the language.

Gently pinch the chain of your pendulum between the index finger and thumb of your dominant hand, so the pendulum is hanging straight down from between your fingers, with your palm facing the table. Place your elbow on the table and prop it with your nondominant hand. Hold the chain between your thumb and forefinger with just enough force to keep from dropping the pendulum. Sit very still and allow the pendulum to settle (this may take a minute). Say *Show me yes* and then be patient as you wait for the pendulum to start moving in a clear direction—it will typically go in a clockwise or counterclockwise circle, swing back and forth in a line, or stay wobbling in one spot.

Once you've established an obvious "yes" direction, still the pendulum with your other hand before saying *Show me no*. Wait for it to start moving in a different way (again, this could take a bit of time).

Then repeat the process one last time as you say *Show me "it's not for me to know."* Once your pendulum is programmed, the movements are set forever. No matter what pendulum I use, my "yes" is always a clockwise circle, "no" is a straight line, and "none of my business" is a quivering in place. When you have your three options—yes, no, and neutral—you're good to go.

Test your pendulum by asking an easy question (*Do I currently live on Jupiter?*) or making simple statements (*My name is Lori.*). This helps sync your energies as you get comfortable working with your new friend. Notice how forceful the swinging is, because that can indicate the strength of your answer. For instance, if you ask *Should I look for a new job?* and the pendulum immediately starts swinging around in a big circle, that's a resounding *YES*.

Work with your pendulum to find lost items by asking questions (*Are my keys in the house? In the basement?*) to narrow down your search. Allow your pendulum to show you what you really want and how you truly feel. When asking whether something (or some*one*) is good for you, ask *Is it for my highest good to eat dairy?* or *Is being in a romantic relationship with Norman in my best interest?* If you just ask *Can I eat dairy?* or *Can I date Norm?*, the answer might be a weak "yes" because, technically, sure you can eat dairy, but that doesn't mean it's good for you (same goes for Norm).

When you ask the pendulum a question, some part of you already knows the answer. It's like how we can be so good at giving advice to others but suck at giving it to ourselves. Having a pendulum on hand can ease your anxiety and hesitation when it comes to making decisions that matter or getting validation—from yourself—when you need it. Pendulums are a wonderful addition to your rituals, especially when you're trying to clarify what needs to be released or finesse what you'd like to manifest.

Writing Wild

Another go-to ritual I've practiced for years works great when you're looking for direction but don't have specific questions. Writing wild (also known as freewriting, psychography, or automatic writing) offers a shortcut to your intuition and doesn't require fancy equipment or specialized training. All you need is a notebook and pen, a quiet table to sit at where nobody will bug you, and the timer on your phone.

Begin by quieting your mind with a few deep breaths. Consider what you'd like clarity on. Make sure it's an open-ended question instead of yes/no. Some examples include: *What are my next steps regarding X? What is X trying to teach me? What do I need to know about X? How can I make X happen easily?* Or you can simply ask, *What does my soul need me to know right now?*

Write your question at the top of the page and set your timer for a minimum of five minutes (I know it seems like a long time, but I promise it will pass quickly once you get going). Soften your gaze, forget about your question, pick up your pen, and start writing. Don't think, just write. Try to let go and write whatever is coming through. Keep writing until the timer goes off, and resist the urge to censor yourself—even if the thoughts are unrelated and the words seem incoherent, write them down. If you're drawing a blank, just write *I don't know what to write* over and over until something else shows up.

You're channeling from a place outside of your conscious awareness, so your handwriting may look different and you may find yourself using words or phrasings that are completely foreign to you. That's okay—it's actually really cool. The wording may read like someone else is advising you (also extremely cool). No matter what comes up, don't stop.

Writing wild can also be done first thing in the morning (see Chapter 7 for more about morning pages), with your question written at the top of the page the night before. As soon as your alarm goes off (or you begin to wake up on your own), grab your pen and notebook to write for a minimum of three pages. Try not to sit up, go to the bathroom, or even open your eyes fully—as your mind awakens, the connection to your subconscious and intuition weakens. (Note: This is also a real exercise in surrendering, because your handwriting will be an overlapping, uneven mess. My morning pages look like they were written by a serial killer.)

Once the timer goes or you've reached your page limit, take a minute to read through what you've written, noting anything that jumps out at you as a new insight. You might receive only a small part of your answer at first, and that's just fine—trust that more information will come through over the next few days, especially if you repeat this practice. Commit to writing wild for at least one week (preferably one month), because consistency is key. Do it every morning before breakfast, last thing at night, or at a different time every day—but do it daily, because you may find yourself receiving guidance on Thursday for something you asked about on Monday. Or you may see answers and opportunities show up in your life that directly relate to what you've written about. This ritual allows you to exercise your psychic powers while giving voice to your highest wisdom. The messages that have been obscured from your conscious mind are revealed. Cravings are conjured and magic is made.

It's also how I do my business planning. Some of the most pivotal moments of my career were conceived when I was half asleep, scribbling in a dollar store notebook at five in the morning. I got booked on Canada's top-ranked daytime talk show with zero contacts in the media and no idea where to start because I wrote (wildly) about it. I didn't question why I'd written *Get on talk show as a guest* in my morning pages, and I tried not to focus on how it would happen (#manifesting101), but I did prioritize visualizing my intention during meditations. When an event planner found me through Google a month later and asked me to be on a segment he was doing for *The Social*, I was weirdly ready because my higher knowing had already given me a heads-up. Not only was I featured in his piece, but I was also asked to give the hosts tarot readings on live TV.

Writing wild creates tiny ripples of inspiration that can become massive waves of transformation. Your intuition is always speaking to you—are you listening?

VIBE PATROL
(PROTECTING YOUR ENERGY)

◇◇◇

You can be the most psychic person in the world, but it won't do you much good if you're an energetic sieve. Every element of our Universe is made of energy that vibrates at certain frequencies, and every interaction we have with people involves an energetic exchange between what mystics call "auras" and scientists label "energy fields." These experiences leave us feeling better, worse, or neutral, depending on the quality of each person's energy.

In 2012, a research team from Bielefeld University in Germany proved that plants are capable of absorbing energy from other plants. Humans are no different. In 2017, researchers from the HeartMath Institute in Boulder Creek, California, determined that we're constantly projecting and picking up electromagnetic signals from each other, to the point that aspects of one person's heart rate can be measured in the brain waves of someone else, which is why health professionals suggest that the key to regulating your own emotional state starts with reviewing the people in your environment. Emotional energy is highly transferable. Whether it's a cheerful Starbucks barista or your cranky coworker, other people's moods are bound to leave you feeling some type of way, especially if you're highly sensitive or empathic.

Science is catching up to what we've instinctively known forever: feelings are contagious, and they leave a distinct aftertaste that lingers. Consistent energetic hygiene needs to be prioritized to remove toxic attachments and clear any emotional residue that might impact your physical, mental, and spiritual health.

Drainers & Dumpers

When you interact with other people, the energetic exchange is like a sunbeam of light connecting your hearts. Once the exchange is over, you have your energy, they have their energy, and that sunbeam of light (sometimes called an "etheric cord") dissipates on its own. But when it comes to friends, parents, coworkers, and lovers, that sunbeam of light can become more like a titanium pipe that gives them free access to either drain your energy or dump theirs all over you. Think about the emotional vampires in your life who leave you so exhausted after a five-minute chat that you need a nap, a drink, and a cry. Or the lifelong pessimists who unload their crappy energy all over you, leaving you so cranky you could punch a wall. This is the power of energetic drainers and dumpers. You might try limiting your proximity to those people, but it's not always possible (for example, you work with them). Sometimes their impact can be felt even when you're not in the same space (thank you, social media/ text messages).

These drainers and dumpers usually aren't aware it's happening, and it's rarely intentional or malicious on their part (kids can be the worst). Regardless of where it's coming from, this energy manipulation needs to be addressed. First, you have to recognize the energetic imbalances so you can rectify them. If you don't deal with these imbalances, they'll start dealing with you—leaving you so depleted or overwhelmed that it will manifest physically, making you sick. As long as these etheric cords are intact, your energy is being manipulated to your detriment. You must restore balance by establishing some energetic boundaries—and I have just the ritual for that.

No Muss, No Fuss, No Energetic Pus (How to Cut Cords)

I've been practicing (and preaching) this ritual for decades because it's so effective. You can do it in a freshly saged space surrounded by your favorite crystals or on a packed subway coming home from work. You don't need a certain day or situation to cut cords. Do it whenever you feel the energy of others encroaching on you.

Close your eyes, ground yourself in breath, and visualize that energetic drainer (or dumper) in your life. Imagine a beautiful sunbeam of light connecting your heart to the other person's heart. Do you see that stream of light shimmering between you? Can you feel the warmth of that golden connection? Good. Now grab an imaginary machete and slice through it like a goddamn ninja. Or hack it with a hatchet. Chop it with a chainsaw. Use your tool of choice to completely sever that cord. You aren't hurting that person or severing your relationship. You're simply saying "There's your energy, and here's my energy. You're welcome." You're doing everyone a favor by recalibrating this energetic imbalance and restoring homeostasis.

If you're stuck in a toxic relationship or situation, make cord-cutting part of your daily ritual until things change—and then be on the lookout. Once you've cut cords and released harmful attachments energetically, opportunities often arise in the physical realm. Sometimes it's a numbers game: if you deal with lots of people in your job—say you're a teacher, customer service agent, tarot reader, etc.—you need to pay particular attention to your energetic hygiene because you have so many interactions with potential dumpers or drainers. Visualize multiple cords coming out of your chest like golden skipping ropes floating out to the ether (not attached to anyone specifically). Now gather them all up, grab your gardening shears, and cut clear through them. This is what I do after every tarot event or speaking engagement, and it's a really effective way to lessen the impact of being around so many people (who may inadvertently be siphoning my energy).

Barricade Your Boundaries (Energetic Upkeep)

Now that your energetic boundaries are in place, you need to maintain them with vigilance. It can be as simple as washing your hands after an interaction (in addition to cutting cords after tarot readings, I scrub up to my elbows like I'm going into surgery). I have friends who work as massage therapists, counselors, or other public-facing professionals, and they all have hand-washing rituals to guard their energy. Some people have a nightly shower and visualize the water washing away the energetic ooze of their workday (this or a ritual bath can be the foundation of an evening ritual, as outlined in Chapter 7). If you need to purge funky mojo after an unpleasant encounter but hopping in the tub isn't practical, simply envision a shower of protective light raining down on you and the funky mojo swirling down the drain. At the very least, shift your energy (and your mood) every day after work by changing your outfit. Even if your commute is from the kitchen to the living room, ditch your professional joggers for casual joggers to avoid lugging yucky energy around (it's like wearing muddy boots to bed).

Get proactive when you're heading into a situation you know will be stressful (for example, facing your ex in court or attending an office holiday party) by surrounding yourself with an energetic shield to repel bad vibes. Close your eyes and envision a white light igniting within your core. Let it grow stronger and brighter as it fills your body; allow it to emanate beyond your physical form to envelop you in a layer of protection. You might also prepare for potential conflicts with a quick zipping up of your energy. You can imagine doing this in your mind, but I find it even more effective to actually reach down to my toes and pretend to pull a zipper up the front of my body, over my head, and down my back, all the way to my heels. As I'm doing this, I say something like *I'm zipping my energy to protect myself from any negativity I may face.* If there's a specific person, I'll say the name: *I'm now zipping my energy to protect me from Bob's negative energy.* When you set the vibrational tone, it will affect how people respond to you as well as how things unfold around you.

Crystals are an incredibly potent tool to protect your energy field (amethyst, smoky quartz, and blue lace agate are great choices; see Chapter 2 for more on crystals). I know I've mentioned sticking some rocks in your bra and hoping for the best, but I seriously used to do it all the time (not as much since receiving my crystal necklaces, but there were many nights when I took my bra off and a bunch of stones tumbled to my feet).

You don't need to stuff your bra with crystals to benefit from their powers. Just go outside and pick up a regular rock that sits comfortably in the palm of your hand and tell it all of your worries (out loud or in your head). Treat it like your bestie or therapist, and spill whatever is on your mind. Keep your rock nearby for the rest of the day, an entire week, or just for that moment of need (but don't hang on to it for longer than a week). Whenever you feel anxious or need to unburden, grab your worry stone and surrender your fears and doubts to it. When you feel the time is right, take it to a nearby pond, lake, river, or ocean and throw it as far into the water as you can, knowing that it will release your fears and wash away your worries. If you're landlocked, bury it in the ground (not in your yard) or give it a mini ritual bath to clear it before putting it back where you found it.

You can smudge negative energy from yourself just like you would your home. Rosemary, cedar, and pine are excellent herbal defenders—just state your intention, spark up your herb, and waft the smoke around your body as you visualize the negative energy ebbing away (see Chapter 3 for detailed smudging instructions). Don't have pine needles handy? Light a white candle as you focus on protective energy infusing your space and soul.

Energetic boundaries also come from how we speak and the company we keep. Watch your words, because they have power. Don't downplay your contributions or dismiss your needs (you're setting your own bar way too low). Stop saying "Yes" to what you don't want, and remember that "No" is a complete sentence. If that's too difficult, try "Let me get back to you," to give yourself some space. Honor your energy by replacing "I don't have time to . . ." with "It's not my priority to . . ." Avoid saying "I'm sorry" when apologies aren't required (this is extra tough for us Canadians; yesterday, I apologized for bumping into an empty chair).

Pay attention to whom you're spending time with and how they make you feel. Are you tired or cranky when you see them, or inspired and fortified? Are your conversations one way versus a true dialogue? Does the other person challenge you to be better or drag you down to their level? Curate your community as a form of energetic self-care—the people you choose to interact with regularly reflect how you feel about yourself.

CHAPTER 12

CIRCLES & SPELLS (THE POWER OF WOMEN GATHERING)

◇◇◇

Although the rituals in this book can be done solo, you can infuse them with even more energy if you grab some kindred spirits and do them together. Group rituals don't have to be in person—every month during Burn Your Sh*t on Instagram I'm reminded just how profound virtual gatherings can be. When you bring people together with intention and sit in a literal or metaphorical circle, the personal empowerment and collective catharsis that occurs is life-changing.

FROM HERSTORY TO HISTORY (AND BACK AGAIN)

◇◇◇

Communing in circles isn't a novel idea, it's primal. The world's oldest temple on record is Göbekli Tepe, in Turkey. Consisting of massive carved megaliths arranged in rings by prehistoric people over 11,000 years ago, these holy circles were used in worship well before the development of tools or pottery. As far back as 800 CE, women were convening in ceremonial circles that connected them to the natural world and each other. Men were often forbidden entry into these mysterious spaces that were believed to connect women with Divine knowledge and healing.

Fire, of course, played a role. Gathering around blazing embers is the most ancient form of social interaction, and women have done it for thousands of years because their survival depended on it. Wisdom was shared as food was prepared, but these conclaves were also tied to Moon and menstrual cycles.

Historically, the Moon Lodge, or menstrual hut, was a sacred space in many Indigenous cultures around the world. It was seen as a place of respite, power, and transformation, and treated with great reverence by the community at large. During women's time in the Moon Lodge, Elders gave teachings, creativity (such as crafting) was encouraged, and energy was restored. By disengaging from daily duties, women in the Moon Lodge were able to nurture themselves.

In First Nations communities throughout North America, the Moon Lodge continues to hold spiritual significance as a sacred refuge for women during their menstrual cycles—a space for rest, renewal, and connection. Within the Moon Lodge, women have an opportunity to share experiences with other women as they honor their relationship with Mother Earth and Grandmother Moon.

In ancient Greece, numerous female-only festivals—including Thesmophoria, Skira, and Haloa—celebrated the power of fertility, while the cult of Athena offered female followers significant independence and opportunities. Rituals performed exclusively by women were crucial to the formation and cohesion of early Greek civilization. The priestesses of the past connected community members by establishing a link between earthly existence, departed ancestors, and the Divine.

Things shifted (that is, went to sh*t) with the rise of patriarchy and the decline of ritualistic, lunar-based practices. The publication of *Malleus Maleficarum* (*Hammer of Witches*) in 1484 incited the persecution and execution of female healers, as well as the systematic destruction of women's spiritual practices—the ramifications of which we're still experiencing today. Circles were rebranded as "covens," and midwives were labeled "witches." Sacred ceremonies became satanic desecrations. But the power of the feminine was never fully extinguished; it was merely hidden from view. Women continued to gather—they just did it in ways that wouldn't offend or challenge patriarchal power structures.

From shrouded covens deep in the woods to ladies' night at a wine bar, from quilting bees to bowling leagues, we're hardwired to gather in communion, which makes sense because there's a clear relationship between conscious conversation and self-esteem.

When a person feels a sense of belonging, that security acts as an antidote to anxiety, depression, and isolation. We yearn for companionship, yet we're forgetting how it's done. Research out of the University of Michigan in 2020 confirmed that our social connections are declining and that, despite being more connected than ever before, we've never felt more alone. The National Institute on Aging asserts that loneliness is worse for our health than smoking, and research out of the University of California San Francisco in 2010 found that the strength of our relationships is a better indicator of life expectancy than exercise, obesity, or air quality. It's no wonder that a growing number of women from all walks of life are reviving ancient ways of connecting in the modern era, recognizing the vital role that assembling with like-minded souls plays in keeping us healthy and making us whole.

Although there is no evidence that women gathered in menstrual huts during Biblical times, the concept was popularized in Anita Diamant's novel *The Red Tent* in 1997. The idea of a dedicated space for women to heal themselves and each other resonated deeply with readers, and a global movement was born. Groups of women began meeting to reclaim the power of their periods.

In their excellent book *Red Tents: Unravelling Our Past and Weaving a Shared Future*, Aisha Hannibal and Mary Ann Clements share the foundations for creating a women's collective that encourages support and community, with an emphasis on fostering inclusive and accessible spaces while refraining from cultural appropriation (for example, incorporating smudging in a respectful manner). At a contemporary Red Tent gathering, women are encouraged to show up as their authentic selves, knowing it is safe to share their greatest fears and deepest desires. Advice is avoided and active listening is implied as women tell their stories. Strength is restored on a physical, emotional, and spiritual level.

Years ago I joined a monthly women's group that was led by a naturopath and focused on different aspects of women's health. I expected to learn about hormones and digestion, but I ended up receiving medicine for my soul that I didn't know I needed. This cultivation of sisterhood and self-care had such an impact on me that I went on to lead my own sessions in her clinic, centered on topics ranging from mindfulness to manifesting. We began and ended each meeting in a circle, checking in with each other and ourselves, and I can see in retrospect how this experience was a precursor for the transformation that awaited me.

COVEN LOVIN'
(MY CIRCLE STORY)

◇◇◇

When I googled "women's spiritual mastermind" in early 2020, I was hoping to meet people working in the woo-woo space. Instead,

I found my soul sisters, thanks to Andrea Bendewald. Andrea has led women's circles for decades, and during the COVID-19 pandemic she expanded her company, Art of Circling, online. The way she leads circles is truly an art. In the years since my first circle with Andrea, gathering with these women has become the foundation for my energetic upkeep and a catalyst for my professional ascension.

I couldn't tell you what the ladies I circle with do for a living or the names of their kids, but I *know* these women—their deepest desires and heaviest burdens—just as they know mine. Through the alchemy of coming together in a circle, we make magic. Like the software consultant who picked up a paintbrush for the first time in a decade and now exhibits her art in galleries around the world. Or the financial dynamo who left her lucrative career in London to get her dream degree at UCLA. (Or the tarot reader who decided to step onto a bigger stage and landed a major book deal.)

The energy Andrea summons in her circles is the antithesis of corporate networking or a boozy brunch—we're compelled to share our true selves, reclaim our power, and remember who we are. There are breakdowns and breakthroughs every single time. The women I circle with are more than a spiritual mastermind: they are my recharging station and cocreators. Whether leaving a marriage or starting a side hustle, all of us have been transformed through the power of circling with Andrea, connecting to the deep well of feminine power and women's wisdom that resides within us. Her circles have helped me and women around the world recognize and step into our potential—shifting us from a place of "Why not *me*?" to one of "Why *not* me?"

Circling is much more than a spiritual sorority. Unlike book clubs or multilevel marketing parties (or even happy hour with your squad), goddess gatherings like Andrea's Art of Circling are specifically designed to nurture the intimacy that comes from vulnerability—and it can't be cultivated organically around the water cooler at work or during school drop-off.

PRIME YOUR INNER PRIESTESS (GATHERING FUNDAMENTALS)

◇◇◇

Circling has been mainstream for the past forty years. Whether you call it a Moon Lodge, Red Tent, women's collective, or goddess circle, let Google be your guide to finding spirit sisters with a shared purpose. In-person gatherings are often held at yoga studios, or you can search meet-up websites to find something near you. Online circles can sometimes provide more options for the right fit. (Pro tip: To ensure everyone gets a chance to speak, skip any gathering with more than twenty participants.) Gatherings can be a one-off or a recurring session with a particular theme (women's health) or occasion (Full Moon). However they're organized and wherever they happen, make no mistake: where there is circling, there is ritual.

If you can't find a gathering in your area, and none of the online options float your boat, try hosting your own circle. Set a clear intention for gathering (more on that soon) and find a dedicated space. You could all meet in the forest, in your living room, or on Zoom. You might provide food and drink to share, have everyone contribute to a potluck, or ask participants to bring a full water bottle and ditch the socializing-with-snacks part altogether. Encourage everyone to bring a journal and pen to record any revelations—taking notes on an app isn't as powerful, plus you can't burn an iPhone during a release ritual (speaking of phones, make sure they're all turned off).

Although there is no "right" way to do it, Jean Shinoda Bolen offers guidance in her book *The Millionth Circle: How to Change Ourselves and the World*. Certain commonalities can be found in every circle, the most obvious being (you guessed it) sitting in a circular formation. Everyone's energy meets in the middle, and having a sacred altar at the center is imperative. It might be as simple as a single candle, a collection of your most potent crystals, or an assortment of natural elements to mark the four directions (as mentioned in Chapter 9, you can align the directions and elements in any way that resonates with you).

Shinoda Bolen suggests symbolically opening the gathering with words or a sound, such as ringing a bell, to get everyone's attention. You can set the mood by burning sage or incense. If you're feeling extra witchy, cast a circle. There are countless ways to do this, but a traditional circle is nine feet in diameter, features either the four directions or natural elements, and is drawn with a ceremonial dagger as participants visualize the energetic boundary being formed. Once the circle is drawn, participants walk around it to concentrate the cosmic power. No matter how you choose to open your circle, this shared ritual marks the space as sacred.

The basic components of a gathering can be found in the work of Christina Baldwin and Ann Linnea. After greeting participants and reaffirming the intention for being there, each woman's voice is heard as she introduces herself to the group, perhaps adding a personal detail such as what drew her to the gathering. For decades, I've started and ended every tarot or manifesting workshop I've ever taught by asking participants for one word to describe their emotional state in that moment, without realizing why I was doing it. I'm telling you, this stuff is embedded in our spiritual DNA.

To ensure that everyone feels comfortable, safe, and respected, always take some time to review the agreements—also known as guidelines. Baldwin and Linnea provide examples, including keeping everything spoken in the circle confidential, listening with compassion rather than criticism, and being mindful of the time (read: don't take an hour to tell your life story).

A talking piece is often introduced as a communication tool. It can be a feather, stone, or any symbolic object. A talking piece serves to identify the speaker and empower her to share whatever is on her mind and in her heart as others honor her with their full attention. Witnessing a woman speak uninterrupted allows her to hear her truth and discover her true self.

What comes next is up to you, but a quick online search will give you loads of ideas that can be adapted to the needs of your group. (If you want to know the secret sauce of my mentor Andrea Bendewald's circles, I suggest joining one yourself to see what all the magic's about.)

It can be auspicious to hold a women's circle around seasonal markers such as an equinox, solstice, or any of the sabbats mentioned in Chapter 8. You might meet weekly, monthly, or quarterly, selecting different themes like social justice, forgiveness, boundaries, creativity, body acceptance, or menopause. You could even circle around a book. What differentiates a book circle from a typical book club is the kind of book you choose, as well as the topics being discussed. For example, Andrea recently led a fantastic circle series for Elise Loehnen's *New York Times* bestselling book *On Our Best Behavior: The Seven Deadly Sins and the Price Women Pay to be Good*. Each week's circle offered a gold mine of reflection and personal growth.

Regardless of the subject matter, you can kick things off with a leading question (also called a prompt) that is related to the intention or topic. Since it can be intimidating to bare your soul in front of other people, even if you know them, consider setting the tone by sharing first. Be willing to get personal and go deep.

If the theme is nature, you might ask what your relationship with nature is (if you have one) or how lunar phases affect your body and mood. If you're discussing intuition, you might ask how you access your intuition, or the consequences of a time you listened to or ignored your inner wisdom. For finances, you could delve into your inherited money story or how your relationship with money has changed over time. Take turns speaking (with the talking piece if you're using one) and let the alchemy unfold.

Closing the circle is as powerful and essential as opening it. It shifts everyone's energy from sacred sharing to easy socializing. Try holding hands with eyes closed as you all take three deep breaths. Or ask everyone to end with a new word that describes their updated emotional state. Sing a song, play an instrument, or get up and dance. If food and drink are being provided, this is the time to enjoy them. Or simply take a few moments to mingle as people prepare to depart. You may be feeling elated or depleted, so pay attention to your needs.

MOON MEETINGS, ASTRAL ASSEMBLIES, & SPIRITUAL SOIRÉES (LUNAR CIRCLES)

◇◇◇

Women commonly gather under a Full Moon or New Moon: the schedule is consistent, the agenda is a no-brainer, and the rituals themselves connect us to the natural world as well as our higher wisdom. Moon circles can be done on the day of a Full or New Moon, or a few days on either side—La Luna's vibes will still pack a cosmic punch.

Full Moon Circle

Every Full Moon is an opportunity for transformation and gathering, and a lunar release ritual can be a catalyst for massive change. Your symbolic center might feature a selection of crystals—smoky quartz, labradorite, and selenite all align beautifully with the mojo of a Full Moon. People can also bring any gems they'd like to charge during the ritual.

During this gathering, the intention is to release what no longer serves. Ask participants to consider what is blocking them from living their fullest, truest, most authentic life. A romantic relationship, work situation, or money mindset may need to change. You may want to lead circle members through the grounding exercise I do during Burn Your Sh*t in Chapter 5 to help them identify what is ready to be relinquished. Have paper and pens available so they can write down *I now choose to release* . . . followed by what (or who) needs to go.

Take turns reading the releases out loud. You can all stand around a firepit or grouping of candles to burn the paper, or use a fireproof container with a lighter. If lighting things on fire won't work in your space (for example, you're indoors), rip up the paper and collect the pieces to burn or bury later. As the paper is burned or ripped, say *And so it is.* The other women can echo this phrase. It sounds a little cultish, but it's very empowering to hear your proclamation repeated back to you.

During my decades leading Full Moon rituals, I usually find myself near the center of the circle, or I move from person to person holding the container and lighter so I can assist with the burning. It can be helpful to hold the container and light the paper for the woman—it allows her to focus on the words as they burn. At the end, ask each woman to share (even if it's just one word) how she's feeling after her release.

A special magic is stirred up when others are present to hear your declaration spoken aloud. The affirmation and accountability bring a fullness to the experience. In bearing witness to one another, we realize we're in this together. In seeing what is possible, success becomes contagious.

New Moon Circle

Manifesting under a New Moon may not seem as witchy as a release ritual, but it's still super juicy—and inherently magical. With the sky unobscured by the light of the Moon, there is a blank canvas of possibility, and our intentions are amplified even more when we summon them in a circle.

Your intention for this gathering is inviting new energy into your life, and in the absence of fire, you can build a New Moon altar with anything that calls to you: fresh-cut flowers, a bowl of oranges, or a variety of crystals (selenite and clear quartz are great New Moon stones, and citrine is perfect for manifesting). Have everyone bring a bottle of water, journal, pen, and any objects for the altar that they would like infused with expansive vibes.

Open the circle with introductions and a grounding exercise, song, or meditation (you can use my New Moon meditation from Chapter 6). Give everyone time to identify their intentions. What seeds are being planted and actions being taken to achieve their goals? Reflect on the internal shifts that are required to bring these dreams to fruition. Turn intentions into affirmations that align with a manifesting mindset. For example, as discussed in Chapter 6, if your intention is to get healthier, an affirmation might be: *I am in a loving relationship with myself and treat my body with the respect and care that it deserves*. If this is too difficult, try something as simple and profound as *I love myself.*

Go around the circle and take turns sharing intentions and affirmations. For the second round of sharing, ask each woman to speak her intentions three times into the water she brought before drinking from her bottle so she can absorb the power of her words. Close the circle by pulling a tarot or oracle card for each woman, or have everyone say one word that epitomizes their vision moving forward.

Invite participants to take their intentions home and keep them somewhere visible (for example, on a vision board), under a crystal (as a mini manifesting altar), or under their pillow to sleep on. If you meet with the same group of women regularly, you can revisit your intentions every New Moon to see where you're all at, determine work that still needs to be done, and identify new directions. Let the power of the collective be fueled by the fertile New Moon.

CELEBRATING SISTERHOOD

◇◇◇

It can be hard to make new friends as an adult. And our oldest confidantes know a particular version of us—based on who we were when we met—that might be at odds with who we become over time. Developing intimate friendships that elevate and celebrate, rather than compare and compete, can seem impossible. What I have found to be true is this: when you sit alongside women who've set an intention to connect with and support each other, enduring relationships are formed, ones built on trust, love, and acceptance.

Our souls crave feminine energy—it nurtures and fuels us. We gather to break the unspoken bonds of silence and expectations of perfection, replacing them with unconditional love and radical collective care. When we meet with intention, we find inspiration. In seeking solace, we discover our strength. We're able to remove barriers to spiritual freedom that we've subconsciously upheld since before we were born. We are all on individual journeys, but we're not meant to do it alone. We can reach out to hold each other's hands along the way, knowing that we're more likely to succeed if we're willing to be seen. Through the stories of others, we discover the depths of our wounds and the salve for our souls. In the feminine, we find the Divine.

The transformative energy that emerges in a circle answers an ancient call. The witches of our past were leaders and healers—mystics and medicine women who understood that when women gather with purpose, they create movements. They were our mothers and our daughters. They were us. They are you.

CONCLUSION

◇◇◇

R ituals aren't therapy, but they're very therapeutic.

When you honor your rituals, you honor yourself. The time you commit to them is time you are dedicating to your growth and healing. As with anything in life, intention is everything. You can be in a traditional Indigenous sweat lodge or the steam room at your gym—if your objective in entering each space is the same, the effects can be just as transformative. Through these sacred moments, you're starting a conversation with the Universe.

My intention in writing this book was to create a guide for your energetic evolution. To help you awaken the natural leader, innate healer, and wise woman within.

These rituals are designed to support you along your path of self-discovery. They can't fix you, because healing comes from within. They won't save you, because you are the hero of your story. They aren't magical—you are.

You always have been.

ACKNOWLEDGMENTS

◇◇◇

Writing a book for publication is not for wimps. It took an enormous team of wonderful people working tirelessly behind the scenes to get this book in your hands, and I'm grateful for their advice, handholding, and expertise.

I won the literary lottery when Alexandra D'Amico became my agent. Alex, thank you for being such a passionate champion of me and my work. Your input made this book better, and you've been instrumental in my transition from writer to author. You are one of the wisest witches I know—kind, intuitive, shrewd, and brilliant—and I'm honored to be your client and friend.

I'm so proud to be with Transatlantic Agency. Thank you to Carolyn Forde for connecting me with Alex, and to Samantha Haywood for assembling such a stellar team.

Thank you to the HarperCollins team for believing in my message and honoring my voice. Julia McDowell, thank you for being my editor and #grammargirlcrush. I'm so fortunate to benefit from your insight, wit, and curiosity—the feedback you provided made these pages sing. Tracy Bordian, I am in awe of your punctuation prowess. Thank you for being a brilliant copy editor; your careful reads and thoughtful contributions carried this book over the finish line. Enormous thanks to Brad Wilson, Janice Zawerbny, Canaan Chu, and everyone else at HarperCollins Canada who contributed in any and every way to bring this book into the world. Working with you has been a joy.

Some people have a personal Board of Directors; I have a Collection of Covens. Most of these special souls have been brought to me in ways that can only be described as magical (or witchy AF). These people have been my safe harbor, rocket fuel, and wise counsel in every aspect of my life, and I'm thrilled for this opportunity to thank them publicly.

To Erica Von Kcaat, my tarot mentor and favorite witch, thank you for . . . all of it. I would not be the tarot reader (or human) I am today if not for you.

MB, thank you for being my trusted confidante; I love our friendship (and walks/forced marches) so much. Meredith Cox, I'm grateful to have you in my corner—thank you for years of delightful dinners and delicious conversations. Reetu Gupta, your support, spiritual counsel, and exuberance for life are essential components of my self-care; thank you for everything. Jane McCann (my sister from an Aussie mister), thank you for being a bright beacon during dark times and encouraging me to Go for It. Dr. Elena Sherwood, reading your wonderful book inspired me to try writing my own—thank you for being a role model to me and so many others.

Trevor Frankfort, thank you for inviting me on national television to do tarot—it remains a key milestone of my career—and every meeting since then (our dates are like Miracle-Gro for manifesting). Brittany Ostofe, my business catapulted when I moved it online, and you were instrumental in that process. You've modeled how to succeed by being unapologetically yourself—thank you for your friendship, guidance, and support (on- and offline). Ryan Ostofe, you are an inspiring leader, and I'm incredibly grateful for your dedication to my ascension (professional and personal). You are both, as the youths say, da bomb.

Jennifer Pastiloff, I'm in awe of the space you create for others to flourish. Thank you for inviting me into your orbit—where vulnerability is wielded like a saber and creativity is nurtured like a newborn—and for reminding me that I get to have this.

Nyakio Grieco—Queen of Wands of my dreams—thank you for being such a generous and effusive supporter of everything I do. You are a true visionary, and your unwavering dedication to your family, community, and business inspires me daily.

I don't know a lot of tarot readers but I LOVE mediums, and I'm fortunate enough to know some of the best in the biz. MaryAnn DiMarco, I feel like I've known you for lifetimes, and I'm so grateful to have you in this one as my soul sister, mentor, and spiritual bestie (there's nobody I'd rather spend an hour cackling with on a call in a Costco parking lot than you). Thank you to Debby Fleming for giving me the guidance I didn't know I needed when I needed it most. Kate King, your artistry is unmatched and I am so honored to wear your mystical crystal pendants—thank you.

Dr. Lauren Wedlock-Brown, thank you for sharing your magic with me (and encouraging me to write a letter to my uterus). Thank you, Dr. Lisa Knapper, for imbuing your witchy ways in the earliest iterations of Burn Your Sh*t. Dr. Michelle Peris, thank you for introducing me to the powerful magic that is conjured when women gather with intention.

To Starbucks staff at store #50088, thank you for letting me nurse my peach tea for hours when I needed to buckle down and finish this book (after realizing that my deadline was June 30, not July 31).

For almost two years, I have hopped on a weekly accountability call with Lisa Davis, Yousra El Alaoui, and Vanessa Gringer to brainstorm projects, vent about annoyances, or take massive leaps (but we're mostly just reveling in each other's company). Lisa, thank you for showing us what happens when you take a chance on yourself—your talent is infinite. Yousra, your courage and brilliance leave me breathless; thank you for sharing your tender, tenacious heart with me. Vanessa, you are an exceptional person (stylist, publicist, editor, etc.) and friend—thank you for being so many things to so many people in ways you'll never understand. Thank you three for making magic with me. I love us so much.

I first met Lisa, Yousra, and Vanessa in a virtual circle led by Andrea Bendewald (we'll get to Drea in a minute), along with so many other women who have become my spiritual family: Eileen King, thank you for our transcendent chick-chats; every conversation changes me for the better. Alex Seidel, you ignite magic in my life whenever we speak—thank you for shining your light my way. Kari Lauritzen, thank you for nourishing my body and spirit (and reminding me I'm TAROT F*CKING LORI when I forget). Emily Kratter, your laughter is medicine and your spirit is spellbinding; thank you for being my energetic spark plug. Cara Hyland, thank you for our healing hangouts; one conversation with you is like a year of therapy. Ronit Cohn, I'm so lucky you were stuck beside me on that two-hour drive to the desert—thank you for your friendship and savvy business advice. Sophie Bushman, thank you for introducing me to King (IYKYK) and holding space for me to voice what I'd been too scared to speak. Cyndi Finkle, thank you for your vulnerable words and photographic witchery. Amy Fields, I'm so happy we chose each other, in friendship and talking sticks. Jaymee Naik, you and your family's love is inspiring and healing to witness. Kat Gana, thank you for letting me see myself through your eyes (hopefully I do the same for you). Amber Goodenough, thank you for always showing up; I promise I'll get to Santa Barbara one day to burn our sh*t in person. Marni Zaifert, thank you for your friendship and support (and Spiritual Ballet . . . which cheers me up whenever I remember it). Robyn Kramer, thank you for being the heart-eyes emoji in human form—I adore you. Andrea Schlegel-Wallace, thank you for your pure heart and unwavering support. Thais Vieira, just thinking about you makes my heart sing and my mouth smile so big it hurts (in a good way). Desiree Dozier, you're the coolest and I want a doggy playdate, stat. Sarah Brownell, your tender heart soothes others in ways you'll never know. Sarah MacGillivray, you are a powerful witch and creative force. Ashley Hinds, thank you for being you; it is more than enough. Ashley Logan, the light you shine in sharing your story illuminates the path for all of us. Francesca Fartaj, thank you for being a role model in living a life of grace, grit, and compassion—you are an angel on Earth.

I would not know any of these women without Andrea Bendewald, circle sorceress and stellar human. Drea, thank you for creating a space for women to realize who they are and what is possible. Thank you for speaking my name in rooms full of opportunity. Thank you for being a spiritual badass. I'm so happy we get to know and learn from each other at this level in this lifetime (#junebugs).

Lisa Badame, thank you for being someone I can trust with my deepest fears and most daring dreams. So much of my personal growth can be traced back to one of the books you've suggested or a reflection you made (or the therapy you insisted I get in my twenties). You and your sweet mom, Ines, are my family.

Treana Peake, thank you for being so many things to me: my first (and favorite) tarot client; my travel buddy; and my employer when I was a writer doing tarot on the side. Most importantly, you are one of my very best friends. You've consoled me at my lowest depths and encouraged me to pursue dreams that seemed preposterous at the time, like doing tarot for a living or writing a book (or both!). I'll meet you on the porch, toots (#rockingchairgoals).

To Lori Bean—my best friend since we were tweens rocking rugby pants and headgear—you know my story more than most because you helped me write so much of it. It's rare to have friendships endure as the individuals evolve, and ours has only grown stronger over the FORTY YEARS we've known each other (I literally figured that out as I wrote this and almost fell off my chair). Thank you for calling me on my bullsh*t, making me laugh until I peed, and holding me when I was broken. I am so lucky to know you and be known by you.

To my mom, Doris Parisan, thank you for surviving. Your story is not an easy one to tell, let alone live, but you have created a life that is beyond our ancestors' wildest dreams. Thank you for supporting my dreams, even when they didn't make much sense, and being the best grandma to my kids.

My sister, Shannon Beavis, is a wonder. In dedicating much of her life to making the world a better and safer place, especially in underserved communities, she has brought healing to so many (including herself). Thank you for being the very best sister (and aunt) and an even better friend.

To Stojan Simeunovic, you are a tremendous father and wonderful partner (in love and life). Our kids are so spectacular in part because of the example you set and the values you've instilled. How we met is a miracle . . . and then we created two more. Volim te.

To my son, Luka Simeunovic, thank you for making me a mom (and thank you to the all-inclusive resort in Cuba that helped make that happen). Watching you live your purpose, always being unapologetically yourself, is inspiring. Your kindness, humor, and curiosity about the world amaze me every day, in every way.

To my daughter, Maia Simeunovic, thank you for teaching me how to love and be loved unconditionally. You are sunshine in human form, and the world is a more beautiful place because you're in it. Your empathy, resilience, and intelligence motivate me to do better and be better every single day.

I've had a library card since I was five years old, and I love librarians like nachos love salsa. I also adore booksellers in all forms (they're the guacamole). Thank you all for being fierce defenders of free speech and unwavering supporters of the written word. I am grateful for everything you do.

Finally, to everyone reading this book—especially if you've ever turned to me for tarot, trusted me to burn your sh*t, manifested with me under the Moon, or mentioned my work to others—thank you. You are my teacher and my guide. Without you, I would not be living this life that I dared not dream was possible. I appreciate and love you all very much.

SCAN THIS QR CODE TO
ACCESS THE RITUAL RECORDINGS
MENTIONED IN THIS BOOK
(OR GO TO WWW.TAROTLORI.COM/
BURN-YOUR-SHT-RECORDINGS)